BIOGRAPHY CONSTANTINE
Grant, Michael, 1914-

Constantine the great :
the man and his times /
1994, c1993

CONSTANTINE THE GREAT

CONSTANTINE THE GREAT

The Man and His Times

MICHAEL GRANT

CHARLES SCRIBNER'S SONS
NEW YORK

MAXWELL MACMILLAN INTERNATIONAL
NEW YORK   OXFORD   SINGAPORE   SYDNEY

Charles Scribner's Sons
Macmillan Publishing Company
866 Third Avenue
New York, NY 10022

Macmillan Publishing Company is part of the Maxwell Communication Group of Companies.

Library of Congress Cataloging-in-Publication Data
Grant, Michael, 1914–
    Constantine the great : the man and his times / Michael Grant.
        p.   cm.
    Includes bibliographical references and index.
    ISBN 0-684-19520-8
    1. Constantine I, Emperor of Rome, d. 337. 2. Roman
emperors—Biography. 3. Christian   saints—Rome—
Biography. 4. Rome—History—Constantine I, the Great,
306–337. 5. Church history—Primitive and early church,
ca. 30–600. I. Title.
DG315.G73   1994
937'.08'092—dc20
[B]   94-714   CIP

Macmillan books are available at special discounts for bulk purchases for sales promotions, premiums, fund-raising, or educational
use. For details, contact:

Special Sales Director
Macmillan Publishing Company
866 Third Avenue
New York, NY 10022

10 9 8 7 6 5 4 3 2 1

Printed in the United States of America

CONTENTS

LIST OF ILLUSTRATIONS

All illustrations come from the Weidenfeld Archive

LIST OF MAPS

ACKNOWLEDGEMENTS

For quotations which appear in this book the author would like to acknowledge and thank the following:

J. L. Creed; Colin Thubron; Ramsay MacMullen; C. Luibhéid; A. H. M. Jones; New American Library and Cambridge University Press for permission to quote from Cambridge Ancient History, Vol. XII (1939).

PREFACE

THE PROBLEM of finding out about Constantine is an acute one, but quite easy and straightforward to formulate. All the ancient historians and other writers are either 100 per cent for him, because he was the first Christian emperor, or 100 per cent against him, for the same reason. And for the same reason, again, much more has been said about the religious developments during his reign than about the secular happenings.

And so, rightly concluded Evelyn Waugh, 'The Age of Constantine is strangely obscure. Most of the dates and hard facts, confidently given in the encyclopaedias, soften and dissolve on examination.'[1] Hundreds of attempts have been made to reconstruct them; here, in this book, is another endeavour to walk over the same treacherous quicksands. And treacherous they indeed are. For Constantine 'is one of the few inescapable figures in Roman history and one of the most intractable'.[2] He 'appears in history as one continuous contradiction'.[3] There is 'irremediable uncertainty about almost every point in Constantine's life'.[4] Or rather, I hope, not totally irremediable. For it is with that optimistic conviction that I have attempted the present study.

I am grateful to Andras Bereznay, Maria Ellis, Malcolm Gerratt, Charmian Hearne, Hilary Laurie, Arabella Pike, Julia Smallbone, Charles Young and Peter James for much assistance with the book. I also want to thank my wife for all the help which, as always, she has given me.

Michael Grant, 1993

PART I:

INTRODUCTORY

CHAPTER 1:

THE SOURCES

IMPARTIALITY, in the later Roman empire, was not generally required of a 'historian'. What people wanted, and needed, was a stereotyped form of history, without too much attention to the truth – which was, in any case, extremely hard to recover. So uncertainty, fiction and falsehood abounded, both on the side of the government and among those who were opposed to it.[1]

The Christian writers, it must be repeated, have little but good to say about Constantine, but they are nevertheless informative about various aspects of his life (of which we should otherwise know little): for this was the great age of the Christian apologists.

First and foremost among them was Eusebius. He came from Caesarea Maritima in Syria Palaestina (Israel), and was born in about AD 260. One of his teachers was the Christian apologist Pamphilus of Berytus (Beirut), who had studied at Alexandria, became presbyter (priest) at Caesarea (Kayseri) in Cappadocia and, after prolonged imprisonment during the persecution launched by Diocletian and Galerius, was martyred in 309/10. Eusebius himself, however, escaped the persecution relatively unscathed, and in about 314, after Christianity had been authorized by Constantine, he was rewarded for his strong support of the emperor by appointment to the bishopric of Caesarea. His sympathies lay, somewhat surreptitiously and vacillatingly, with the leading Alexandrian presbyter Arius, whose doctrines, described as Arianism, argued that the Son was separate in essence from the Father. But, when Arius was declared a heretic by the Council of Nicaea (325), Eusebius accepted this decision. However, he also attended the Synod of Tyre (335), which condemned Arius' opponent Athanasius, the bishop of Alexandria. He died in *c.*339/40.

He wrote in Greek and was the author of many works. His *History of the Church*, divided into ten books, virtually created ecclesiastical history as a subject. It gives a consecutive story of Christianity from its beginnings until the early fourth century AD. The climax of Christian martyrdoms is reached in Book VIII, which describes the persecution of Diocletian and Galerius. The last book celebrates the Peace of the Church, supposedly established by Constantine. The emperor's eldest son Crispus was still in favour. He was executed in 326, so the publication of the work must have been completed before that date, probably during the year or two immediately preceding it.

If we are to understand Constantine at all, we have to read Eusebius – with a grain of salt. We read much praise of the emperor; and in his *Life*, which was Eusebius' last work, the praise swells into full-scale, highly coloured, romantic encomium, marred further by interpolations and additions. These eulogies are echoed in another work, the *Praise of Constantine*. The ruler appears as a man of superhuman qualities, directed by God. And Eusebius, much too hopefully, believed that Constantine had created unity – not only unity between church and state, but unity *within* the church as well. In his *History of the Church* he appends imperial letters which showed how disgusted and horrified Constantine was by the divisions he had proved unable to prevent.

Unfortunately, however, Eusebius was not only a mediocre stylist but a depressingly unobjective historian.[2] Despite his occasional touches of scholarly caution, and his refusals from time to time to believe improbabilities and lies (notably in the matter of Constantine's 'vision'), he falsified the emperor into a mere sanctimonious devotee, which he was not, and showed himself guilty of numerous contradictions and dishonest suppressions, and indeed erroneous statements of fact, or untruths. For, even if not deliberately fraudulent, Eusebius was indifferent to precision, for example in relation to chronology, and his quotations from sources are often inaccurate and garbled.

Eusebius was learned enough, but incapable of assimilating what he had learnt. But no matter, for the works that he wrote were, in fact, intended as colourful romances, and that is what they were. However, he not only lacked insight but the results of his efforts were dull. Nevertheless, he himself was not altogether unaware of his own deficiencies; and, besides, these faults and prejudices are by no means useless to modern students of the period, for his attitudes are likely to have been much the same as the attitudes of many of his Christian contemporaries, and consequently reveal what went on in their minds: what Eusebius thought about the emperor was not very different from what the bishops of his day were also thinking, so these thoughts are valuable to the historian.

Moreover, his creation of ecclesiastical history (under various influences, but written mainly for the east) was a massive achievement. The first edition of his *Church History*, containing Books I–VII, was published in c.295 (or 303 or 312), the second (revised and extended, with VIII and IX) in c.313–14, the third (containing ten books) in c.315/17, and the fourth in c.325. The last edition shows a sharp transformation of Licinius from hero to villain (though Eusebius left his earlier encomia unaltered).

The *Life of Constantine* (containing edicts which have now been proved genuine by papyrus discoveries)[3] was published after Constantine's death, and remained unfinished when Eusebius died (hence doublets, fictitious reduplications and irrelevancies). Though extremely valuable, it is well on the way from biography to hagiography. *Praise of Constantine* and *On Christ's Sepulchre*, though joined in the 'Tricennial Oration', are, in fact, two separate speeches.

Like Constantine himself, Eusebius attacks divisive Christian schematics. He has been interpreted as the emperor's chief theological adviser before and after the Council of Nicaea (328), but against this it has been argued that he really did not know Constantine very well, and met him on only about four occasions.

Lactantius (*c*.240–320) came from north Africa, and was a pupil of Arnobius, a Christian apologist. Under Diocletian he was summoned to the imperial capital Nicomedia (Izmit) to teach rhetoric there. It is uncertain when he was converted to Christianity, but he was a Christian by 303, and lost his academic position when persecution of the Christians began in that year. He remained in Nicomedia till 305, and then moved to the west; in *c*.317 he became tutor to Crispus, the eldest son of Constantine.

Lactantius wrote numerous works on various subjects, but only Christian writings survive. His *Divine Institutions* (*Divinae Institutiones*, *c*.303–13), in seven books, are dedicated to Constantine, whom he saw as the embodiment of traditional virtues and may have accompanied in Gaul in 318–19 (perhaps they had met when Lactantius was summoned to Nicomedia). The *Divine Institutions* were intended to be a refutation of all opponents of Christianity, past, present and future – and, in the process, the work emphasizes the indissoluble union of philosophy and religion. *On the Anger of God* (*De Ira Dei*, 314?) demonstrates, against certain philosophers, that anger was a necessary element in God's character – a belief which was also held by Constantine, who, as we shall see, went continually in fear of this wrath.

On the Deaths of the Persecutors (*De Mortibus Persecutorum*) is probably an authentic work by Lactantius, in spite of arguments to the contrary. It has been attributed by some to *c*.310, or may have been written in 313 and finished late in 314, or was entirely written before and during the winter of 314/15, or a little later, perhaps at Nicomedia. It is a pamphlet designed to show how all persecutors of the Christians, and particularly those of Lactantius' own times, came to a bad end, and how good prevails over evil, God over the

Devil. The work displays a savagely vengeful tone (much more so than his other writings), and, although accurate in many of its facts, must be suspected of having tailored and distorted others.

Lactantius' violent hostility to paganism overflowed into secular affairs, so that in retrospect he attacked Diocletian's tax system, for example, as ruinous. His work is favourable to Licinius, and *may* originally have been intended as propaganda on his behalf. It does not show much philosophical knowledge or ability, and has little of importance to say on Christian doctrine or institutions.

Orosius, a Spanish presbyter, fled before German invaders, the Vandals, to Africa in 414 and became a pupil of St Augustine, at whose request he wrote a seven-book Christian chronicle, the *Histories against the Pagans* (*Historiae Adversus Paganos*), from the creation of the world to the story of Rome, which he pursues until the year 417. He wrote to contradict the pagan view that conversion to Christianity was the cause of the empire's disasters.

Socrates Scholasticus (*c.*380–*c.*450), a lawyer of Constantinople, continued Eusebius' *History of the Church* from 305 to 439, trying to give an objective account based on documents and first-hand testimony. He made some bad mistakes and did not always understand theological issues. But he is generally sensible and straightforward, plain in style, interesting for his lay outlook (for instance, his dislike of episcopal squabbles), and useful because of his quotation of sources verbatim. In principle, he saw the necessity of relating ecclesiastical to secular affairs: though he did not always succeed in doing so effectively.

Sozomen (died *c.*AD 450), another Constantinopolitan lawyer (from near Gaza), wrote a history of the church from 324 to 439 (the conclusion seems to be lost). It depends heavily on Socrates, whom he never mentions, and resembles him in style and content, except that he is less critical but a better stylist and is able to offer a certain amount of additional information, particularly on monasticism.

Theodoretus (*c.*393–466) became a monk and bishop of Cyrrhus (Kurus) in northern Syria. His *Church History* from Constantine to 428, dealing with the lives of ascetics, contains some valuable material. The *Excerpta Valesiana* are two historiographical texts, which owe their name to H. Valesius, who edited them in 1636. Their authors were once again Christians. The first *Excerptum*, dating from the fifth century, offers a sketch of the life of Constantine, which goes back to *c*.350. (The second, of sixth-century date, deals with the period 474–526.)[4]

There are also certain other Christian historians who ought not to be left out of account. Philostorgius (*c*.368–430/40), a Cappadocian, compiled a continuation of Eusebius' *Church History* to 425. It is not extant, but was epitomized by Photius in the ninth century. Johannes Laurentius Lydus (died *c*.490) described governmental posts. Evagrius (*c*.536–600) wrote a *Church History* covering the period from 431 to 594. George Cedrenus wrote a *History* up to 1057. Johannes Zonaras' twelfth-century *Universal History* went as far as 1118. In addition, *Lives* of Constantine abounded, many of them full of unreliable legends.[5]

There are also twelve *Panegyrics*, in Latin, which give a clear picture of the western view of the Tetrarchic system of Diocletian and what followed. IV(X) is Nazarius' speech to Constantine (in his absence) on an imperial anniversary. V and VI, again to Constantine, are by anonymous Gallic orators, speaking at Augusta Treverorum (Trier). VII, delivered at the same place, is addressed to Maximian and Constantine, on the occasion of Constantine's wedding to Maximian's daughter Fausta. XII(IX) is an anonymous orator's eulogy of Constantine, again at Augusta Trevirorum, after his defeat of Maxentius at the Milvian Bridge. The *Panegyrics*, composed in the rhetorical schools of Gaul, were ceremonial, theatrical, cloyingly fulsome set-pieces, flattering Constantine to the point of adulation. Nevertheless, they furnish important facts about him and his life.

Nor were these the only literary source, apart from historiography, from which one can derive information about Constantine. For example, on the Christian side, Publilius Optatianus Porphy-

rius, too, dispatched from exile (before 325) his own verse encomium to Constantine, and after his recall became prefect of Rome.
His poems are full of ingenuities, such as acrostics, and were
pressed into the shapes of water-organs, altars and so on; it is
unfortunate that Constantine expressed his approval of such
feeble trifles.[6]

Optatus of Milev, in the time of Valentinian I (364–75), wrote
against the Donatist 'heretics', and their own case is presented in
the *Sermo de Passione Donati* and the *Donatist Acts of Martyrs*. Hilary of
Limonium (Poitiers; died 367) and Gregory of Nyssa (between
Ancyra [Ankara] and Caesarea [Kayseri]; died 395) were bishops
who wrote against another 'heresy', that of the Arians; and another
bishop was Synesius, who infused his Christianity with Neoplatonism. Bishop Athanasius (*c.*295–373) wrote voluminously, as did
his opponent Arius, founder of the movement mentioned above.

There is a good deal of relevant legislation in the *Codex Theodosianus* of Theodosius II (438) and the *Codex Justinianus* of Justinian
I, supervised by Tribonian (534).

And for those who want a deliberate statement of Constantine's
point of view there is his coinage. His coins, and medallions, offer
a wide diversity of types and inscriptions showing (though with
due caution, because he did not want to cause too much offence)
what he wanted his people to think he had done and what his
policies were, and putting forward the ostensible keynotes of his
actions.

His successful civil wars are mentioned only in the most general
terms (since the killing of Romans by Romans was not a popular
theme), by reference to 'blessed calm', 'perpetual peace' and so
on.[7] But emphasis is laid upon his victories against the northern
'barbarians', which were not as notable or final as the coins and
medallions liked to indicate.

Constantine's dynastic hopes for his sons also receive full
numismatic treatment, though without, of course, providing any
explanations why his oldest son Crispus so suddenly disappeared
from the coinage – after his father had arranged for him to be put

to death. The coins and medallions of the period also display a very wide variety of Constantinian portraiture, mostly adhering to the more or less hieratic interpretations displayed by portrait-busts, though with occasional touches of realism.

As for the reverse types, how far can they be ascribed to the emperor's direct decision? At least the general instructions must have been issued by high authority, perhaps at the level of the praetorian prefects.[8] Mint history is a significant historical instrument, and so is the degree of attention (or sometimes deliberate lack of it) which emperors producing coins afforded to their colleagues. Issues inscribed 'Constantinopolis', at the mint of Rome, deserve special attention, and so do those of transient Augusti (such as Aurelius Valerius Valens and Martinian under Licinius) and rebels (such as Domitius Domitianus against Diocletian, and Domitius Alexander against Maxentius).

An even more probing view of what Constantine thought, and wanted to be seen to be thinking, is supplied by the surviving range of his own edicts, not to speak of his letters – which he utilized to deliver orders and impose novel principles, as had rarely been done before. Certainly, many of these documents may have been drawn up for him by members of his secretariat and other advisers (such as Ossius of Corduba [Cordova], a good Greek scholar), because Constantine's own Greek was not too good and he had not the time to polish his Latin up to official standards. Nevertheless, these edicts and letters may sometimes have been written in his own hand,[9] and, in any case, manifestly reflect his points of view. In particular, they have a lot to say about his attitudes to religion.

His *Oration to the Assembly of Saints*, probably delivered at Antioch in 325, is a key document; and it is the most extensive surviving statement by any emperor between Marcus Aurelius (161–80) and Julian (361–3). This *Oration*, like Constantine's other utterances, shows how keen he was to achieve imperial unity, and how contemptuous and impatient of the theological dissensions that made this impossible. The *Oration* also confirms his conviction that he himself was a man, *the* man, of God, who spoke to him directly, he believed, and told him what he must do. And it shows how sure he was that God would be angry with him if he did not do the right thing.

Constantine's outpourings – for, as has been said, these pronouncements bear his own stamp, even if they were trimmed by others – indicated, or concealed, a personality which, as will be suggested elsewhere, could be reserved and devious. Moreover, his literary style, even after such trimmings had taken place, emerges not only as stiff and clumsy, but also as more than a little muddled, as in this letter of 330:[10]

Perhaps it may appear a mystery to you, what on earth this prologue to my address means.... From the collision of the disputants sparks and flames result. As I would please both God and yourselves and as I would like to enjoy your prayers, I love you and the haven of your gentleness.

Since you expelled that source of corruption, you have brought in concord in its place by your usual goodness, planting a secure trophy, running a celestial course towards the light, and, so to speak, with an iron rudder. For this cause, take on board the incorruptible cargo; for all that defiled the ship is bailed out like bilgewater.

All the sources that have so far been mentioned are unsatisfactory, because they concentrate too much on giving us Constantine's own point of view. His own utterances and coins and medallions, of course, do this quite directly, if carefully. And the literary sources that were mentioned earlier display similar attitudes, from a simple enough motive, because they are pro-Christian, and acclaim him as the first Christian emperor – who could therefore do no wrong.

Conversely, and just as simply, there is an array of sources that maintain he could do no right – for the same reason, because he made Christianity the religion of the empire – and they are, of course, the work of writers who are pagans.

On this pagan side, Libanius (314–*c.*393) was a Greek rhetorician and man of letters who became professor of rhetoric at his native Antioch (354) under the Christian emperor Constantius II

(337–61), but greatly admired Constantius' pagan successor Julian the Apostate (361–3; whose *Caesars* have interesting criticisms of Constantine). Nevertheless, the Christian emperor Theodosius I (379–95) granted Libanius the honorary title of praetorian prefect.

Julius Firmicus Maternus (who became a Christian only in later life) wrote a rather confused and turgid treatise on astrology – which he identified with sun-worship – called the *Mathesis*, in eight books (334–7). Themistius from Paphlagonia (*c.*317–88), a pagan who opened a school at Constantinople, delivered official speeches and wrote paraphrases of philosophical doctrine. A pagan who strongly criticized Constantine was Eunapius (*c.*345–*c.*420), a Greek from Sardes (Sart) who wrote *The Lives of the Sophists* – of which he was one. An admirer of the pagan emperor Julian the Apostate (361–3) and, like Julian, a convinced opponent of Christianity, he wrote to defend the old pagan religion. His *History* contained fourteen books, covering the period from 270 to 404; it is lost, except for fragments.

Another pagan was Aurelius Victor – governor of Pannonia Secunda (under the anti-Christian emperor Julian the Apostate, 361) and prefect of the city of Rome (389) – who published *The Caesars*, from Augustus to Constantius II, based on Suetonius. His sources are useful, and he does not copy them slavishly, but the observations which he intersperses, notably on literature and morality, are banal; and he is too interested in prodigies.

Zosimus wrote at the beginning of the sixth century. A Greek historian who held senior official posts, he wrote a *New History* (*Historia Nova*) of the Roman empire from Augustus to AD 410, although his use of sources is hurried and careless. A pagan, like Eunapius, on whom he draws, he sees the decline of the empire as a consequence of its rejection of the pagan religion. He is therefore favourable to Julian and hostile to Constantine, his enmity to whom spills over into criticism of some of that emperor's non-religious measures, for example in relation to the army. Edward Gibbon, therefore, accurately enough, described Zosimus as the exact opposite of Eusebius.[11]

Among the writers who have been summarized here it is hard to find many who are impartial to Constantine, because, as has been seen, they either welcome his conversion to Christianity or deplore it.

Some attempt at impartiality, however, was made by the Latin author Ammianus Marcellinus (*c.*330–95) – from whose distinguished history, a continuation of Tacitus, a narrative of the period from 353 survives – and by another Latin historian Eutropius, who was in an unusually good position to adopt a balanced viewpoint because he had taken part in the Persian campaigns of the pagan Julian and had then served the Christian emperor Valens (364–78) as a senior official (*magister memoriae*). Eutropius' judgment of Constantine, therefore, as far as it goes, is impartial. It appears in his survey of Roman history (*Breviarium Ab Urbe Condita*), a work of ten books covering the story of Rome down to the death of the emperor Jovian (364). This *Breviarium* was destined to become a favourite in schools. But, although it was based on a series of imperial biographies (now lost), as well as being founded, to some extent, on personal knowledge, its independent value is limited to the filling of a few small gaps in our information.

This brief survey confirms what was said earlier: that our sources for Constantine are wholly inadequate, a poor lot. Although, as we have seen, a few writers were relatively impartial (though not very distinguished), the inadequacy of the rest was largely due to the fact that his religious attitudes biased them either for or against him. For religious feelings among such writers and their readership were intense, and biased the historical record: without a great deal of regard for the truth. That is to say, falsification and the creation of legends were freely mobilized to buttress whatever point of view one chose to maintain. The modern student of history, then, has to do everything that he or she can to find out what really happened: by scrutinizing documents, by trying to see through the prejudices of writers in order to recover the historical core beneath, and by discounting the insincerities and untruthfulnesses of panegyrics and the personal attacks which formed their counterweight. Even so, however, the general concentration on religious aspects means that we are usually left in the dark about secular developments – which are, therefore, peculiarly hard to reconstruct.

So Constantine's reign confronts the historian with a singular challenge. What sort of man was he, and what did he achieve? That is what we have to find out: by piecing together whatever material we can track down, and reading between the lines of what the ancient historians and other writers say.

CHAPTER 2:

THE RISE TO SUPREMACY

THE DATE of the birth of Flavius Valerius Constantinus (Constantine the Great), like so much else, is disputed.

What we do know is that his birthday was on 27 February of some year or other. But whether that year was *c.*280 (282?) or *c.*272 (273?) remains uncertain. On the whole, however, the earlier date can be favoured. The later alternatives were supported by Constantine's panegyrists and admirers, who succumbed to the influence of his own propaganda, since he wanted to stress his youthfulness at the time of his accession in 306. However, this looks rather like an invention or adjustment, since there is more to be said for the view that he was an older man, born in *c.*272 or 273. Admittedly this interpretation is based on evidence that is not contemporary, but it is rather solid, as most scholars nowadays agree: almost all the secure information about his age at his death presents him as between sixty-two and sixty-five years old, which takes us back to the years immediately following 270. That, then, was probably the time when Constantine was born.

His birthplace, too, has been variously stated. Naissus (Niš), in Upper Moesia on the River Nišava nine miles from its junction with the Margus (Morava), is the favourite candidate – named for this distinction by Firmicus Maternus – the principal argument to the contrary being the suggestion that the place was chosen, retrospectively, for this role because it had been the site of an alleged famous victory (over the Goths) by Claudius II Gothicus (269), whom, as we shall see later, Constantine subsequently and fictitiously claimed as an ancestor. But it is possible to turn that argument upside down, and to suppose that one of the reasons why Constantine selected Claudius Gothicus as his alleged ancestor was just because Claudius had won his alleged victory (which Constantine claimed he had repeated) at Constantine's own birthplace: which Naissus seems to have been.

His father Constantius I Chlorus, however, came from a more easterly region of the same area, subsequently known as Dacia Ripensis. A powerful, stout, rough and red-faced man, Constantius could not boast an 'aristocratic' origin, as flatterers maintained later, but was the son of a goat-herd and of a freedman's daughter. At first an unsophisticated soldier, later he became an officer and pursued a distinguished military career, rising to the position of the praetorian prefect and deputy (Caesar) of Maximian (Augustus from 286). Constantius ranked as a 'Roman', but was really a Danubian provincial, like most of the friends of Maximian and Diocletian and their successors. Constantius seems to have been not only a fine general – he put down the usurper Allectus in Britain – but also generous and kind (unless this is a myth), and, despite his own lack of education, he was reported to have had some concern for culture, including philosophy. He was also apparently interested in monotheism. The name of his daughter, Anastasia, suggests Christian sympathies, but one should not accept later claims that Constantius had ever been a fully fledged Christian.

Constantine's mother Helena, supposedly a *stabularia* (a barmaid or landlady of a tavern, perhaps the owner of a guest-house), may not have been married to Constantius I Chlorus – who as a high officer could have found it difficult to marry a non-Roman wife – although some modern authorities refuse to accept this view, out of a pious determination to regard Constantine as legitimate. In their favour it must be conceded that it was the commonest form of abuse to call someone a bastard, even if he was not. Nevertheless, Constantius I Chlorus abandoned or supplemented his connection with Helena promptly enough in 293, when a politically correct marriage to Flavia Maximiana Theodora, the stepdaughter of Maximian, was offered him. We do not know whether he kept Helena with him or not, but Theodora gave him six children (including, as we have seen, Anastasia, a name which has suggested to some that Theodora, as well as Constantius, may have been inclined to Christianity). But Helena, as we shall see later, rose to prominence again in subsequent years as the mother of the emperor Constantine. A head in the Louvre is believed to represent her, and she is portrayed on Constantine's coinage, and perhaps a fresco.[1]

When Constantine was still very young, he was taken to the court of Diocletian. Diocletian, a Dalmatian of humble origin, had risen to be commander of the bodyguard of Numerian (283–4), the younger brother and fellow emperor of Carinus (they had divided the empire between them, like Marcus Aurelius and Lucius Verus [161–9], and Valerian and his son Gallienus [253–60]). Numerian, however, was found lifeless in his carriage, whereupon Diocletian murdered the dead man's father-in-law and praetorian prefect Lucius Flavius (?) Aper, on the pretext that he had been responsible for Numerian's death. Diocletian then defeated Carinus in the valley of the River Margus (Morava), and gained supreme power (284–305).

His classic achievement was to establish the Tetrarchy, dividing the control of the empire between two Augusti and two Caesars. He had evidently decided that the increasing, simultaneous pressure on the frontiers from the Germans in the north and the Persians in the east made it impossible for a single man to dominate the entire situation: whereas from now onwards, after this change, every potential trouble-spot had a commander with imperial authority within a few days' riding. Moreover, the Tetrarchic division, with its military implications, was a safeguard against internal usurpers, of whom, during the past half-century of political upheaval, there had been far too many. As was mentioned above, earlier arrangements had envisaged a twofold division, but Diocletian added two Caesars to the two Augusti so as to multiply the rulership still further.

He himself was a man of unusual administrative talent, and a passion not only for order, which his plans went to elaborate and detailed lengths to secure, but also, in particular, for tradition, which he sought to defend and maintain, as we shall see, by persecuting the Christians. As his fellow Augustus he selected Maximian, from a family of farm labourers near Sirmium (Sremska Mitrovica). While Diocletian reigned at Nicomedia (Izmit) in western Asia Minor, Maximian was made Caesar on 1 March 286 to look after the west. After proceeding to Gaul to suppress the 'bandits' known as Bagaudae (Bacaudae), he became 'the son of the Augustus', and was Augustus himself by the end of the year: the Augustus of the west, reigning at Mediolanum (Milan), while Diocletian was the Augustus of the east, with his capital at Nicomedia (Izmit).

Maximian was an able general, and fought successfully to protect the Rhine frontier, but he did not succeed in defeating the usurper Carausius in Britain (whose successor Allectus was suppressed by Constantius), although Diocletian – since despite the Tetrarchy *coups d'état* by local commanders still persisted – put down Domitius Domitianus (identified with, or supported by, a certain Achilleus) in Egypt (296–7). Nevertheless, Maximian felt able to honour the powerful recruiting base that constituted his homeland by the coin-type 'The Courage of Illyricum' ('VIRTVS ILLVRICI').[2]

Constantine's father Constantius I Chlorus, who (as governor of Dalmatia) had been a very early backer of Diocletian, became Maximian's Caesar in 293, with his headquarters at Augusta Trevirorum. Diocletian's Caesar, based on Sirmium, was Galerius, appointed three months after Constantinus. Born at Serdica (Sofia), Galerius was, like Maximian, the son of a land-worker, and became known as *armentarius*, the herdsman.[3] He proved a tough, arrogant and ambitious right-hand man to Diocletian.

The Tetrarchy has been subsequently described as one of the causes of the eventual downfall of the empire, which it split into four parts, but at the time its establishment seemed a necessary response to crisis, and so probably it was. It was a sort of mixture between elective and hereditary rulership. For, although chosen on grounds of merit (mainly military ability), Constantius I Chlorus and Galerius were married off into the families of their Augusti, Constantius, as we have seen, marrying Maximian's stepdaughter Flavia Theodora – in favour of whom he put Helena away – and Galerius putting away his wife to marry Galeria Valeria, the daughter of Diocletian.

This Tetrarchy, despite later charges against it, was a remarkable, if short-lived, expedient for dealing with the military emergencies of the day. It was primarily based upon Diocletian's reliance on Maximian; and their concord was celebrated on coins, and by panegyrists.[4] But it was Diocletian, the senior emperor, who directed policy, and Maximian who carried it out. And this proved the weakness and death of the system. Its temporary success was due to Diocletian's ascendancy and personality, and once he was gone the Tetrarchy could not last.

Yet it was while this arrangement was at its height that Constantine grew up in the palace of its principal creator, and it exercised an indelible influence on his development and thinking – which was both appreciative and critical of all that he saw. After his father's appointment as Caesar, the boy Constantine had been kept by Diocletian at his own travelling court; it was later suggested that he served a political purpose there, as hostage for his father's continued loyalty. Anyway, Constantine accompanied Diocletian against the usurper Domitius Domitianus in Egypt. And he acquired some education, as well as preliminary training in what a prospective ruler ought to know. Nor need we disagree with Edward Gibbon when he conjectures that, in the process, he learnt the art of keeping his views to himself. Gibbon saw the court of Diocletian, at which Constantine spent his early years, as a school of dissimulation, at which the young man, surrounded by jealous and hostile courtiers, mastered all the skills of deception and duplicity.[5]

When old enough, Constantine became a successful officer (military tribune), serving as a member of the bodyguard first of Diocletian and then of Galerius, under whom he fought against the Persians (297–8), probably accompanying him to the conquered capital Ctesiphon (Taysafun) in Mesopotamia.

Then came the sensational event of Diocletian's abdication, in 305. Perhaps he had decided to take this step before the end of 303. The conjectures that he foresaw a general crash – and hoped by his withdrawal to prevent civil war – and the view of Christian writers, fostered by Constantine himself, that the failure of the persecution of the Christians (of which more will be said later on) played a part in Diocletian's abdication, are both unlikely. And as for the suggestion that Galerius pushed the ailing Diocletian into taking this unprecedented step, it is impossible, at this distance of time, to determine whether it is true or not.

But what is clear is that Diocletian, despite his own retirement, envisaged the Tetrarchy as a permanent institution in which, at approximately twenty-year intervals, the two Augusti were to abdicate in favour of the two Caesars, who would then become Augusti in their turn, and appoint two new Caesars: and so on into perpetuity. It was a vain and hopeless dream, as has already been suggested – since the Tetrarchy had only held together because of Diocletian's predominance. But, evidently, it was a dream in which Diocletian himself believed, buoyed up by his belief that he himself had saved the world, which must now, even after his abdication, bow to his wishes. And so he and Maximian withdrew to what the coinage described as their 'rest', 'QVIES AVGG.' (Augustorum),[6] Diocletian to Spalatum (Split) near Salonae, and Maximian to Lucania in south Italy (the suggestion that Philosophiana [Piazza Armerina] in Sicily was one of the places of his retirement is unlikely).

The Augusti, now, were Constantius I Chlorus and Galerius – who was much the more important of the two. It appears, however, that there was some uncertainty about who the two new Caesars were to be. Lactantius maintained that everyone in Galerius' army expected Constantine, the son of Constantius I Chlorus, to be one of them, and that there was great disappointment and surprise when this turned out not to be so. In the words of Lactantius:

The gaze of all was upon Constantine. No one had any doubt; the soldiers who were present, the military officers who had been chosen and summoned from the legions, had eyes only for him; they were delighted with him, they wanted him, they were making their prayers for him. There was some high ground just under three miles out of the city, on whose summit Maximian himself had assumed the purple, and on which a column had been put up with a statue of Jupiter. It was to this point that they proceeded.

A meeting of the troops was called there, at which the old man [Diocletian] addressed them in tears. He was frail, he said, and was seeking rest after his labours; so he was handing over the imperial power to men who were more robust, and was appointing other Caesars in their place.

There was tremendous excitement on all sides as to what he was going to tell them. Then suddenly he proclaimed Severus and Maximinus [Daia] as Caesars. Everyone was thunderstruck. Constantine was standing up on the platform, and people hesitated, wondering whether his name had been changed. But then in view of everybody Galerius stretched his hand back and drew Daia out from behind him, pushing Constantine away....[7]

Probably Lactantius is exaggerating the melodramatic surprise at this development. Certainly, Constantine was a possible choice for the Caesarship, but there is no particular evidence that Galerius liked him, whereas Flavius Valerius Severus, another Illyrian of undistinguished birth, was Galerius' friend and companion (although he had little practical experience, except as a commander of some military unit), and Galerius Valerius Maximinus II Daia was the son of Galerius' sister.

The mint of Alexandria had betted wrongly, or mirrored an

unsuccessful attempt to push Constantine into action, by calling him 'Caesar' at a premature stage. Perhaps one of the reasons why Galerius rejected him was a disapproval of heredity (he being sonless himself). At the same time, and possibly for the same reason, Diocletian rejected Marcus Aurelius Valerius Maxentius, the son of Maximian and Eutropia, as one of the new Caesars. The mint of Serdica (Sofia) celebrated the new order which had rejected Constantine and Maxentius by calling one of the two new appointees, Maximinus II Daia, 'the prince of youth' ('PRINCIPI IVVENTVTIS').[8]

Constantine, passed over, decided to depart from the east and rejoin his father Constantius I Chlorus in the west. Lactantius tells a highly coloured, too highly coloured, story of how he managed to get away from Galerius' court:

A message soon arrived from Constantius, pleading ill-health and asking that his son be released to him. Galerius delayed, thinking no kind thoughts of the young hostage. Legends describe the plots against Constantine's life, through convenient boars or barbarians, hunts or wars.

At last Galerius consented to his leaving; the congé was official. Taking no chances of the emperor's change of mind, Constantine anticipated a more ceremonious departure by a wild nighttime flight, in his bolt for freedom killing the post-horses behind him and no doubt half killing those he rode himself. When Galerius woke up next day, the bird had flown, and pursuit was impossible.[9]

A lot of this is traditional propaganda (perhaps derived from as many as four different sources), and need not be believed. What is true, however, is that Constantine left Galerius' eastern domains and went to his father Constantius I Chlorus in the west. Probably his journey was anxious, because Severus – who was unlikely to forget that he had made the rejected Constantine his enemy – could have intercepted him while he was on his way.

It may well be true that Constantius I Chlorus, in asking Galerius for his son, 'pleaded ill-health'. Indeed, the Christian writers repeated the story that he was on his death-bed when

Constantine reached him. This cannot be entirely true, since he lived long enough to fight victoriously against the Picts, with Constantine, in Caledonia (Scotland). Yet the account of Constantius' ill-health may not be wholly untrue either, since he did die only a short time after his son's arrival (at Eburacum [York] – of which he had enlarged the fortifications – on 25 July 306).

Thereupon the troops in Britain, following the bad old precedents of such military coups, hailed Constantine as Augustus – perhaps in accordance with his dying father's request, and with the support of a German (Alamannic) king who was present as their ally, Crocus or Erocus. Galerius, although Constantine formally sought his recognition, was not at all pleased with this application, but (hiding his resentment, no doubt) conceded him the rank of Caesar – granting Severus, however, the superior position in the west, as his own fellow Augustus. Constantine, with diplomatic circumspection, ostensibly accepted this arrangement, because he did not yet feel strong enough to dispute it; and the title of 'Caesar', as well as 'Prince of Youth', is accorded to him on coins issued at Augusta Trevirorum and Rome.

But meanwhile, at Rome too, the son of Maximian, Maxentius – who had likewise been passed over (and did not get on with Galerius, although the latter's daughter Maximilla was his wife) – had asserted himself by a rebellion, on 28 October 306. His revolt was prompted, in part, by jealousy of Constantine. And it was also encouraged by the support of the praetorian guardsmen, who were angry because their camp at Rome had been abolished by Galerius: evidently he blamed and feared them because of their taste for emperor-making, whereas Maxentius, on the other hand, now saw the opportunity to regard and treat them as a possible nucleus and demonstration of the 'Romanness' with which he publicly identified himself. Maxentius also used the unpopular taxation policy of the recognized western Augustus, Severus, as a useful stick to beat his rivals with. At first, cautiously, he just called himself *princeps*, but then, very soon afterwards, Augustus.[10]

Even though jealous of Constantine, Maxentius soon appealed

to him for help – and coins show that they extended recognition to one another. Meanwhile Maximian, also, had resumed the throne (which he had so reluctantly abandoned in 305) – allegedly in support of his son Maxentius – and he, too, proclaimed his alliance with Constantine, whom he declared to be yet another Augustus. This proclamation probably took place on 31 March 307 (or possibly on 25 July), though Constantine did not use the title of Augustus until some date late in the year, perhaps 25 December[11] (and subsequently, after he had fallen out with both father and son, he preferred to disregard the event and treat 25 July 306 as the date of his accession, *dies imperii*). To stress further his friendship with Constantine, Maximian gave him his daughter Fausta in marriage (they had been betrothed since 293).

All this proved convenient in 307/8 when Maximian temporarily quarrelled with his son Maxentius, who had refused him obeisance (*adoratio*) – we need not accept the view that the quarrel was only a pretence. As a result of this quarrel, Maximian sought refuge with Constantine, by whom he was duly given shelter. And Galerius, too, not unnaturally turned against Maxentius, when first Severus, on Galerius' instigation, and then Galerius himself, invaded Italy in order to depose him – in both cases in vain.

Severus' invasion in 307 is variously and dubiously told, but what apparently happened was this. Marching south from Mediolanum (Milan), he failed to capture Rome from Maxentius. Then he retired to Ravenna, surrendered to Maximian on the promise of his life (at this point Maximian, now reconciled with Maxentius, resumed the title Augustus), but was put to death at Tres Tabernae on the Via Appia by Maxentius, who took over what remained of his army. As for Galerius' invasion later in the same year, this proved equally unsuccessful, because he halted at Interamna (Terni), out of nervous fear of Constantine, and then had to retreat.

It is uncertain, however, how Constantine, in fact, had reacted to these two setbacks in Italy, suffered successively by Severus and Galerius. But it does seem clear that he avoided helping Maxentius to crush them (mindful, no doubt, that his father Constantius I had seen himself as the spiritual father of Severus, named Flavius Valerius like himself), so that both were able to withdraw; and indeed Maxentius himself refrained from pursuing them as they retreated, perhaps owing to the influence of his wife Maximilla, who, as we have seen, was Galerius' daughter.

Despairing, in consequence of these failures, of a military solution, Galerius next proceeded to summon the various leaders (other than Maxentius) to the Conference of Carnuntum (Petronell) on the Danube (18 November 308) – the culmination, probably, of a long period of negotiation. At this conference, Galerius suggested that Diocletian should return to the throne, but Diocletian refused (and died a few years later, probably in 311/12, though some believe that he lived on, until 316).

But otherwise Galerius had his way. He persuaded or compelled the unwilling Maximian to resign for a second time (though Maximian, it was said, thought of killing him). And then thought had to be given to replacing Severus, who, as we have seen, was dead. So what Galerius did, on 26 December 308, was to appoint Licinius in Severus' place, as Augustus in the east. Licinius was a comrade-in-arms of Galerius, but it was a controversial appointment, since Licinius had never served as Caesar. Nevertheless, he was chosen as the second of the two Augusti, in an attempt, apparently, to revive the system of two joint emperors.

This meant, however, that Constantine had to abandon the title of Augustus and become merely Caesar again, with the inducement of the not very distinguished or exciting title of 'son of the Augusti' (*filius Augustorum*), which was also conferred on Maximinus II Daia.[12]

Constantine, for the time being, accepted the title, as a coin of Antioch shows. But both he and Daia resented the expedient and were, indeed, so disconcerted with this whole new situation that they soon claimed to resume the rank of Augustus. Whereupon Galerius was grudgingly obliged to acknowledge their claims, and Licinius, too, did not contest Constantine's self-assertion – which implied the rulership of the west (in its entirety, after Spain came under his control in 308 or 310), with the result that Licinius himself, shut in between Constantine and Daia, was left in control only of the Illyrian provinces (though they formed a valuable recruitment area). As for Constantine, he ignored the consulship which Galerius gave him for 309, and the Sixth Panegyric, delivered at Augusta Trevirorum, did not mention Galerius at all.

In 310 the restless Maximian caused trouble again. As we saw, after breaking with his son Maxentius, he had sought sanctuary with Constantine. But now, while Constantine was away on the Rhine, he rashly revolted against him at Arelate (Arles), annexing the funds that were lodged there, and seized Massilia (Marseille), perhaps hoping to use it as a base for a maritime invasion of Italy. At Massilia, however, he was quickly forced to surrender to Constantine's forces and compelled to commit suicide. His plot against Constantine was said to have been disclosed to the latter by his wife Fausta, who was Maximian's daughter. Maximian's death was described to the public in various contradictory ways, partly mendacious.

Constantine had hitherto laid stress on his connection with Maximian – claiming, indeed, that he ruled legitimately owing to Maximian's recognition – but these new events had obviously discredited the link, which should now be forgotten. True, Maximian's posthumous memory, though assailed by Lactantius, was not permanently vilified by Constantine, who, in 314 and 324, included him among glorious predecessors celebrated by the coinage at various mints, since Constantine wanted, inaccurately, to demonstrate the 'clemency' with which he had treated Maximian. But the immediate aftermath of the latter's revolt and death was not yet the moment for recalling this connection.

So Constantine instead decided to make a shift in his propaganda, and to base his position on something altogether different, in which Maximian had no part. That is to say, he claimed to be the descendant of the emperor Claudius II Gothicus (268–70), as his coins proceeded to proclaim[13] – implying the renunciation of the

Tetrarchy and the creation of a new Claudian and Constantinian dynasty (sometimes described as the Second Flavian House, Vespasian's in the first century having been the first). The claim was entirely fictitious. And the nature of the alleged relationship was even variously stated: it was alternatively declared that Constantine was Claudius II's grandson or grand-nephew – the propagandists did not seem able to make up their minds.

Claudius II had become famous as a great general, who had reputedly begun the revival of the Roman empire by winning a great victory over the Goths at Naissus (Niš) in 268. It seems possible, indeed probable, that he had done nothing of the kind, because the real victor had been his predecessor Gallienus earlier in the same year.[14] But that version was disregarded: and it was Claudius II who had gone down to history as the restorer of Roman unity and discipline. Now Naissus, where he had won this supposed victory, was believed to have been Constantine's birthplace. True, it has been conjectured that the town was said to be his birthplace only because of Claudius' alleged victory there, but, as I have said, it seems equally, or more, likely that Constantine *was* born at Naissus, and that one of the reasons why he chose Claudius II as his ancestor was the supposition (encouraged or even invented by Constantine himself) that Claudius had gained his triumph at the place of Constantine's birth.

In any case, Constantine's proclamation of his descent from Claudius II reveals that he was prepared to disregard one of the main principles of Diocletian's Tetrarchy, which was promotion to imperial status by merit. For from now on, instead, Constantine based his claim to legitimate rule on heredity, which was henceforward held to rank above Tetrarchic considerations – and was stressed by the Panegyrists.

By this alleged descent, Constantine implicitly claimed to be sole emperor. Yet that implicit claim was contested by Licinius, and he too invented an imperial ancestry to justify his claim, asserting that he, for his part, was the descendant of another ruler, Philip the Arab (244–9).[15] As for Maxentius, on the other hand, he, of course, based his rule on his sonship of Maximian. And it was Maxentius, ruling like Constantine in the west, who seemed to him to present the most immediate danger, so that it was against him that Constantine now felt impelled to act.

PART II:

CONSTANTINE AT WAR

CHAPTER 3:

CIVIL WARS

MAXENTIUS was now Constantine's most obvious and gravest enemy. Constantine was the Augustus of the west, and yet Maxentius ruled, independently of him, in Italy, having rebuffed invasions both by Severus (incited by Galerius) and by Galerius, whom Constantine once again did not apparently either help or hinder. Maxentius ruled in north Africa as well, where in *c.* 310 he successfully put down the rebellion of Lucius Domitius Alexander. This man, a Phrygian, may well have been secretly in touch with Constantine, and the latter is likely to have become alarmed by his defeat at the hands of Maxentius, whom he was, therefore, determined to attack quickly before his new African resources made him too strong.

And Maxentius, it would appear, like Constantine, claimed the whole western empire, so that a clash was inevitable. This is not a book about Maxentius, but it may be observed that it is virtually impossible to find out any true facts about him, since he was the defeated foe of Constantine, whose version inevitably prevailed.

Yet something can be said about Maxentius, all the same. His coinage shows that he laid enormous stress on Rome and his own Romanness – not a bad publicity line, since for some decades now emperors had preferred to reign elsewhere, and yet the prestige of the eternal city remained huge. Maxentius' pro-Roman attitude ought to have endeared him to the senate and upper class of Rome, and indeed to the city's population in general. And so ought the fact that he called his son (died 309) Romulus, in honour of Rome and its traditions (the boy's grandmother had been called Romula). Moreover, Maxentius launched an abundant construction programme in and around the city, where his buildings included not only his Circus but the 'Temple of Romulus' (perhaps really of Jupiter, or the audience hall of the city prefect), and a restored Temple of Venus at Rome, which had been burnt down (with the consequence that there was a riot); Maxentius' *cella* still survives.

Yet he managed to lose much of his popularity in Rome all the same, because all this building required money, and so did other aspects of his regime, and these funds were collected by oppressive taxation and seizures of property – accompanied by a shortage of food, since although north Africa, which he had reconquered, proved an invaluable granary for his troops, civilians did not get much of the proceeds.

Constantine and his eulogists, of course, said everything that they could against Maxentius (even suggesting that his father was not Maximian at all, but a Syrian), and liked to see the strife between the two leaders as a battle between Christianity and paganism (represented by vice and sorcery at Maxentius' court). But that is really not quite accurate, since Maxentius was no enemy to the Christians. Early in his reign, however, he had treated them rather well, and they had quite liked him. For example, he annulled the decrees of Diocletian and Galerius which had prompted their persecution (and did the same in north Africa, after he had defeated Domitius Alexander). When the papacy was disputed, he settled the matter as a mere internal police problem, rather than a pretext for heavy-handed intervention. And when a new pope was finally appointed, Maxentius gave him back the churches and cemeteries which Diocletian had seized.

Nevertheless, in the end the Christians were not, apparently, sorry to see the end of Maxentius: he seems to have alienated many of them, probably because (like others) he blew hot and cold about Christianity, and because Constantine outbid his claims to be its protector.

After the conquest of north Africa, Maxentius had issued coins for his deified father, their period of hostility forgotten. His relations, however, with other Roman rulers who were still living presented delicate problems. After the death of Galerius in 311 he drew closer to Maximinus II Daia (for whom he had already coined in 306) – because Constantine and Licinius had shown signs of a closer relationship binding them to each other, and Maxentius felt that the two of them were like pincers threatening to crush him.

Thus he and Constantine became enemies. It was really a struggle between two power-hungry men, each asserting heredity (in un-Diocletianic fashion) as his justification, and each making the best of whatever propaganda assets he could mobilize. As has already been mentioned, it is hard to reconstruct a true picture of what Maxentius was like, because he lost the subsequent war, and we only have the winner's version. But, like Constantine, he seems to have been a clever leader, with some innovative ideas. Constantine was possibly the more murderous of the two, even if Eusebius ascribed similar crimes to Maxentius; and indeed Christian and pagan writers alike speak badly of his character – although Lactantius took a favourable view of him, and modern attempts have been made to rehabilitate his reputation.[1]

And so hostilities broke out between Constantine and Maxentius. We are furnished with two versions concerning the outbreak of the struggle,[2] corresponding, it would appear, to successive phases of the publicity issued by Constantine's own entourage. The first version claimed that Maxentius provoked and began the war, on the ground that he needed to avenge the murder of his father Maximian by Constantine. The second version, on the contrary, although still Constantinian, depicts Constantine himself as virtuously initiating the war, in order to liberate Rome from what was described as Maxentius' tyranny.

We can, in fact, legitimately ascribe the outbreak of hostilities to both sides. Maxentius had been jealous of Constantine's successes on the northern frontier, and moreover claimed – as we saw – that he had murdered his (Maxentius') father Maximian, while Constantine, for his part, in addition to his general unwillingness to tolerate another rival ruler in the west (a feeling fully shared by Maxentius), had reason to object to the disfigurement or destruction of his statues which took place in Maxentius' territory.

Both were nervous of the possibility that Licinius, from the east, might intervene to help the other. This was a particular source of anxiety to Maxentius, since Licinius saw himself as the heir of Maxentius' failed enemy Severus. It may well be that Maxentius felt in a better position to gamble on the prospect of a quick war with Constantine at a time when Licinius, as it happened, was fully occupied with the Persians across his eastern frontier. Moreover, Maxentius may well have been worried, surmising, perhaps rightly, that Constantine had made a secret pact with Licinius not to impede his (Constantine's) invasion of the Italian peninsula; so that he, Maxentius, fearing the worst, may have felt that war was inevitable, and that he had better start it and win.

And so, in 312 (more probably then 311, which has also been suggested), Constantine struck across the Alps into Italy. In doing so, he disregarded advice that these hostilities were rash: so that subsequently his flatterers attributed his apparently overbold initiative to divine inspiration. When this move forward made it clear that the final crisis had arrived, Maxentius, unwisely it would seem, failed to occupy the Alpine passes in the hope of blocking Constantine's invasion, but sent his praetorian prefect Ruricius Pompeianus – a man who was loyal to him and unlikely to change sides – from Rome to the north of the peninsula.

Pompeianus fortified the north Italian cities, and constructed or reinforced a line of strongpoints on the Alpine passes, as well as along the Mediterranean and Adriatic coasts. The troops under his command were reinforced by transfers from north Africa, where an extensive army was no longer needed, now that Domitius Alexander had been put down.

The total number of soldiers available to both sides remains uncertain, especially as Constantine's spokesmen (including a flattering Panegyrist)[3] chose to minimize his numerical strength, in order to cast an even more glorious light on the victories that lay ahead. It is true, however, that he did not use all the troops he might have, because he could not leave the Rhine frontier unprotected. It does seem, therefore, that he commanded no more than 90,000 infantry and 8,000 cavalry, and was greatly outnumbered by the forces of Maxentius, although the latter, too, did not commit anything like all his soldiers to north Italy. Instead, he kept many men at Rome under his own command, partly because he needed to keep an eye on Licinius, and partly because Rome was where he himself decided to stay, defending the capital and prepared to create a second line of defence in case Pompeianus' resistance crumbled in the north. But it seemed unlikely that this would happen, especially as Pompeianus' cavalry included mail-clad *cataphractarii* or *clibanarii*, forerunners of the medieval knights, who borrowed their heavy armour and tactics from the Persians and were a formidable force.

Constantine's entrance into Italy through the Cottian Alps (Mont Genèvre) was unopposed. This, as has been said, seems an unaccountable failure on the part of Maxentius, but it was perhaps partly because he was turning his eye, as we have also seen, in an eastern direction, in case Italy was assaulted by Licinius from the east while Constantine came from the north and west.

Maxentius had, however, reinforced the garrison at Segusio (Susa). But Constantine marched on the place and took it by storm. He then refused to allow his army to plunder the town. This was unusual, but also very sensible. It emphasized that he claimed to be fighting a war of liberation, not of conquest, and it encouraged other Italian cities to view his invasion with greater favour.

But then, soon afterwards, there was serious fighting not far from Augusta Taurinorum (Turin) – perhaps between Alpignano and Rivoli. During the engagement, Constantine's centre gave way before the enemy's *clibanarii*, which then, however, found themselves assailed and encircled from the wings by special groups of Constantinian soldiers armed with iron-bound clubs. These units wrought havoc among horses and men alike, and when the *clibanarii* retreated towards Augusta Taurinorum it became clear that their local commander had made a serious error by committing his whole force to fighting outside the walls. For when he tried to withdraw into the town, its citizens shut their gates to him and his fellow fugitives who, in consequence, had to fight outside the walls, with their backs to them, until surrender became inevitable. Once again, Constantine would not permit the city to be looted; and once again this paid useful dividends.

For Mediolanum (Milan), as well as other centres, now surrendered to his invading army, which then, after resting and regrouping, pushed on towards the principal enemy force at Verona, commanded by Pompeianus. Near Brixia (Brescia), Constantine at first nearly experienced a setback, because he miscalculated the strength of the opposition, but in the end, following a battle in which he fought bravely at the head of his men, he broke the strength of the *clibanarii* ranged against him, who fled after a single charge.

Next he advanced on Verona from the west, but realizing that from this side the city was defended by powerful fortifications he decided to cross, by night, the River Atesis (Adige) – which flanked Verona on the other three sides – and thus encircle the city by the traditional kind of siege. Pompeianus waited until Constantine's troops were moving across the river and then attacked, but suffered a heavy defeat, and lost the crossing point. He himself slipped away to collect reinforcements, but when he came up with them again he was killed; in the morning the garrison capitulated, and many prisoners were taken.

In spite of Pompeianus' death stubborn fighting went on, but the Maxentians continued to lose ground. The next towns to fall were Aquileia and, after a short siege, Mutina (Modena). By the middle of October the road to Rome lay open. There Maxentius remained. He had stayed in his capital, the centre of his lines of communication, relying on Pompeianus in the north to keep the invaders away. But now Pompeianus was dead and Constantine was approaching Rome, and Maxentius had to take command himself. What Constantine must have been afraid of was that Maxentius would not leave the capital. For it was too heavily fortified to be easy for him to capture, as Severus had recently found out to his cost, when he was forced to retreat without success. And Maxentius' army, as we saw, was well equipped with grain recently transported from north Africa.

Nevertheless, he decided to move out of the city to confront Constantine. It has been suggested that he first made a stand at Saxa Rubra, on the Via Flaminia as much as nine miles out of Rome, because he could not ignore the local landowners' appeals for protection. But the alleged engagement there does not seem to be historical, the account of it being based on a confusion with events that had taken place 119 years earlier.[4] Nevertheless, Maxentius did come out of Rome. And his decision to do so, in spite of all the reasons why he should stay inside the city, proved completely disastrous – so disastrous that pro-Constantinian writers later ascribed it to divine intervention.

Yet Maxentius, it was said, felt that there were two adequate justifications for taking this catastrophic step. The first was that 28 October, the day of the Battle of the Milvian Bridge that followed, was the sixth anniversary of his accession, and therefore, in his view, a lucky day to force an encounter. The second thing that prompted his departure from Rome, it was asserted, was the fact that the Sibylline Books, which he had consulted, declared that on that day 'the enemy of the Romans would perish'. This advice, which proved, in the end, to mean that Maxentius would be the one to die, was replete with an ambiguity fully worthy of the diplomatic oracular tradition. The story may not be true. But one must not underestimate the ancient reliance on omens and oracles, which Maxentius is likely to have shared.

Nevertheless, his decision to leave Rome could have been prompted by political considerations as well, or instead. For he may have become, by now, distrustful of the attitude of certain Romans. A number of them may, earlier, have supported Domitius Alexander in north Africa. Moreover, when Maxentius visited the Circus Maximus the crowd had shouted that Constantine could not be conquered. So Maxentius may well have felt that if he stayed within the walls of Rome some of its inhabitants might be willing to betray him, so that his resistance would be weakened and undermined. Anyway, he did decide to leave his capital, and to fight the decisive battle against Constantine outside the walls of the city.

This engagement took place near the Milvian Bridge (a stone bridge since AD 109) spanning the River Tiber – *across* the bridge, that is to say on the north bank of the river, the bank away from Rome, which was two miles away to the south. Maxentius had destroyed the bridge before Constantine ever arrived, so as to leave his enemy no possibility of eventually marching over it to Rome. But in its place he himself constructed another bridge of boats, consisting of two halves linked by iron bolts which could be unfastened if the enemy tried to cross; and between the river and city he built a network of trenches and forts, to cover his own retreat into Rome should this, eventually, become necessary.

What proved fatally mistaken, however, was Maxentius' decision to move north of the Tiber at all. True, there was a ferocious struggle, in which his praetorian guard and Constantine's Gallic cavalry (led by Constantine himself) were prominent, but in the end Maxentius' left flank was turned, and his troops were forced back to the Tiber. The bridge of boats broke under their weight, and many soldiers fell into the river and were drowned. Among them was Maxentius himself. His body was recovered, and his head, mounted on a lance, was carried into the city, when Constantine entered it in triumph.

Although the whole engagement had shown Maxentius to be a less than competent general, for Constantine it had been a wonderful, brilliant campaign. The victory was pronounced a miracle, in line with the traditions of other imperial military 'miracles', notably the rainstorm which had 'enabled' Marcus Aurelius' Legio XII Fulminata to defeat the Quadi in AD 172. Reference was also made to the miraculous appearance of the Dioscuri at the Battle of Lake Regillus in *c.*496 BC, and to the divine intervention which drowned the armies of the Pharaoh seeking to prevent Moses' crossing of the Red Sea, in order to lead the Israelites out of bondage.

Moreover, although one would not gather the fact from the coinage, this victory over Maxentius made Constantine's name more effectively than his various struggles on the Rhine and Danube. And Constantine tried to show the Romans, after he had entered their city, that his 'Romanness' was no less than that of Maxentius. For, despite the delicate rarity of direct civil war references on coins, he allowed some to be inscribed 'RECV-PERATORI VRBIS SVAE', 'to the Recoverer of his own city',[5] and issued a series of later pieces with the inscription 'VRBS ROMA', 'the city of Rome';[6] while a painting of Constantinian date (*c.*325–330?) in the Palazzo Barberini shows a frontal seated figure of Roma, and there were many traditions of Constantine's friendly relations with Pope Silvester I (314–35).

Moreover, besides calling himself 'liberator' of Rome and Italy, Constantine had now become master of the entire west. Yet the eastern provinces still remained outside his control, in the realms of Maximinus II Daia, who was hostile, and of Licinius, who had annoyed Daia by becoming engaged to Constantine's half-sister Constantia in 310 – and marrying her in 313 – an act which Licinius regarded as virtually an indication that he, with Constantine's agreement, could believe himself to be heir to the western empire. Daia had another reason, too, for disliking Constantine: when the latter entered Rome, the senate proclaimed him 'Maximus Augustus':[7] first of the three Augusti, the senior emperor.

(Nor, naturally, did this salutation endear him to Licinius, who after the death of Galerius regarded *himself* as the senior Augustus – so that Constantine's new title cancelled out, as far as Licinius was concerned, the amicable effects of his marriage to Constantia.)

However, the immediate problem was that Licinius shared the control of the east with Daia: an arrangement that was precarious, because each wanted the other removed. It proved, in fact, to be Licinius, in 313, who eliminated Daia. Daia's position was already weakened by famine, and Licinius defeated him in a battle at Campus Serenus in Thrace (between Tzirallum and Druzipara) though the engagement lies beyond the scope of this book, since Constantine, although his relations with Daia were cool, did not get himself involved. Anyway, Daia was defeated and lost his life (leaving his memory to be sharply vilified by those who had hated him, including Lactantius, who accused him of womanizing). And, as a result, Licinius ruled over the entire eastern part of the Roman world, from Illyricum to the Euphrates.

What is significant, too, is the singularly ruthless bloodbath with which Licinius was said to have followed up his victory. Before the end of 313, many of Daia's principal ministers had been executed, and the proscription (conducted especially at Tarsus) covered all his relatives as well. Even Galerius' widow Galeria Valeria was put to death, and Galerius' mother-in-law Prisca, who was the widow of Diocletian. Except for Constantine, there was no one left to compete with Licinius.

And an event now occurred, in 316, which precipitated the rupture between the two rulers. What had happened was that Constantine, setting out to seem friendly, had designated as Caesar a certain Bassianus who, although married to another half-sister of Constantine, Anastasia, was closely associated with Licinius. But the 'friendship' between the two leaders – which may not have gone very far, since there are no coins of Bassianus – soon broke down. For it was declared that Bassianus' brother

Senecio (the man who was largely responsible for Bassianus' close link with Licinius) was behind a plot against the life of Constantine, possibly in association with the latter's half-brothers, the sons of Constantine I Chlorus by Theodora: and Licinius, justly or unjustly, was accused of instigating the plot. Caught, it was said, red-handed, Bassianus was confronted with his guilt and put to death.

But it is doubtful whether the 'conspiracy' was authentic; it seems more probable that Constantine just wanted Bassianus out of the way. For Constantine already had a son of his own, Crispus, who in his view would really be preferable to Bassianus as his heir. And moreover, his current wife, Fausta, was now pregnant (the child eventually born was Constantine II), so the desirability of having Bassianus as Caesar became even smaller still. In other words Bassianus, even though he was Constantine's brother-in-law, assumed the position of a rival to Constantine's own sons, and was therefore unwelcome and expendable. And this, of course, made him subject to attack. Possibly he had said something unwise, or had even been reported, not necessarily with accuracy, as uttering potentially seditious words. He may have been totally innocent; but perhaps he had people around him who were not. Anyway, he was charged with sedition and executed. It looks rather like the death of Maximian all over again – a rival killed, and killed, it was said, because he had planned to assassinate Constantine.[8]

Should the 'plot' – if there was one – have succeeded, Licinius would then have been the one and only emperor, with Bassianus as his Caesar in the west. However, the secret plan – so Constantine claimed – was detected. And after he had had Bassianus put to death, he demanded that Senecio, too, who was in Licinius' territory, should be handed over. Licinius, however, refused, and the repaired relationship between the two leaders was broken:[9] all the more so because Constantine's coins declared that he himself was 'ruler over the whole world' ('RECTOR TOTIVS ORBIS').[10]

It was inevitable, therefore, that before long the two men

should clash with one another. So in the same year, 316, it would appear (some prefer the date 314, but probably wrongly – though the dating of all these events is much disputed), Licinius moved his staff up to the borders separating their territories. War was evidently imminent, and became inevitable when, at Aemona (Ljubljana in Slovenia), Licinius did not save Constantine's statues from being hurled to the ground. Numbers are unreliable, but it was reported that Licinius had 35,000 infantry and cavalry under his command, and Constantine 20,000 – these troops apparently consisting, for the most part, of the two emperors' personal bodyguards. Licinius occupied a useful defensive position on dry ground in the middle of the Hiucla marshes in the valley of the Savus (Save) – between that river and the Dravus (Drave) – near Cibalae (Vinkovci), on the road leading to Sirmium (Sremska Mitrovica).

Nevertheless, it was Constantine – although the odds seemed to be against him – who moved to the attack: thus allowing his enemy to brand him as the aggressor. What Constantine did was to launch an assault under cover of darkness. The consequent, unpleasant battle was fought before dawn on the morning of 8 October 316. Licinius proved the loser, after failure to resist a cavalry attack, and 20,000 of his infantrymen were said to have been killed. He rapidly retreated eastwards, pursued by Constantine, and rejoined the main body of his army at Hadrianopolis (Edirne, Adrianople) in Thrace. There he prepared to stand fast, having, on the way, at Serdica (Sofia), declared that Constantine had been deposed and that his own frontier commander (*dux*), Gaius Aurelius Valerius Valens, was appointed Augustus in his place (a few of his coins have survived – not all forgeries, as has sometimes been stated).

Meanwhile Constantine had advanced to Philippopolis (Plovdiv) a hundred miles west-north-west of Hadrianopolis, and there envoys came from Licinius to negotiate with him after all. Licinius' intention was probably to keep him talking until his own forces in Asia Minor could be moved over into Europe to help defeat him.

But, if so, that plan did not work. For before long the two confronting armies lurched into a second battle in the plain of Iarba or Arda (probably not Mardia) in the valley of the River Hebrus (Maritsa), which lay between their two headquarters. This time the engagement was not decisive, and Licinius slipped away northwards in the direction of Beroe Augusta Trajana (Stara Zagora). But, although Constantine was slow to notice that this had happened, Licinius' withdrawal proved a serious strategic error, because it gave his enemy an almost unopposed south-eastern march to Byzantium (Istanbul), which he duly captured.

This meant the end of the war, because Europe and Asia alike were now at Constantine's disposal. Yet he still could not afford to relax, since Licinius and his army remained in his rear. So when Licinius once again sent him a deputation, he received it with suitable formalities – though he kept its leader, Mestrianus, a hostage, until the first two of his demands were met. These were, one, the deposition of Aurelius Valerius Valens, and, two, his own recognition as Maximus Augustus, the senior emperor. These demands were both accepted. Licinius not only deposed Valens, but, for good measure, executed him as well.

And a territorial adjustment was arranged at Serdica on 1 March 317, according to which, although Licinius remained master of the east, he ceded a large part of the Balkan peninsula to Constantine. He kept Thrace, but gave up half of Moesia and the whole of Pannonia: five provinces altogether, comprising a major recruiting area, and including the mints of Siscia (Šišak) and Thessalonica (Salonica) – although Licinius could, perhaps, comfort himself by reflecting that the provinces he had lost were too remote from his headquarters and capital to have been readily defensible in the event that war was renewed.

This territorial change meant that the Balkan region was now divided – as it is, increasingly, today. It also meant that Constantine was now unmistakably the senior emperor (as Licinius had conceded). On these terms, friendly relations with Licinius were ostensibly restored; and Constantine might claim that one of his favourite numismatic slogans, 'BEATA TRANQVILLITAS',[11] was justified. Moreover, the new friendship was celebrated by the declaration, in 317, that the sons of the two emperors were Caesars. Licinius' son, now briefly given the additional name of Constantine,[12] was the infant Licinius Licinianus (born in *c.*315), whose mother was his Syrian concubine Mamertina. Constantine's sons were now Crispus, whose mother was Minervina, and the newborn Constantine junior (Constantine II), born to Fausta.

This seemed an amicable enough arrangement. Nevertheless, a renewed deterioration of the relationship between the two rulers was soon on the way. It is illustrated by the lists of Roman consuls. In 315 the two emperors themselves had shared the consulship together; it was the fourth occasion that each of them had held the office. But now things looked distinctly different. Not only had the two protagonists fought a serious war, but Constantine's announcement for 320, in which the consuls were to be himself and his second son of the same name, seemed directed against Licinius, who was excluded. And even more unfriendly was his declaration that the consuls in 321 were to be his own two eldest sons, Crispus and Constantine junior – once again without any mention of Licinius Licinianus, the son of Licinius, who on this occasion refused to allow the publication of the Constantinian consuls' names in his provinces. Henceforward, the two emperors, in their appointment of consuls, went their separate ways: their revived 'friendship' was no longer in existence.

And meanwhile, in 317 or 318, Constantine had moved his capital eastwards from Sirmium, where he had been residing up to now, to Serdica – a centre well placed for the surveillance of the Thracian territory which was Licinius' surviving outpost in Europe. A renewal of the war between the two men now appeared inevitable, and followed after a short interval, in 324. The war was between the two men who shared the leadership of the Roman world, and found the presence of the other uncomfortable and intolerable, since each wanted the entire empire for himself. Constantine's supporters made out that it was a religious war, of

Christianity against paganism: but Licinius only incurred the reputation of being anti-Christian because he suspected his Christian subjects of being too friendly to Constantine. This meant that Constantine's favour to the Christians made it almost imperative for Licinius to take the opposite course. At the same time, however, he did try to please both parties – without much success, as the adverse judgment of the pagan Julian the Apostate suggests. Nevertheless, despite Julian's verdict, it had been true that the ultra-pagan Jupiter figured very prominently on Licinius' coinage.

One factor connected with this religious situation was Constantine's alliance with the Armenians (recently Christianized), which Licinius – who had earlier had to fight on that eastern frontier – believed was intended to encircle him; and so he finally did start to harry the Christians near the empire's eastern frontier, and thus gave Constantine a good excuse to become his enemy.

A further serious cause for friction between the two rulers was provided by the northern, Danube frontier. For in 323 the Visigoths had crossed that river into the empire, where they did a great deal of damage. It was Constantine, not Licinius, who threw them back across the Danube. Then he returned to Thessalonica (Salonica), where he was constructing a new harbour. But in order to deal with the Visigoths he had moved over into the Thracian provinces which belonged to Licinius, and Licinius complained (suspecting, indeed, that Constantine had actually prompted the Visigothic invasion, so as to pick a fight with himself). Constantine answered that his incursion had been accidental and that, in any case, it was justified, since it had resulted in the rescue of Roman citizens from their barbarian captors.

Licinius rejected this explanation, preferring to interpret Constantine's action as the preliminary to a full-scale invasion of his own portion of the empire. So he brought most of his army up to Hadrianopolis (Edirne), at the western extremity of his territory. And Constantine, also, took preparatory measures, massing an army on his frontiers with Licinius – not far from his new capital at Serdica – and sending his navy south from Thessalonica, under his eldest son Crispus, to join forces with a transport fleet at the Piraeus, in anticipation of a major war in which both soldiers and ships would be needed.

For a new war was now quite evidently on the way. The first one had been little more than a probe, a 'shadow war' which was merely the preliminary to another. Now that the precarious renewal of 'friendship' had come to nothing, and the time for the second, principal war had arrived, it was clear that it would be the largest for hundreds of years. The forces involved on both sides were substantial. As always, we cannot estimate them with certainty, but it would not be a bad guess to suggest that Licinius commanded 150,000 infantry and 15,000 cavalry, against a Constantinian force of about 120,000 infantry and 10,000 horse – though Constantine compensated for this inferiority by his possession of the Illyrian recruiting ground, which Licinius had been obliged to cede to him after the earlier war.

On 3 July 324 the two armies clashed outside Hadrianopolis, and in one of the biggest battles of the entire fourth century Constantine won. Licinius lost 34,000 dead, and many of the survivors on his side deserted. But he successfully directed a fighting retreat, getting his main force across the River Hebrus (Maritza) by an ingenious feint, and falling back on Byzantium (Istanbul), where both sides prepared for a siege. Licinius, as in the last campaign, declared Constantine deposed, appointing his own Master of Offices Martinian Caesar and then Augustus in his enemy's place,[13] as he had earlier appointed Valens. Martinian was sent to Lampsacus (Lapseki), on the southern shore of the Hellespont (Dardanelles), to collect Licinius' Asian army and bring it up to the coast. And Martinian was also supposed to help Licinius' navy in the adjoining waters of the strait.

For it was there that the situation now developed. Licinius' naval commander Abantus (or Amandus) had charge of 350 warships on the strait, and, against him, Constantine's eldest son Crispus had brought up 200 vessels, including transports, from Greece. Licinius' admiral ought to have been able to stop or destroy them, but, acting weakly on the defensive, he failed to do so. Not contriving either to intercept them *en route*, he did, nevertheless, manage to hold them up for two days near the western entrance of the Hellespont. But he lost heavily in the process. Moreover, on the second night his anchored fleet was wrecked by a storm, and that was the end of him. One hundred and thirty of the Licinian ships were destroyed, and 5,000 sailors were pitched into the sea and drowned. When day broke, the surviving vessels and men of the wrecked fleet surrendered. And Crispus was able to sail on, unimpeded, to Byzantium.

Licinius, after a holding operation to cover the retreat, was compelled to evacuate the city, which Constantine occupied (as he had occupied it in the First Licinian War). After leaving Byzantium, Licinius withdrew across the Thracian Bosphorus to Calchedon (Kadiköy). He had lost his last foothold in Europe. But even Calchedon was too dangerously close to Constantine, who now commanded the sea, and Licinius soon retreated again, in a south-easterly direction, to Chrysopolis (Üsküdar, Scutari), which was on the way to his capital Nicomedia (Izmit). At Chrysopolis he learnt that Constantine, too, had found it possible to cross over to Asia, disembarking in the neighbourhood of Calchedon. So Licinius saw that the time had come to summon Martinian back from Lampsacus to reinforce his depleted army. And, in addition, he ordered up the Visigoth Aliquaca or Alica to fulfil the same purpose (p. 57).

By mid-September 323, Constantine was encamped outside Chrysopolis, and it was here that the decisive engagement took place, on the 18th of that month. He decided to take the initiative, and once again he won an enormous battle. Licinius was said to have lost 25,000 or 30,000 dead, and thousands more broke and ran. He still did not, however, give up the struggle, but moved back to his capital Nicomedia – despite further desertions on the way – with the intention of making a last stand.

Yet this intention was undermined, because of the action of his wife Constantia, the half-sister of Constantine, whom he found waiting for him in his Nicomedian palace. In the course of a single night, we are told, she persuaded Licinius that further resistance would be useless, and on the next day she went to Constantine's camp to negotiate what terms she could. Her efforts were at least successful in saving her husband's life – for the time being – and on that very same evening he dined at Constantine's table, before going off to a comfortable internment at Thessalonica, while Martinian was dispatched to a similar house arrest in Cappadocia.

They were deprived of all their offices, and Licinius' acts were annulled. Nor, in fact, did either of them survive. For they were both executed, probably in spring 325. Later, the Christian historian Socrates Scholasticus asserted that this was because Licinius conspired with the Goths, whereupon the outraged Roman army demanded his execution,[14] with which demand Constantine reluctantly complied. Later still it was again said that Licinius had conspired, but with the alternative tale that he actually escaped to the Visigoths in the Southern Carpathians, but met his death at their hands.[15] But these are fictitious or at best doubtful stories (which even Eusebius does not trouble to include), invented to whitewash Constantine's memory by getting away from the simple fact that, contrary to his original promises, he had the two men killed.

Presumably he felt that while they lived they remained a danger, to himself and the peace of the world – in other words, that they *might* engage in a plot in the future – and that this justified his murderous actions. Moreover, Licinius' son Licinius Licinianus was executed with his father (though his half-brother, legitimized by rescript, survived, only to be reduced to slave status in 336 on suspicion of involvement in the rebellion of Calocaerus in Cyprus, and sent to work in women's quarters at Carthage, or killed).

Licinius' final quarrel with Constantine, and downfall, are illustrated by a remarkable change in Eusebius' attitude to him: Book IX of the *Church History* views him with favour, but in Book X he is a villain. Which version is the more truthful it is hard to tell. For it is as difficult to find out the truth about Licinius as about

Maxentius, and for the same reason, because he was the enemy of Constantine who survived and won, so that the sources favourable to him, and unfavourable to Licinius, are almost all that we have. As regards religion, like Maxentius, Licinius seems, as we saw, to have vacillated and veered, mainly with an eye on Constantine and in order to avoid being worsted by Constantinian propaganda. So our verdict on his religious policy must be neutral.

On the credit side, however, it does appear that he possessed some vigour and discernment, and that he had a genuine interest in the small farmers and the poor and did his best for them – alienating the landed interest, inevitably, in the process, by raising the land tax. He was also said to have 'made the cities flourish'.[16] On the debit side, he was inferior to Constantine as a general, and it looks as though he was tolerant of corruption, inclined to the practice of tying people hereditarily to their land, and self-seeking, ill-tempered, anti-cultural, coldly cruel. In particular, he was believed guilty of a series of horrifying murders after his defeat of Maximinus II Daia. Other national leaders, including Constantine, were likewise murderous, but Licinius' holocaust seems to have been exceptionally bloodthirsty, and left a blot on the character and record that cannot be wiped out.

Weigh the two men against each other as we will, it was Constantine who won, and this is what he had to say shortly afterwards, in obviously one-sided fashion, about the civil wars in which he had been so overwhelmingly victorious:

Who could obtain any good who neither recognizes God the author of good things nor will pay him proper reverence?...

All who dishonoured and neglected justice and knew not the Supreme Power, but dared to subject its faithful followers to injury and irremediable penalties, and did not think themselves wretched in that they inflicted penalties for such a cause....

Their armies have many of them fallen and many turned to flight, and all their array of war has ended in shameful defeat.[17]

Moreover, the serpent or dragon (Satan) on coins of Constantine,[18] the traditional emblem of the powers of darkness, was probably intended to represent Licinius.

And so Constantine was now the only Roman emperor. There had not been a sole, single emperor since the first two years of Diocletian (284–6), before he gave himself a colleague. Now Constantine reigned unchallenged. His title of *victor* was thoroughly and universally vindicated, even though it was in civil rather than foreign wars that he had gained the greatest military distinction (and Julian later commented that his foreign enemies had been less than impressive).[19]

The empire was one and at peace, and Constantine's greatest desire was that it should be a unity. As we shall see elsewhere, it was with this aim in mind that he favoured the Christians. But that proved a snare and a delusion, since the Christianity that he favoured was sharply and irremediably divided, and produced the very opposite to the unity for which he longed: as we shall see in a later chapter.

CHAPTER 4:

FOREIGN WARS[1]

THE NORTHERN frontier of the Roman empire, comprising the lines of the Rhine and the Danube, had presented new and alarming dangers during the period preceding the birth of Constantine. These were displayed in c.AD 263 by the permanent Roman evacuation of the Agri Decumates, the protruding part of Upper Germany, of which the Roman occupation had been intended to shorten communications between the two rivers: but the region had now proved untenable.

In the Rhineland, new German confederacies had been formed, notably the Rhenish Franks (adjoined by Salian Franks, behind whom were the Burgundians) north of the River Menus (Main), and the Alamanni on the Upper and Middle Rhine south of the Menus. The Franks were a league consisting of various tribes, who are first mentioned after c.250, when they showed a desire to break across the Rhine frontier: but they may have appeared on the scene a generation or two earlier. However, in 288 we find the Romans supporting a Frankish king (Gennoboudes), who had sued for peace, as a bulwark against other invaders from further east. The Alamanni, a relatively advanced group which, although the Germans were primarily a warrior society, employed slaves for agriculture (but were convulsed by and immobilized by internal strife, which is impossible, now, to reconstruct), had moved from the banks of the upper River Albis (Elbe) and appeared as a loose confederacy in south-western Germany in around AD 200 (they are first mentioned in 213). It was the Alamanni who impelled the Romans to evacuate the Agri Decumates, although they themselves did not settle the region in any strength until *c.*300. We know something about their habits and movements, because the historian Ammianus Marcellinus happened to be well informed about them.

Under Diocletian's Tetrarchy, Maximian and Constantius I Chlorus were repeatedly active against Franks, Alamanni and other Germans, especially in 285–9 and 300–4. Constantine, in 306, repelled Frankish raids – which were prompted by the desire to take advantage of a change of emperor – and exhibited two captured kings in Games at Augusta Trevirorum (Trier). He also refortified frontier cities, rebuilt the Rhine bridge at Colonia Agrippinensis (Köln) in 307/8, defeated a hostile coalition which sought to take advantage of the war against Maxentius, in 314 constructed a fort on the east bank of the Rhine, spent three years after the first war against Licinius reorganizing and consolidating the frontier, and in the Second Licinian War was helped by the Frankish monarch Bonitus.

We also hear of Roman armies pushing across the Rhine for attacks or counter-attacks against the Bructeri north of the River Rura (Ruhr). And it is clear that Constantine claimed victories over the Alamanni as well. They were celebrated by triumphal Games, recorded on his coinage.[2]

The Germans who did manage to cross the Rhine were mostly not invaders – although some of them were – but displaced persons. Driven in destitution and desperation from their own lands, by the hostilities and raids and plunderings by which the whole region was convulsed, they were not very difficult for the disciplined Roman legions in the frontier area to deal with. A hundred years later, the pressure of Germans on the river frontier was to become perilous and uncontrollable. But in the time of Constantine the Rhine border was still a virtually effective barrier, beyond which death or enslavement were all that awaited those who had managed to penetrate it.

True, Constantine had to raise taxes in the empire in order to confront the Alamanni and Bructeri, and this was obviously unpopular in the empire. But the money was sensibly spent. A good deal of it was employed to maintain a Roman river fleet, and to construct a line of fortresses along the bank of the Rhine, including the camp of Divitia (Deutz), near Colonia Agrippinensis (Köln), where a spectacular bridge was also built, across which the Roman troops could march straight into the heart of Frankish territory.

It was clear that these measures helped to keep the flocks and herds of Gaul safe from being stolen and driven off, and prevented farms and homes from being burnt down by German invaders or 'bandits'. In fact, although nothing was done to scotch the German threat which would be so violently revived in the future, the immediate task of defending the river frontier was easier than it had been for a good many years, because every German tribe or tribal group was at war with its neighbours, or under pressure from the east. For this reason no full-scale invasions of Gaul from across the Rhine occurred for several years, and Constantine's measures of protection seemed almost entirely successful.

It all looked good, and Constantine's triumphal salutations (and his son of the same name was hailed Alamannicus in 330 or 331), and his victorious coin-types, made the most of it. Yet, in spite of the optimistic celebrations, no very important victories were won, and the results were not permanent, since later, in the dying days of Rome – after Valentinian I, too (364–75), had conducted spectacular operations – this Rhine frontier was destined to crumble. All that could be said was that Constantine had stabilized the frontier for a time. But grandiloquent boasts of advancing the frontier to the River Albis (Elbe) were bound to come to nothing, just as they had always come to nothing hitherto.

Constantine really had more reason to fear the Danube than the Rhine frontier – and he knew it. The Via Egnatia, which ran east through the Balkans, was vulnerable. And Constantine rightly appreciated that the *Lower* Danube (Scythia Minor) was the principal danger-point.

We are not however, very well informed about the 'barbarian' activities in the Danube region during this period. 'A great deal of interesting history has been lost for ever along this Danube frontier'[3] – including, very probably, information about German movements that alarmed the Romans, but have not been recorded.

The Carpi, in Rumania (whom Galerius had fought four times), were ceasing to be a direct threat, the last imperial salutation as 'Carpicus Maximus' dating from 317. But the people whom Constantine, above all, had to fear were the Goths. These were people who had begun their migration from the Lower Vistula and Oder and Jutland in the later second century, and completed the movement in *c*.250–60. The victory of Gallienus (or, as was believed, Claudius II 'Gothicus') at Naissus (Niş) in 268 halted the immediate threat from the Goths, but their menace revived, and this renewed threat was now beginning to be, and would increasingly become, the outstanding strategic problem of the empire. However, the Goths largely focused on internal affairs during Diocletian's reign, and the Tetrarchs' policy of playing off mutually hostile 'barbarians' against one another kept them from becoming a very serious menace. Nevertheless, the peril was perceived. It is uncertain whether Diocletian adopted the title 'Gothicus', but the Panegyrists claimed that he and Maximian had forced the Goths to make peace – although this claim was later mocked by Christian writers.

It was, indeed, fortunate for Rome that the Goths, like other Germans, were disunited and disorganized: every geographical unit of Gothic territory had its own separate markets, selling goods to whoever was prepared to buy, whatever race they belonged to.[4] But what was especially crippling for the Goths was that the fragmentation that was so characteristic of them had long extended to political life, for Gothic society normally had no real leader or leaders, no one capable of introducing or enforcing any degree of centralization.

This lack of centralization was particularly apparent in their relationship to the Romans. Local chiefs, strong enough in their parochial environments, competitively desired access to Roman goods, and to the capacity for doling out prestigious largesse which these goods afforded them. As a result, they were not averse to acquiring favourable positions in relation to Roman frontier communities, and often jostled one another, as well as engaging in petty border raids and retaliations against the Romans, in order to gain or seize this type of benefit.

And so the Goths have been described as 'a weak, uncertain wall between the empire and the true barbarians'.[5] Yet, despite their weaknesses, they were, in reality, not all that weak. They had become settled, and were partly Romanized, having assimilated, in particular, Roman military techniques. That is to say, they were not weak enough for Constantine to disregard them. On the contrary, 'unless the whole of the Gothic frontier could be grappled with and held, the old danger was not removed, but only suspended'.[6]

A decisive moment had occurred when the emperor Aurelian, not long after the evacuation of the Agri Decumates, also abandoned Dacia, the modern Rumania, north of the Danube (274). Rich in slaves though the region was, he led the Romans out of it partly because it could no longer be held, and partly because his frontier troops in the area were needed elsewhere, to fight Sassanian Persians and usurpers. After the withdrawal of the Romans from Dacia, while the northern part of that country fell into the hands of a tribe known as the Gepids, its southern portion was occupied by the Visigoths, who settled as far as the River Alutus (Olt) to the west, and the Damastris or Tyras (Dniester) to the north.

The Gepids also helped to divide the Goths, by the end of the third century, into two separate units: the Visigoths (descended, to some extent, from the Tervingi) beyond the Danube,[7] and, farther away from the Roman empire, the Ostrogoths (originating among the Greutungi), east of the Damastris in the Ukraine, where they built up an empire of their own – the walls of Slava Rusa (Libida?) date from the early fourth century. (Later, in the sixth century, the two groups were called 'western' and 'eastern' Goths respectively.)

As for the Visigoths, they had experienced enough contacts with the Roman empire to change and modernize some of their traditional German habits as well.[8] For example, they, or some of them, had become literate: the time was approaching when Ulfilas, who had already visited Constantinople with a delegation in the lifetime of Constantine, would devise a Gothic alphabet to translate the Bible. Moreover, as a prop to the increasing military efficiency they had absorbed by contact with the Roman army, they were learning metal-working techniques from their Sarmatian neighbours. That made for an increase in the Visigoths' wealth, and this was becoming concentrated in the hands of a few of their individuals, who even possessed slaves of their own and lived lavishly, relying upon consumer goods that they were obliged to import – selling slaves as the principal export that they offered in exchange.

Moreover, although the society of the Visigoths maintained its basically tribal structure, there were developments in regard to leadership among them, reducing or eliminating their traditional fragmentation. That is to say, in times of emergency, their tribes now tended to gravitate towards a single leader, and since emergencies were so frequent this leader began to assume something not far short of a durable monarchical position. His military forces were primarily the foot-soldiers on whom the Goths had customarily relied, but their cavalry too rose rapidly in strength, borrowing its methods from the nomad lance riders of their neighbours in the eastern interior.

Thus strengthened, the Visigoths organized incursions into the Roman empire from time to time, and began to be recognized as a major threat: particularly, it would appear, in 315 – and then again in late 322 or January 323, when they crossed the frozen Danube. The marauders were in large numbers, indicating a recent rapid expansion, and comprised a new generation that had forgotten the defeat of 268, and was keen to take advantage of the quarrel between Constantine and Licinius, which destroyed the unity of the Roman frontier defence line.

When they crowded over the Danube into Roman territory Constantine undertook a retaliation which assumed a massive scale, attacking the invaders over a front that extended for some 300 miles. Battles at Campona (which had fallen into Visigothic hands), and on the River Margus (Morava), and at Bononia (Widin), marked the points where the Romans defeated the Visigoths and broke through – the second of these engagements, apparently, being the most decisive of the three. Constantine's advance, made possible by the successful outcome of these battles, took him deep into the territory of Dacia, which had for so many years been abandoned by the forces of Rome. And after vigorous fighting he gained his principal objective: that is to say, the Visigoths surrendered, although Constantine may have had to offer concessions in order to persuade them to do so. He adopted the title 'Gothicus' in 315 and 319, partly because of his successes and partly to recall his alleged descent from Claudius II Gothicus. And in 323 he threatened that anyone who collaborated with the Goths would be burnt to death.

Licinius, as we saw earlier, objected that Constantine's reprisals caused him to trespass into Licinius' own territory (with a view to which, he suspected, Constantine had created the entire crisis). Then, in the subsequent war between the two men, Visigoths were mobilized to fight on both sides. Prisoners of war from this source were employed by Constantine to construct the harbour at Thessalonica (Salonica). Visigothic auxiliaries joined the army of Licinius' deputy Martinian in Asia Minor, and the Visigothic royal judge Aliquaca or Alica[9] fought for Licinius at Chrysopolis. Later traditions maintained that Licinius conspired with the Visigoths, or escaped to them in the South Carpathians, but met his death at their hands (or was arrested and killed at Thessalonica).[10] But, until he was finally defeated and met his death, Constantine never felt able to forget the potential threat from him while he himself was fighting on the northern frontier; effective defence against the Visigoths was impossible if Constantine and Licinius quarrelled.

On that frontier facing them, as we have seen, two essential points stand out. The first is that, as the sites of the battlefields indicate, the Visigoths had succeeded in penetrating deep into Roman territory. And the second is that Constantine employed the occasion to move north of the Danube – and attempt to retake (with the help of a client system) at least the southern half of the old province of Dacia, conquered by Trajan and abandoned by Aurelian.[11]

The information about Constantine's campaign across that river is obscure and untrustworthy. The question, therefore, of what he achieved by this enterprise was, and is, subject to contradictory interpretations. On the one hand, the Panegyrists claimed that he had repeated the triumphs of Trajan. On the other, his own nephew, Julian the Apostate, spoke for many when he expressed the view that this second 'conquest' of Dacia was incomplete and extremely brief.[12] The probability is that there had been a menacing movement of the Visigoths, such as was not uncommon among the 'barbarian' tribes at this time, and that Constantine beat it off, and gained victories which allowed him to advance across the river.

Nevertheless, the subsequent treaty with the Visigoths, in which they probably committed themselves to help defend the Roman Balkans, may have been facilitated by an unpublished undertaking by Constantine not to attempt to occupy Dacia permanently. According to some, that is what he should have done, instead of concentrating so keenly on internal religious affairs. As it was, however, he had been a party to a compromise; confrontation with the Visigoths ended in what was virtually a draw. That is to say, he had won victories which looked impressive enough at the moment, but were in no way decisive – because decisive finality was out of his reach.[13]

However, Constantine returned to the attack in 328, launching the most serious northern campaigns undertaken by the Romans for sixty years. It was now, apparently, that the bridge over the Danube and its marshes from Oescus (Gigen) to Sucidava (Celeiu) – 2,437 metres in length, said to be the longest bridge in the world – was completed, linking the empire with the former, but no longer, imperial region of Dacia Inferior (Oltenia, Little Wallachia). The event was celebrated by a bronze medallion, displaying the three-arched bridge, figures of the emperor and of Victory, and a kneeling captive or suppliant;[14] and milestones reveal that Constantine also built a road running north from Sucidava to Romula-Malva (Rechka, near Caracal).

Further monetary commemoration was accorded to the building, at about the same time, of the river frontier fortress of Constantiniana Dafne (Spanţov, near Olteniţa),[15] linked by a large ferry to Transmarisca (Tutrakan), opposite the mouth of the River Marisca: so that the concentration of Roman troops at this point protruded like a thorn into Germanic territory (a start had been made with the process in 304/5, when Constantia was built across the river from Margum). And equally threatening were Constantine's other frontier fortifications on the Danube, which were perhaps completed at the same time, although their inception may well have dated back to 323, or earlier. There are also traces of his camps and defences in the Transdanubian area.

Driven away from the Danube, the Visigoths began, increasingly, to infiltrate central Transylvania instead, notably the basin of the River Maros (Mureş) (where their presence has been interpreted as an expansion of what is known as the Sintana de Mureş culture). Constantine, however, having expelled them from the Danube area, made the most of this success, since he was eager to be seen as a victor over foreigners, and not just in civil wars: 'VICTORIA GOTHICA', therefore, appears on his coins.[16]

Next, too, in *c*.332–4, ostensibly in response to an appeal (so often invoked by invaders at all periods) – the 'appeal' against the Visigoths was said to have come from the Sarmatians, of whom more will be said later[17] – Constantine sent his eldest, adolescent surviving son, of the same name (later Constantine II), to fight the Visigoths again across the Danube, where they were possibly led by a certain Vidigoia, or if it was not they whom the younger Constantine fought it was their nomadic horse-riding allies the Taifali.

For all these peoples blamed the Sarmatians for the setbacks they had received at the hands of the Romans, and the Sarmatians were alarmed at their threatening attitude, which was why they asked the emperor for help. The Roman intervention was impressive, since the advisers of Constantine junior, after inflicting heavy casualties (greatly added to by cold and starvation) and capturing the son of the Tervingian royal judge Ariaric – the captive was probably Aoric, father of the later Visigothic monarch Athanaric – compelled his enemies to sign a treaty which abrogated earlier agreements and relegated them to the subordinate status of 'Federates' (*foederati*).

The treaty, which also committed them to help in the defence of Constantinople, was something of a landmark, instituting a new sort of relationship. Many of the Taifali were deported to Phrygia, and the rest became allies of the Romans instead of their enemies. Constantine the Great reassumed the title of 'Gothicus Maximus' (he was three times proclaimed 'Germanicus Maximus'), and his son of the same name was declared Germanicus or Gothicus. Gothic Games were celebrated at Constantinople.

One of the results of the treaty was increased trade at the fortified crossings of the Danube. In other respects, however, the results were not entirely impressive, a fact which did not pass unnoticed, either at the time or later, when Constantine's 'successes' were, as has been said, sometimes derided. True, there was peace for a period, and the Visigoths respected Constantine, who regarded the area as so safe that, when he divided the empire among his heirs, he gave the 'Gothic bank' (Thrace) to the lowest of the Caesars, Delmatius.

Yet the Visigoths renounced the treaty not long after he was dead, thus shattering all his efforts. Valentinian I had to spend a lot of time on the crumbling northern frontiers, and when Valens allowed some of these people to settle on Roman territory he suffered one of the most appalling Roman defeats of all time at Hadrianopolis (Edirne, Adrianople) and lost his life.

That was in 378 (perhaps about three years after the death of the legendary Visigothic ruler Ermanaric), and it seems unfair to blame Constantine for something that occurred forty-one years after his death. But the disaster at Hadrianopolis was a sign that, despite all Constantine's propaganda and his attempt to initiate an accommodation with the non-classical world, his victories over the Visigoths were not, in the long run, decisive, and his expansion policy was doomed to failure.

As for the Ostrogoths, in the Ukraine, their links with Constantine were not very important, although their commercial relations with the Roman empire were, it now appears, much larger than had been supposed, and they had significant relations with the Greek city of Chersonesus (Sevastopol) in the Crimean peninsula – which helped the Romans to win their victory in 332.[18]

The other group of peoples with whom Constantine had to contend on the Danube was the tribe or tribes of the Sarmatae (Sarmatians), nomads who, although to some extent intermingled with the Visigoths (or, in border areas, absorbed by them), were not Germans but spoke an Indo-European (Iranian) language related to Scythian. A large number of the Dacian slaves imported into the empire were Sarmatians.

Although many Sarmatians remained further east, their two main branches in more westerly lands were the Roxolani and the Jazyges. Centuries earlier, the Roxolani had advanced westwards and southwards to the Danube estuary, while the Jazyges crossed the Carpathians and occupied the plain between the middle Danube and Pathisus (Theiss, Tisza).

Both peoples had become Roman clients, but in the second and third centuries AD they were set moving again by the pressure of other tribes behind them. And so the Jazyges, pushed forward, invaded Dacia and Pannonia in the 250s, and the Roxolani joined the Visigoths in raiding Moesia. Carus (282–3) and Diocletian fought against the Sarmatians, and Diocletian was hailed as 'Sarmaticus' on no less than three occasions. Although there is some confusion, among writers, between Sarmatians and the Germanic Vandals, it is clear that Galerius conducted further Sarmatian wars; and so did Licinius.

To the west of Licinius, and in order to fight against him, Constantine withdrew detachments from the Danube frontier, thus offering a weakened defence that offered a tempting invitation to the Sarmatian Jazyges under their king Rausimondus (if, as is not certain, he was a Sarmatian, and not a Goth), luring him to cross the river. This, therefore, he did – all the more willingly because he was suffering from Visigothic pressure. So Rausimondus, it would appear, invaded Pannonia in the spring of 322, although the dates of all these military operations are disputed.[19] But Rausimondus did not get very far into the empire, where he was held up by the resistance of some town to his besieging army. Thereupon Constantine took him by surprise, drove him back across the Danube, and pursued him right into his own kingdom, where Rausimondus sought in vain to resist, and was killed. Constantine returned home victorious.

Nevertheless, the victory was surrounded by controversy. In particular, as was suggested on an earlier page, this entire campaign against the Sarmatians was claimed by Licinius – into whose territory the pursuing army had penetrated – as a provocation deliberately designed by Constantine to bring Licinius into war against him. Nevertheless, no less than five of Constantine's mints coined with the inscription 'Sarmatia Conquered' ('SARMATIA DEVICTA').[20] Moreover, a young poet Publilius Optatianus Por-

phyrius, who had served in the campaign, commemorated its successful conclusion in verse.

Some Sarmatians emigrated into the Caucasus, but those who remained in more westerly lands subsequently thought it best to be on the Roman side, and, as we saw earlier, appealed to them in 332 for help against the Visigoths, which Constantine's son of the same name (Constantine II) and his advisers duly provided (although he too displayed a Sarmatian captive on his coins).[21]

In order to deal with this Visigothic threat, however, the Sarmatian Jazyges on the River Pathisus (Theiss, Tisza), ruled by a group known as the Agaragantes, had also armed a subject tribe, the Limigantes, 'slaves' dependent on themselves; and after the defeat of the Visigoths these 'slaves' rose against their masters, whose king they killed, driving his compatriots away. Some of the exiles took refuge with another Germanic people, the Vandals, but many others belonged to a group which appealed to Constantine for help.

He responded by welcoming them as farmer–settlers into imperial territories, including Macedonia, Thrace, Gaul and even Italy, and mobilizing a number of them to form tribal regiments in his army. Moreover, in order to support their cause still further, he again crossed the Danube himself in 334, and apparently claimed further Sarmatian victories (assisted by the subjugation of the Jazyges by the Roxolani). And two years later he assumed the title 'Dacicus Maximus', thus reiterating once again his claim to have repeated the conquests of Trajan.

This he had not, however, done, since his own conquests proved so ephemeral: thus in 375 Valentinian I had to cope with a Sarmatian invasion of Illyricum. But at least, for the time being, Constantine had both the Sarmatians and the Visigoths under his control, with consequent benefits for the agriculturalists in Roman frontier areas. Eusebius gave lyrical voice to this achievement, rather vaguely linking the Sarmatians with their Scythian cousins in the Ukraine:

Do I need to describe, however briefly, the way in which he subjected barbarian peoples to the authority of Rome? He was the first to subdue the Scythian and Sarmatian tribes, which never before had known servitude.... Previous emperors had actually paid tribute to the Scythians.... But this would have been intolerable to Constantine....

The Scythians learnt to be subject to Rome....

It was God himself who drove the Sarmatians under Constantine's yoke.... During a Scythian attack, they had armed their slaves in order to drive off the enemy. The slaves repelled the invaders but then turned their weapons against their masters. They drove all of them from the country.

The exiles could find no refuge except with Constantine; and since he was accustomed to providing sanctuary he allowed them all to come into Roman territory.

He enrolled the men of military age in his army, *and to others he gave lands to provide for their needs.*[22]

That last sentence of Eusebius' flattering passage raises a matter of importance. For the fact was – as we saw – that Constantine, in addition to his importation of Visigoths, settled very many Sarmatians indeed, men and women and children, within the frontiers of the empire, and especially on the Lower Danube accompanied and followed by further settlements of Talfali and Vandals, in Asia Minor and Pannonia respectively. As for the Sarmatians, there may have been as many as 300,000 of their settlers, including women and children.

Now this was not an entirely new policy. From the beginning of the empire, and even before, one Roman ruler and general after another had imported northern foreigners, 'barbarians', not only as hostages but as settlers, in very large numbers: most recently the same policy had been followed by Aurelian, Probus and Constantius I Chlorus. And now Constantine was doing the same.

It was an enterprise which had obvious advantages. It immobilized, indeed removed, potential enemies and trouble-makers across the frontiers. It helped to farm deserted or inadequately cultivated lands within the empire. It also strengthened depleted garrisons by adding further recruits, and provided much needed frontier guards. Yet there were also marked dangers, which became more ominous still when the importations, such as Constantine's, were on an exceptionally massive scale. For one thing, he was accelerating the process by which 'barbarians' ceased to be nomads, and became settled, agricultural peoples, developing mixed cultures with other peoples (for example at Intercisa [Dunapentele]). Moreover, Constantine took this action at a time when the whole concept of Romanness as a barrier against foreignness (barbarism), often stridently asserted, was at risk, since the frontiers were in danger of collapsing. Thirdly, as was seen in connection with the Visigoths, 'there were simply too many barbarians to be assimilated once the barriers were down: there was no finality, because no finality was possible'.[23] Moreover, in the army in particular – as we shall shortly see – the Roman element was already rapidly diminishing, and now it was certain to diminish further.

The true extent of these perils was to become evident not long after Constantine's death, and they were directly derived from what he had done: for 'it would be hard to imagine the massive, really uncontrolled and fateful admissions ... to the empire in the 370s, had precedents on a large scale not been established in the 330s'.[24] It is impossible, that is to say, to avoid the conclusion that Constantine's massive settlements of Germans, even if they had short-term advantages, contributed substantially to the collapse of the western empire that was to follow so soon.

Constantine also had other methods for keeping the 'barbarians' quiet. One of them was the handing over to them of huge subsidies – the Visigoths are especially mentioned, but the Sarmatians, too, were no doubt included: 'gift payments',[25] especially in gold, in return for assistance with defence, and as a reward for favourable trade. This, too, had long been a standard instrument of Roman diplomacy, but once again Constantine carried it to novel and dangerous lengths.

Northern envoys, also (often bringing gifts themselves, as a counterweight to what they were receiving), found themselves treated with honour – and attracted attention:

We ourselves sometimes happening to be at the gates of the palace have seen lines of barbarians of remarkable aspect standing there, with distinctive costumes and with different types of appearance, hair and beards, grim faces, terrifying glance, and surpassing bodily size; some with red complexions, some pale as snow, some blacker than ebony or pitch. . . .

Each in turn, as in a painting, brought to the emperor what was of value to each, some bearing gold crowns or diadems set with precious gems, or blonde children [as slaves], or clothing embroidered in gold and flowers, or horses, shields, long spears, bow and arrows, showing that they offered by these means their service and alliance to the emperor, if he would accept them.

Indeed, a statue of an eminent barbarian, probably the Visigoth Aoric, father of the future monarch Athanaric, was even to be found in the antechamber of the Constantinople senate house.[26] Besides, Constantine endeavoured to link these foreigners to himself and the Roman state by converting them to Christianity.

It is hardly surprising, then, that he was criticized for a too pro-barbarian attitude to Goths and Sarmatians, in spite of all the much trumpeted victories – and additional reasons were put forward for such a charge against him, such as the (doubtful) accusation that he raised 'barbarians' to consulships; and we may note the depiction of one of his sons, probably Constantius (II), in Sarmatian dress on a silver plate of the Gotho-Sarmatian city Panticapaeum.[27]

But what Constantine himself stressed was his military victory over these northern foreigners. Victory figured very largely in his publicity. The goddess of that name was said to have accompanied Apollo in Constantine's alleged vision in which, as we shall see elsewhere, the god was believed to have appeared to him; the same message was rammed home by Constantinian propaganda of all kinds, which made the utmost of these victories. 'In the Constantinian period military coin-types predominated, some of them notably harsh in conception.'[28] Figures of Victory abound in visual and artistic representations of every kind, not least the Arch of Constantine. This victoriousness was also celebrated by an inscription over the chancel-arch of the new St Peter's. The sarcophagus of his mother Helena (now in the Vatican), originally intended for his own body, is covered with reliefs celebrating military triumphs; and 'Victory'(Nike) was the meaning of Nicaea, where Constantine held his great church Council.

Moreover, victory was essentially and indissolubly associated with the person of the emperor. It was his principal job. 'Wars had raised the military duties of the emperor to an importance high above any others.'[29] And that had never been more the case than it was now, when the holding of the northern frontier had become the most important and urgent of military tasks. What this meant (and the putting down of rivals was not forgotten, either) was that Constantine had to present himself as the very embodiment of victory; which was envisaged as God's special gift to him.

And so his military glory was proclaimed on a thousand coins and medallions. Thus a fortified camp-gate, and one or two standards accompanied by soldiers and inscribed 'The Glory of the Army' ('GLORIA EXERCITVS'), are very frequent types.[30] And coins refer to the 'innumerable triumphs of the Augustus'. 'Always victorious' they called him, and 'Author of joyful victories', and 'Conqueror of all races' ('VICTOR OMNIVM GENTIVM' and 'EXVPERATOR OMNIVM GENTIVM'), and 'Triumpher over the barbarian races' ('TRIVMFATOR, DEBELLATOR, GENTIVM BARBARARVM'),[31] and the stabber of one of the fallen 'barbarians'.[32]

These, incidentally, in accordance with widespread Roman rhetoric and thinking, were vaguely and conveniently lumped together for this sort of purpose, in an 'identikit' stereotype of uncouth, beer-swilling, promiscuous, destructive natives[33] (though, occasionally, distinctions were made, for example between the skin-clad, noisily gregarious Goths and the fair-haired, clean-shaven Franks).

There was some basic justification for this chorus of praises of Constantine's victoriousness, since one thing that must be said unequivocally about him was that he was an extremely fine general: there was universal agreement about this, and it was his outstanding characteristic. He owed his position to military service – and he became the most notable general of his age: as the Christians, of course, emphasized, and even pagan writers (followed by Gibbon) had to admit.[34] There were many comparisons with Alexander the Great, and the terms *victor* and *triumphator*, of which appearances on the coinage have been noted, became parts of the imperial title. In fact, the picture of emperor as victor became the fundamental image of his rule, and that of his successors.[35]

But an embarrassment also lurked here. Constantine fought both civil and foreign wars. Wars of the latter kind made for the most convincing publicity, and it is they that are celebrated, *ad nauseam*, on the coinage. Yet, despite all those triumphant messages, they had not been all that terribly or permanently decisive. It was in the civil wars that Constantine had most distinguished himself as a soldier, but, although his victory over Maxentius gave him a hero's prestige, it still remained true that the slaying of one Roman by another did not make an immensely valuable impression. True, it earned Constantine his Arch, and he assumed the title 'victor' after the Second Licinian War, but for the rest it was upon the foreign wars, despite their somewhat inconclusive character, that he chose to base his reputation.

And victory, he declared, brought peace – 'BEATA TRANQVILLITAS' – which does not say whether his enemies had been foreigners or Roman: the peace which, on his behalf, writers praised, and of which Constantine could call himself the Founder ('FVNDAT [*or*] PACIS'), although it proved a painful exaggeration to describe it as 'Perpetual Peace' ('PAX PERPETVA').[36]

It is a curious paradox that this emperor who so loudly claimed to have suppressed the 'barbarians' did more than anyone else to advance the already existing tendency to appoint German generals in the Roman army and to strengthen it by the addition of numerous German soldiers.

As to generals, 'barbarians' had already reached high rank in the army by the time of Gallienus (253–68), and the process had continued; indeed, the Tetrarchs were mostly of semi- 'barbarian' origin themselves. But it was a process which Constantine – whose accession had been supported by a Frankish chieftain, Crocus or Erocus – carried much further.

Indeed, the military men who stood nearest to him, as to Licinius, were almost all 'barbarians', especially Franks – who became increasingly prominent in this role as the century progressed. To move into the realms of conjecture, it would be interesting to know how such men reacted to Constantine's cruel treatment of their captive countrymen, and what they thought of the coins that showed him dragging recumbent 'barbarians' by the hair. Probably this left them completely unmoved, and they did not think of these 'barbarians' as their own people any longer, as such commanders had become pretty thoroughly Romanized. That, for example, was no doubt the situation of Aurelius Januarius, the German *dux* of the province of Pannonia Secunda.

No doubt Constantine found these 'barbarian' commanders useful and indispensable (especially in dealing with their compatriots who threatened the frontiers), and he may even, given his own largely un-Roman origins, have seen them as congenial – more congenial, perhaps, than many Roman senators. But one can see why, as was noted earlier, he came to be called too pro- 'barbarian'. And indeed his appointment of German generals looked forward uncomfortably to the time when such men could control the western empire, and bring it down.

The two top military officers, who were now so often Germans, held the posts, from the early 320s, of Masters of Cavalry and Infantry. The fact that there were two of these generals rather than one – and indeed they were supplemented by a third, the *magister militum praesentalis*, who commanded the field force – made usurpation of the imperial throne more difficult and less likely. And so did Constantine's completion of the already growing cleavage between senior military and civilian (administrative) posts (of which something will be said later).

A very large proportion of the ordinary soldiers fighting in Constantine's army were likewise northern 'barbarians'.

This, too, was by no means new. For many years past there had been Roman complaints about the strong foreign element in the armed forces. And now Constantine's army which invaded Italy and conquered Maxentius was very largely German (his Arch gives prominence to the German contingent of the Cornuti). Usurpers had employed Germans, Aurelian and Galerius (297) had already engaged units of them, and they were regularly employed from c.300.

But Constantine, who like his father Constantius I Chlorus used German troops in Britain, greatly increased their number (as did Licinius), so that whole regiments were more and more made up of Germans – a frequent condition of Constantine's treaties with German tribes was that they should send auxiliaries when needed. And he probably incorporated some Germans into the legions as well. How many, in this way, became legionaries is disputable, but the proportion was, in all likelihood, by no means small – and on the increase. In any case, however, the legions (now only 1,000 strong, that is to say much smaller than in previous centuries) had largely been superseded by *auxilia*. And, in the *auxilia*, Germans were very numerous indeed.

Constantine's bodyguard, too, was almost wholly 'barbarian'. This was a cavalry unit known as the *scholae palatinae*. It is probable that this bodyguard had originally been formed by Diocletian. He had greatly reduced the size of the praetorian guard, whose camp, as we saw, Galerius abolished, so that the praetorians joined his enemy Maxentius, and joined him against Constantine as well, which caused their extinction when Maxentius was defeated. Constantine was also attended by an inner bodyguard, the *protec-*

tores, who had been brought into existence, it appears, by Gallienus and are known to have accompanied Diocletian.

These German soldiers attracted a good deal of comment, and created a vivid impression:

Such lean, harsh giants, these Gaulish and German soldiers! It disturbs me to look at them. Barely one among them has known the soft shores of our Mediterranean. Their heads are covered in manes of brown or yellow hair, which the weight of their helmets has compressed into moist sheaths.

I confess they amaze me. They camp here, a thousand miles from home, and are paid a pittance to attack an emperor they have never seen.... It seems they regard Italy as a kind of paradise.... Their dialect sounds like stones grating together....

I suppose these tribes to be safe recruits for our armies, since they hate each other more than they hate us.[37]

There was some truth in this, but in any case the commanders – who were themselves so often 'barbarians' – preferred German soldiers to Romans and provincials, who were, moreover, increasingly hard to get. So 'by the mid-fourth century the typical fighting force appears to have been half imported. The army [was] ever more dependent on immigrants for its actual fighting capacity.'[38] That was largely due to the initiative of Constantine, and so, therefore, was the subsequent transformation of the western empire into a German state.

Constantine found himself in command of an army which Diocletian had greatly increased in size, perhaps doubling it (even if not quadrupling it as Lactantius implied), equating the increase with the establishment of the four Tetrarchs.[39] That is to say, Diocletian and his colleagues possessed sixty-seven legions, as against thirty in the time of Septimius Severus (193–211). Admittedly, as we have seen, the legions were now smaller, but the auxiliaries were now more numerous, so that the army which Constantine inherited amounted to at least 435,000 men, and probably a good deal more, perhaps in the neighbourhood of 600,000. This large increase was one of the principal reasons why taxation, of which something will be said later, was so severe, especially as Constantine was so generous to the army, notably in distributing quinquennial bonuses (*donativa*).

As regards military organization, his major contribution and innovation was the division of this large army into two parts, the *limitanei* who guarded the frontiers, and the *comitatenses* who were stationed further back, and acted as a striking (field) force available at any point where the need arose. There had been moves towards this sort of division before. But its ultimate creation was mainly due to Constantine, who had the new striking force under his command at least as early as 312. Constantine built it out of the *comitatus*, which had been brought into existence by Diocletian and Maximian (or, more probably, by one of their predecessors) by transferring units from other branches of the army. The *comitatus* had started as a sort of imperial escort, supplementary to the bodyguard units, and part of it still continued to serve that purpose. Once again the formation consisted, to a considerable extent, of Germans, whose mobility made them particularly useful for the purposes of this striking force of *comitatenses* which had developed out of the *comitatus*.

The *limitanei* were obviously more static and less mobile than the *comitatenses*, and more difficult to detach when specific operations were needed. Consisting, mainly, of agriculturally minded soldier–settlers (often 'barbarians') these *limitanei* were less well paid and served longer, and were regarded with less esteem and respect, than the striking force, whose members were given superior privileges by a law of 325. However, a very large proportion, perhaps two-thirds, of the entire imperial army consisted of *limitanei*. Yet the striking force of *comitatenses* suffered such serious casualties in foreign and civil wars that more and more soldiers had to be transferred to it from the *limitanei* in order to keep up its total numbers. This was especially noteworthy, and damaging, on the northern rivers, where the strength of the imperial frontier defences was seriously diminished as a result.

Nor was the benefit to the *comitatenses* all that remarkable, and indeed the contrary was the case, since they had been obliged to fill up their numerical strength by so many frontier soldiers of inferior quality. Besides, the *comitatenses* were faced by other problems as well. To take a single example, their units in north Africa were deprived of the mobility which should have been their most important feature, because of the overriding need that the grain of the area which was due to be sent to Rome should receive military protection in order to prevent it from being diverted to some other place and purpose.[40]

The pagan historian Zosimus was extremely hostile to this division of the army by Constantine. He emphasized the bad morale caused among civilians in the bulk of the empire because of the posting of the striking force among them. And he also felt that the weakening of the frontier army, to which reference has been made, was inexcusable: so that he blamed Constantine for the subsequent downfall of the western empire, which he ascribed to this division of its military strength into two unsatisfactory parts. He wrote:

Constantine abolished security by removing the greater part of the soldiery from the frontiers to cities that needed no auxiliary forces. He thus deprived of help the people who were harassed by the barbarians and burdened tranquil cities with the pest of the military, so that several straightaway were deserted. Moreover, he softened the soldiers, who treated themselves to shows and luxuries.

Indeed (to speak plainly) he personally planted the first seeds of our present devastated state of affairs.[41]

It has lately been argued that Zosimus' criticism was largely justified, and it appears that this is right. For one thing, as he suggested, the striking force, well behind the river boundaries of the empire, succeeded in irritating the populations among whom it was stationed, causing widespread disloyalty. Nor was the militia-like frontier force strong or effective enough, or of high enough quality, to resist the determined barbarian incursions which remained, in fact, the principal danger to the empire, as the gradual western movement of the Germans continued, despite the reconstructed defences.

On a short-term view, Constantine's striking force, relying on speed, had originally been brought into existence to fight civil rather than frontier wars, and was no doubt useful for this purpose, and, besides, at least suspended the collapse of the northern frontier in the face of barbarian incursions. But from a longer-term viewpoint his twofold division of the army undermined its capability, as grave defeats after his death made clear. And so the accusation that this division helped to bring about the downfall of the western empire seems justified.

Meanwhile, however, Constantine, benefiting by his annexation of the Illyrian recruitment area from Licinius, did his best to encourage his soldiers, not only by incessant propaganda in their favour, but by generous treatment which became legendary (it is displayed in his letters and edicts of 311 and 320 or 326). This generosity was partly intended, no doubt, to ensure that the army, although pagan, would continue to support him. But it was also accompanied by efforts to stamp out its corrupt treatment at the hands of its officers. Such steps were all the more necessary because of his insistence on conscription: in 313 he assumed military service to be legally obligatory, and later reiterated and justified this conclusion.

In view of the numerous and mostly unresolved hazards presented by the northern frontiers, it is all the more surprising that in his very last years Constantine decided upon full-scale war against the Roman empire's eastern neighbour, Sassanian Persia.

Persia was the only substantial state on any of Rome's frontiers, and it seems unwise of Constantine to have embroiled himself with it at a time when the northern frontiers were so uncertain. Presumably his principal motive was simple autocratic megalomania, and a desire to emulate Alexander the Great, with whom flatterers were ready enough to compare him.

There was, of course, an extensive past history. In 298 Galerius had won a huge victory over Narses of Persia, redeeming an earlier defeat, and in the following year a treaty was signed according to which Narses was compelled to surrender seven satrapies north of the Tigris: it was the greatest success Rome had gained in the east since the time of Trajan (98–117). A long line of frontier fortresses was established, and to celebrate the victory Diocletian and Maximian led thirteen elephants and 250 horses into Rome; and Diocletian assumed the title 'Persicus'(indeed he did so on five occasions).

But Armenia remained a bone of contention, and in c.310 fighting with Persia was resumed. However, although Galerius' Edict of Toleration to the Christians may have been partly due to the resumption of these hostilities, and all the emperors became 'Persici Maximi', the campaign did not amount to much. What proved confrontational, however, was that Armenia became Christian, the first country officially to take this step, and this induced the anti-Christian Maximinus II Daia to launch an invasion of Armenia, which seemed, he felt, to be ganging up with other Christians against him.

Moreover, Armenia's Christianity looked like provocation to the Persians as well. And so, very shortly afterwards, did Constantine's subsequent alliance with the Armenians – although this was, in fact, not primarily directed against the Persians, but was intended to encircle Licinius, who had been conducting campaigns near Rome's eastern frontier (313/14), and harrying Christians in the area. Then in c.324 – or at any rate shortly after the final defeat of Licinius – Constantine wrote a letter to King Sapor (Shapur) II of Persia (309–79), making it clear that he was only too ready to interfere with the numerous Christians on Persian territory. 'I come now also to the lands of the east', he declared in his own writing, 'which, in their bitter pains, require my earnest aid.'[42]

The background to this curious letter is somewhat obscure, as indeed is the background to most of Constantine's actions in regard to Persia. What is clear, however, is that the whole situation on this eastern frontier appeared to him, as to other Romans, worryingly precarious and unstable. The successes of Galerius had won Rome massive advances in Mesopotamia, confirmed by a peace treaty of 299. But the Persian king Sapor II was not likely to continue to submit to the treaty – which had dictated Roman annexations and instituted a Roman protectorate – unless continual diplomatic and military pressure was maintained by the Romans.

Licinius kept a watchful and suspicious eye on the Armenians, whom he believed to be in secret touch with Constantine. With similar suspicions, no doubt, in mind, Persian envoys visited Constantine in *c*.320. Yet the Persian prince Hormisdas fled in 324 from his brother Sapor II and arrived at Constantine's court, and shortly afterwards Publilius Optatianus Porphyrius was writing as if Constantine was on the point of launching a military attack on Persia.[43] It was probably at this time, and in alarm at the situation which was developing, that Sapor dispatched a deputation to Constantine, which brought him gifts and tokens of friendship, and arranged a renewal of the treaty of 299.

At the same time, however, the Persian king cannot have been pleased, and must have remained displeased, by Constantine's evident readiness (displayed in his letter) to intervene as the protector of Sapor's Christian subjects. And so, despite Sapor's inability (owing to technological deficiencies) to mount a large force it was not long before he formed plans to win back the lands Narses had lost in the last years of the previous century.

With this in mind, in 334, Sapor broke the peace by invading Armenia, deposing its king and attempting to enthrone one of his own brothers: who was killed, however, by Constantine's son Constantius (II) in the following year, after Constantius had fortified the frontier strongholds of Amida (Diyarbakir) and Antoninopolis (Tela Maximianopolis, Constantia), which lay to its south-west.

Actual war, however, between Constantine and Sapor still did not officially exist. But it was possible for the Romans to proclaim that Sapor, in hostile response to Constantine's letter, was persecuting the Christians in his dominions, even though he did not want war with the empire. Constantine, on the other hand, seemed to be eager for war; and so a fantastic pretext was invented and brought forward.

It concerned a certain Metrodorus,[44] who was stated to have made a journey to the remotest Indies as part of a plan to go round the world. Gaining the goodwill of the Brahmins and securing admission to their shrines, he stole many pearls and other jewels. The king of the Indi, it was said, also presented him with many valuable precious stones, on the understanding that he was to pass them on to Constantine, as a gift from the monarch. When, however, Metrodorus got back to Constantinople, he presented these gems to Constantine *as his own gift*, and added that he himself had dispatched many more priceless objects overland, but that they had all been appropriated *en route* by the Persians. When Constantine wrote to Sapor requesting that they should be handed over, he did not receive any answer; and that is why and how the peace between the Romans and Persians came to an end, and war was provoked by Constantine.

But this whole preposterous story was a fiction, intended to give the Romans a case. As the historian Ammianus Marcellinus observed, Constantine never ought to have believed what Metrodorus told him – if indeed he did believe it, as we can never know. But what we do know is that this tale, believed or not, served to back Constantine's decision, already made, to make war on the Persians – and thus, despite all his embroilments in the north, to become a second Alexander the Great, the world-conqueror proclaimed on his coins ('RECTOR TOTIVS ORBIS').[45] For 'world-embracing plans and mighty dreams led him by an easy road to the streams of blood of slaughtered enemies'.[46]

He had made his decision, and was not deterred, although he pretended to be, by a Persian delegation in 336. Despite the delegation, Constantine continued to prepare for war. His appointment of Hannibalianus as 'king of kings' in the east[47] was a further provocation to the Persians, declaring his intention that this kinsman of his should replace Sapor after the latter had been removed: although Constantine, it would appear, did not press the Persians to recognize Hannibalianus, and did not actually enthrone him himself.

Nevertheless, war against Persia was approaching, and in 336/7 Constantine personally supervised the mobilization of his field army (*comitatenses*) in Asia Minor. But in 337, before he could launch hostilities, he died. All he had achieved was to bequeath Rome a long, ugly and costly eastern war in the future. For Sapor II profited by his death to lead an immediate Persian invasion of the eastern provinces of the Roman empire, and what followed was the fault of Constantine, now dead,

who kindled the Persian fires.

[The result was] the annihilation of our armies, the capture so often of whole companies of soldiers, the destruction of cities, the seizure or overthrow of fortresses, the exhaustion of our provinces by heavy expenses, and the threats of the Persians which were soon brought into effect, as they claimed everything as far as Bithynia and the shores of the Propontis [Sea of Marmara].[48]

PART III:

——

CONSTANTINE AND
THE STATE

══

CHAPTER 5:

THE GOVERNMENT AND CHARACTER OF CONSTANTINE

CONSTANTINE was a more openly autocratic ruler than the early Roman emperors had been. The difference is summed up by the description of this later empire as the 'dominate'. It had already been advisable to address Caligula and Domitian as *domine* (lord). Yet the designation does not appear on coins until the time of Aurelian (270–5),[1] and not long afterwards coins were dedicated to Probus (276–82 and Carns 283–3) as *deus et dominus*.[2]

But it was under Diocletian (284–305) that the title *dominus* was formally and publicly assumed. Indeed, Diocletian, although in practice little, if at all, more absolute than the emperors who preceded him, made a point of adopting orientalizing symbols, taken from Persia, and introducing elaborate court rituals. 'The simplicity of Roman manners', remarked Edward Gibbon, 'was insensibly corrupted by the stately affectation of the courts of Asia'.[3] For example; Diocletian wore sumptuous robes of silk and gold, and gemmed shoes. And in place of the traditional greeting (*salutatio*), he insisted upon the grovelling *adoratio*, the Persian *proskynesis*: though this may not have been entirely new, and was also seen as a practical safeguard against assassination, to make sure that no one could get near the person of the emperor.

Although Constantine's father Constantius I Chlorus was probably more or less unconcerned with such matters, Constantine himself took a rather different view. Eusebius, for his benefit, refashioned the Hellenistic philosophy of kingship, which was now portrayed as a direct reflection of the Christian God's heavenly court. 'Sacred' and 'divine' had long been synonyms for 'imperial', and this tendency was intensified: *sacrum* appears frequently in Constantinian ceremonial, and his palace was the *domus divina*, likened to a temple.

Constantine wore long, shoulder-length hair (recalling Alexander the Great) – some of it false. He also covered himself with bracelets and other jewellery, and put on elaborate jewelled robes with flowery designs. Eusebius, somewhat disingenuously, said he did this only because the people enjoyed it, like children 'wondering at a hobgoblin', whereas Constantine's attitude was merely one of detached amusement.[4] However, from *c.*315/16 a gemmed, high-crested helmet, foreshadowing the Byzantine crown, appeared on his coins,[5] replaced ten years later by a pearl-decked diadem[6] consisting in its final form of a double strand of pearls: a sign that amounted, it might be said, to the deliberate elevation of the emperor far above other mortals (and even his sons began to wear diadems from *c.*325).

Constantine was not averse to this kind of display, as Gibbon disapprovingly noted,[7] contradicting Eusebius. But at the same time the emperor was also, consciously, putting forward a new theocratic concept of kingship, of which we learn from Eusebius as well. And, while dutifully protesting against the remote, inaccessible isolation which this elaborateness was in danger of imposing, the emperor, imitating and even exceeding Diocletian, made the fullest use of this autocratic power, 'a man happily at one with the role of colossus'.[8] Like his prose, his architecture, his costume and his manners, his coinage presses the point home.[9]

As for the administration of the empire, one retains the general impression that it had largely been Diocletian, a very able and industrious administrator, who cast the government in a new, orderly and stable (though top-heavy and over-centralized) form, which Constantine, on the whole, was content to preserve.

But there were certain changes, or at least developments, during his reign. For one thing, Diocletian had begun the separation of civil and military commands (a military governor was exceptional), and Constantine completed the process, so that there was an ever-growing cleavage between civilian and military careers. From now onwards, provincial governors very rarely held military commands in their province – these went to others, generals known as *duces*. This meant that governors and generals were both less powerful and of more limited authority than before: they were therefore less likely to rebel against the emperor.

And for similar reasons, so that provincial governors, once again, should not be powerful enough to think of sedition, Constantine accepted Diocletian's conversion of provinces into more numerous and smaller geographical units, so that it even remains uncertain whether he continued and accelerated this evolution, or, conversely, felt that it had already gone a little too far. At any rate, the process was not substantially reversed, since there was a tendency to reduce units of secular government to a size suitable for episcopal sees. To take specific instances of changes for which Constantine was responsible, he divided Moesia, but reunited Numidia, and suppressed certain other small provinces (which were later reinstated).

He also innovated by making public office in the expanded civil service very much a replica of the military career, so that it became a sort of *militia*, on a par with the *militia armata* which was the army. The purpose, in this case, was to bind the civil service more tightly to the emperor's person, so that it was clearly understood to be under his direct command; and this militarization came naturally to Constantine, since he was a military man himself.

As will be recalled, however, he abolished the praetorian guard, because it had supported Maxentius: and this meant that the praetorian prefects, although retaining supply and recruitment functions in connection with the army, lost the direct command of soldiery that might have prompted them to institute an uprising. Thus even the most famous of Constantine's prefects, the Cretan

Flavius Ablabius, despite a marked capacity for intrigue, never presented him with any threat (although he was killed shortly after the emperor's death). So when pagan writers complained that the abolition of the prefects' military power caused the ruin of the administration[10] they are not telling the whole story, because they do not explain why this was done.

It is a fact, however, that as a result the prefects became virtually civilians. They were still very important men, it is true – so important that Constantine admitted no appeal from them to himself, and Christian writers (with dubious theology) compared their relation to him to the relation of God the Son to the Father.[11] However, their functions were now basically fiscal, administrative and juridical.

Moreover, as their duties were thus reinterpreted, they were allotted a further, special task as well. In 313–17 there had been only two prefects (as there may have been previously under the Tetrarchy), but as Constantine groomed his sons for ever higher duties, each had an additional prefect attached to him – with particularly large powers after the death, in 326, of the emperor's eldest son Crispus (which will be described later), when his remaining sons were too young to take control themselves. There was also a senior prefect on the personal staff of Constantine (Evagrius at the end of his reign), and another from 333 in Africa (in 337 he was Nestorius Timonianus). When the emperor died, therefore, there seem to have been five praetorian prefects, although some prefer a slightly later date for parts of this development.

Constantine's new arrangements regarding the prefects were accompanied by further reorganizations of the central government. A Master of Offices (*magister officiorum*) now controlled not only the emperor's personal bodyguard (*scholae*) – largely German as we have seen – but also the four principal imperial bureaux (*scrinia*); and he was also in general charge of personnel. Moreover, there was a corps euphemistically described as Men of Affairs (*agentes in rebus*), probably not entirely new but expanded by

Constantine. These were men who, while officially couriers, also acted as imperial spies, reporting any sign of subversiveness to the emperor. The *quaestor sacri palatii* (attributed to Constantine by Zosimus,[12] though no holder of the office is known until the mid-fourth century) was the chief legal officer, concerned with the drafting of edicts, rescripts and petitions. The *comes rei privatae*, in consultation with the *comes sacrarum largitionum*, handled the revenues and expenditures in gold and silver. And the Chief Chamberlain was a eunuch (and therefore unable to harbour dynastic ambitions) who was set over the staff in the apartments of the emperor and empress, to make sure that nothing went wrong there.

These officials helped to ensure that Constantine maintained tight control. But his most spectacular innovation was to create a new Order of Imperial Companions (*comites*), who largely replaced the old governing aristocracy as the emperor's principal subordinates. This *comitiva*, consisting partly, but not entirely, of senators (who secured most of the consulships, but did not exercise anything like a monopoly among the *comites*), was organized, formally, into three grades. The *comites*, foreshadowed like so much else by an arrangement of Diocletian, were employed, flexibly, for a wide variety of tasks (Felicianus' appointment as *comes orientis*, early in 335, was a special move, prompted by the coming Persian War). The *comites* were 'friends', like the other *amici principis*, but often found themselves disgraced and executed on very insubstantial grounds.

The essential feature of the *comites* was that this new hereditary 'aristocracy of service' owed its allegiance to the person of the emperor rather than to the state, thus paving the way for medieval vassalage. But so that senators who belonged to the *comitiva* should not feel outgunned, and those who did not belong to it should not feel excluded and disgruntled either, Constantine reopened a number of official posts to senators, of whom a number, as individuals, began to recover a portion of the prestige they had lost during the past century. And he also greatly increased the number of those entitled to claim senatorial rank, so that the new senate was increased from 600 members to at least 2,000. 'The emperor', as Eusebius observed, 'created dignities of every kind so that more and more could receive honours from him.'[13] Fond of pomp and ceremony himself, and willing to endow those whom he promoted with pompous trappings, he created many new titles. And, while so doing, he revised the ancient order of the patricians, as a highly select and prestigious body.

The emperor's council was the *sacrum consistorium*, so called because its members stood in his presence. But it was also a 'standing' committee in the other sense, derived from Diocletian's *consilia sacra*. It was later reduplicated at Constantinople. Constantine's administration largely depended on co-operation between the praetorian prefectures and this *consistorium*, which also retained close links with the Offices – and, once again, ensured personal control by the ruler himself.

'Public Utility', 'VTILITAS PVBLICA' was what Constantine, on his coinage, described as the keynote of his administration.[14]

But its multiplicity, increased further by a huge bureaucracy, was tremendously expensive, as was the army – especially when engaged, as it frequently was, in military operations. Taxes had already been high in the time of Diocletian, but Constantine added not only the vast administrative machine that has been mentioned, but extravagant building programmes – which, as we shall see, were needed both for the new faith and for Constantinople. And there was also his famous, much commented on, excessive personal lavishness, in many different directions, which his eagerness for popularity increasingly demanded.

This general extravagance of Constantine was stressed by a number of writers as a cause of the empire's subsequent decline.[15] No ruler, it was declared, had spent so liberally since the last year of Alexander the Great. Eusebius also emphasized Constantine's generous almsgiving to widows, orphans and beggars; which was costly, since the number of economically idle mouths had greatly increased in recent times. Constantine also, as we saw, gave extensive payments to the army – and provided huge subventions in gold to the 'barbarians'. In addition, he provided subsidies in grain and wine to Italian cities for services to Rome and Portus, the harbour at Ostia. Moreover, his associates imitated his extravagance, as well as gladly accepting it: 'he opened their jaws' (*proximorum fauces aperuit*).[16] And his own benevolence, we are told, was frequently imposed upon, especially in his later years.

All this expenditure created a burden which meant that taxation had to be fixed at an extremely high level. Diocletian, already finding that his needs were greater than his utilizable resources, had tried to grapple with the problem that this situation had created by introducing a change of capital importance, an *annual* announcement of tax requirements; and he established a single common unit (*iugum*), based on agriculture, so that everything seemed to become simpler. All the same, Lactantius believed that Diocletian's exactions had been insupportable.[17] But he may have been prejudiced against this pagan emperor, who had at least done something to bridge the growing gap between expenditure and receipts.

As for the other rulers of the time, it may have been believed that Constantius I Chlorus did not collect taxes strictly enough. Maxentius, though particularly short of money, let it be understood that his enemy Severus was a fiercer extortioner of taxes than himself, and helped to inspire a revolt against him on these lines: but then Maxentius stringently taxed the rich himself, and indeed gained a bad name for his unscrupulous confiscations. Licinius, too, tightened the taxes and, in the same vein as Maxentius, since he particularly disliked rich men, not only undertook compulsory purchases but raised the land tax, thereby causing widespread annoyance among influential people. Maximinus II Daia sought favour by remitting eastern taxation.

But emperors were in something of a dilemma: if they tightened taxes they were obviously considered oppressive, but if they diminished them they not only failed to raise enough money but were accused of seeking cheap popularity for themselves.

As for Constantine, impelled to a severe taxation policy not only by his own extravagance but by the expenses of the army, court, official posts and church, he maintained the taxes he had inherited, perhaps with minor changes, and instituted others as well: adding a *caput*, poll tax, to Diocletian's *iugum*. There was also a new *collatio glebalis* or *follis*, a surtax or supertax on senators, who were graded into three categories for the purpose. The poorer victims naturally grumbled, but to the detriment of the treasury the taxes imposed on the senators were relatively low. Indeed, although 'wealthy men' (undefined), if late paying their taxes, had to pay fivefold – and failure to pay could even be a capital offence – the argument that Constantine slashed private wealth is invalid, since, on the contrary, his policy favoured the landed class, and justified the suggestion that there was one law for the rich and one for the poor. As Eusebius observed, 'he remitted a quarter of the annual land taxes and gave it to the landowners'.[18]

Far more serious than the *collatio glebalis* was the *collatio lustralis*, also known as *chrysargyron*, the gold and silver tax, because it could be paid in either metal. It was imposed on manufacturers and merchants, and apparently assessed on their own persons, and on the persons of their families and staff (including slaves and apprentices), and on their capital equipment: tools, implements and milling requisites in the case of manufacturers, and ships, waggons and draught animals in the case of merchants.[19] It is true that the *chrysargyron* may have been no more than the extension of a tax originally devised by Maxentius. But its employment by Constantine was more drastic, and did mark a shift in the balance of taxation from the upper class to a lower level.

This imposition of the *chrysargyron* provoked a loud and unusually widespread fuss, and produced dismal scenes, which were eloquently described by contemporary and later writers. Even the Christian Lactantius, usually a supporter of Constantine, describes for us the survey as summoning the people of the town and of the country to the public squares and applying torture, making children give evidence against their masters: extorting from them by means of blows exaggerated returns which they then made still higher, placing on the register children and old men.[20]

And Libanius painted an equally gloomy picture:

Gold and silver tax, intolerable tax which makes everyone shiver when the fifth year approaches. . . . While merchants can recoup themselves by speculations, those for whom the work of their hands scarcely furnishes a livelihood are crushed beneath the burden.

The lowest cobbler cannot escape from it. I have seen some who, raising their hands to heaven and holding up their shoe-knife, swore that they would pay nothing more. But their protests did not abate the greed of their cruel oppressors, who pursued them with their threatening shouts and seemed quite ready to devour them.

It is the time when slavery is multiplied, when fathers barter away the liberty of their children, not in order to enrich themselves with the price of the sale, but in order to hand it over to their persecutors.[21]

Egypt, in particular, was a country on which the *chrysargyron* inflicted grave hardships. Indeed the Egyptians, we are told, often refused to pay altogether until they had been subjected to physical violence. A papyrus of the time of Constantine records the sort of thing that happened:

Pamonthius, a wine dealer in Egypt, being long importuned by the magistrates of his native place with exactions beyond his means, and being asked for this and not being able to meet his liabilities, was compelled by his creditors to sell all that he had, even to the garment that covered his shame.

And when these were sold, scarcely could he get together the half of the money for his creditors, who, those pitiless and godless men, carried off all his children.[22]

Zosimus, too (although the *chrysargyron* had been abolished by his time, in 498), is thoroughly critical and melodramatic about what the emperor had done.

He imposed a tribute of gold and silver on all who engaged in commerce, even on the pettiest tradesmen in the towns; wretched courtesans even were not exempt from the tax.

On the return of the fourth year, as the fatal time approached, all the towns were seen in tears and grief. When the period had arrived, the scourge and the rack were used against those whose extreme poverty could not support this unjust tax.

Mothers sold their children, and fathers prostituted their daughters, obliged to obtain by this sorry trade the money which the collectors of the *chrysargyron* came to snatch from them.[23]

Gibbon felt that Zosimus, although so often prejudiced, is not too far wrong here: the *chrysargyron* was assessed in too arbitrary a manner, and collected with excessive brutality.[24] He goes on to stress the hardships which the tax imposed on the townsmen who had to pay, pointing out that the 'secret wealth of commerce, and the precarious profits of labour' were hard to evaluate accurately, and were sadly susceptible to unfair valuation by the financial authorities. Unlike landowners, whose property could be seized as a security, manufacturers and merchants could provide no acceptable security other than their own persons, which meant that the only way for the treasury to get hold of their money was to torture them or beat them up.

And yet, although it might have seemed, and Gibbon apparently felt, that the urban middle class would be the worst hit by this tax, it was, in fact, the populations of the countryside who were the worst sufferers. For the merchants and traders in the cities, needing to raise money to satisfy the treasury's needs, extracted the highest possible rents from the rural areas. Such wealth, therefore, as the rustics possessed was diverted to the towns, and the rural populations were reduced to extreme poverty, increasingly fleeing, as time went on, to the refuge from the extortionate imperial authorities offered by rich men's large estates. With the consequence that not only trade but agriculture suffered.

Constantine was evidently aware of the hardships the *chrysargyron* was causing, since he issued an edict forbidding the employment of racks and scourges (which were evidently used to enforce these extortions) and insisting that the imprisonment, which was an inevitable alternative to these methods, should at least be in spacious and well-ventilated conditions.

Moreover, he also specifically authorized certain tax remissions. For example, he cut nearly a quarter of the taxes of Augustodunum (Autun, for which one of the Panegyrists seems to have been speaking), and he cancelled its arrears. Elsewhere, now that cash was more abundant, an effort was made to mitigate tax hardships by commuting payments in kind into money payments (*adaeratio*) – although this did not, in fact, do much to diminish oppression, since the assessments of money values of goods could be notoriously arbitrary.

However, Constantine attempted further measures of relief as well. Thus he passed a general law in 320 against oppressive tax extortions, and created a special official, the *peraequator census*, to hear appeals against tax liability (and to show how different he was from Licinius, some of whose toughest measures, which had been deplored by influential people, he rescinded).

And Constantine tried to keep an eye on the decurions (*curiales*), the town councillors throughout the empire whose duty it was to assess taxes: to fix, that is to say, what each proprietor had to pay, according to the property census drawn up by the *tabellarii*.

The decurions suffered from an initial disadvantage, because of Constantine's tendency to take a proportion of civil, local taxation for himself, in order to meet his own expensive needs. Moreover, at the end of his reign all municipal indirect taxation was confiscated by the government; and, in addition, civic taxes were often channelled into the lavish construction of churches.

But quite apart from these particular difficulties, the position of the decurions was a miserable one. Indeed, the ruin which these enforced taxation duties brought upon them, largely as a result of the policies of Constantine, meant the virtual destruction of the entire middle class of which they were the backbone – the class to which the Roman world had owed so much.

In Roman Africa in the 320s there were still popular elections of city officials; but they may have been merely a formality, since genuine elections scarcely existed. The offices and duties of these decurions were handed down to their sons and daughters, so that their families tended to become hereditary groups. This was, it might seem, a distinction, but in fact wealthy men had long since become unwilling to serve as councillors: which is why the function, instead, devolved upon the classes below them, who sometimes appointed an elite executive committee of ten or twenty of the more influential men among them to get the dirty work done.

Seeing that the collection of taxes was their principal task, it was not surprising that, to the people below them, they looked like oppressors, who were merely, it would appear, transferring powerful people's taxes to the poor. But they were shot at from the other side as well, since the government, too, leant on them very heavily in its attempt to collect sufficient taxes. Thus the Code of Theodosius II (*Codex Theodosianus*) includes as many as 192 edicts browbeating the decurions and threatening them with every sort of penalty.

These official menaces created a terrifying atmosphere of intimidation as far as the decurions were concerned. The government and the decurions were incessantly at daggers drawn, and in order to enforce its will the administration was perfectly prepared to have recourse to savage physical violence. The only redeeming feature was the fact that the authorities were not wholly efficient in their efforts to get what they wanted. The perpetual repetitions and reiterations of imperial pronouncements, and the sharp stridency of their tone, indicate clearly that the provisions of these orders were not being completely enforced, and could, somehow, be got round.

Nevertheless, the lot of the decurions remained lamentable: Maxentius recognized this when he condemned a Christian to be a town councillor! It was only to be expected, therefore, that, despite the attempts to enforce heredity, the councillors should wish to leave their jobs. But everything possible was done by the imperial authorities to prevent this by legal action. The decurions

were stopped from fleeing into the army or the civil service or the clergy (326) (whose status seemed particularly desirable to the decurions, since, as a letter from Constantine to Anullinus, proconsul of Africa (313), shows, they were granted immunity from decurional office).

To sum up, it must be concluded that Constantine's arrangements for taxation, although partially inherited and no doubt urgently required by the costly policies on which he had embarked, contributed largely to the failure of trade and agriculture, and caused widespread hostility to the state – an alienation which in turn proved to play a large part in the downfall of the western empire. It was a crushing tax system, which ultimately defeated its own purpose, because it destroyed the very people who had to pay the taxes.

It was therefore imperative, if too much damage was not to be done, that Constantine's taxation policy should be backed up by efficient monetary plans, and this was only partially achieved, or rather, *was* achieved, but at the expense of the poorer population.

Throughout the crises of the later third century everything had gone wrong with the currency. Gold and silver coins had become much too scarce, and the bronze pieces (*folles*), silver-washed but still allotted artificial values which made large profits for the government, had suffered from galloping inflation, so that a huge number of these coins had been needed to pay for anything at all, with consequent hardships and miseries that can only be imagined.

Diocletian's Edict on Prices (301) had attempted to limit the size of this inflation. Yet, although the Edict went into elaborate detail, and was, it must be admitted, epoch-making in its ambitious intentions, it had proved totally ineffective, and, indeed, was never adequately implemented at all. For traders and merchants ignored its provisions, which were virtually abandoned after a very short time. The flight from money to goods continued – in so far as goods were available, that is to say in so far as they were not driven off the market – and prices rose still higher. Diocletian had acted according to his view that 'uncontrolled economic activity is a religion of the godless'.[25] But his alternative, based on a brutally schematic concept of universal welfare in which the rights and concerns of the individual were brushed aside, proved unworkable and soon, as we saw, died a natural death.

Diocletian did, however, manage to produce a gold coinage, struck to an exact standard, at sixty (occasionally fifty) to the pound.[26] But these *aurei*, which were moderately, even if not sufficiently, abundant, did not achieve any satisfactory ratio relationship with his silver-washed bronze *folles*, which continued to create inflation at a fantastic and increasing rate.

Then Constantine, deriving windfalls from his defeat of Licinius – resulting in confiscations and compulsory purchases (like those of Licinius) – and later from the plundering of pagan temples, strengthened and amplified the gold coinage, which he found very useful. He preferred, however, to issue these pieces at a slightly lower weight than those fixed by his predecessors, that is at seventy-two not sixty to the pound. This new coin was the *solidus*, which was introduced in *c.*310, and replaced the *aureus* in Italy in 312 and in the east in 324. Of higher quality than its predecessors, it was at first, perhaps, not so much a coin as a piece of bullion stamped with a seal. But people soon felt it advisable to accept it at its declared value, even if this may have been regarded as excessively high.

In 317 Constantine legislated severely against the operation of varying exchange rates. He used the *solidus* for the annual payment of salaries to his senior officials, and for his five-yearly donatives to the troops, and for providing subventions to his barbarian allies. And he also timed its minting with tax requirements in mind. This *solidus* was one of Constantine's most lasting achievements, because it continued to maintain its weight and purity for seven centuries to come, being employed by many nations (even in the east) for trading, so that this 'dollar of the Middle Ages' played a large part in preventing the reversion of the west to a barter economy.

Constantine's silver coinage was not very abundant, although he issued a series of silver multiples in *c.*310 and *c.*330. Greater abundance would have been convenient for the public, to bridge the gulf between gold and bronze; but the convenience of the public was scarcely considered. Silver coins were employed by the emperor to pay salaries that were not paid in gold – for example to act as paymaster for the army. Silver pieces were also employed to buy supplies, and to conduct transactions which were on a medium scale. But they did not play a major part.

However, his silver-washed bronze coinage remained as feeble as it had been before, and indeed it became worse, and its damaging results increased. In particular, these issues continued to fuel an ever-increasing inflation. The weight of the bronze *follis* was persistently and unremittingly reduced, declining from thirty-two to the pound in 307 to seventy-two in 313. In 324 Constantine partially arrested the fall of the (notional) *denarius* at 172,800 to the pound (a far cry from the 60,000, itself very high, of AD 300), though later this figure could no longer be maintained, and became inflated to 275,000. But in Egypt the rise was much larger, and the rate amounted to millions; probably the same phenomenon occurred elsewhere.

Arguments that the inflation had less serious effects than we might suppose, because there was no large class with fixed money incomes, and that it did not therefore substantially undermine social stability, seem unacceptable. On the contrary, this perpetual inflationary tendency, involving, among much else, the inevitable restriction of all exchanged and imported goods, caused widespread destitution and misery.

In other words, Constantine's coinage favoured the rich, who possessed and dealt in *solidi*, and disqualified the poor, who possessed no gold coins and had to conduct their transactions with this ludicrously valueless and inflationary token currency. Constantine, as we saw, managed to acquire a reputation for almsgiving to the poor, and his legislation dutifully drew attention to such underprivileged groups, but in this vital matter of the currency they – and what might be called the 'lower-middle class' – were mercilessly and inhumanely discriminated against. His coinage, in other words, was principally designed – in accordance with established tradition – as a medium of state expenditure, and not to meet social requirements at all.

For most of the population never laid hands on any coins at all except these silvered bronze pieces – and as time went on, as we saw, they constantly diminished in value. But the government continued to issue more and more of them (without siphoning them into taxes, which had to be paid to it in other metals), so that there was a glut of these worthless coins on the market. This did not worry the authorities, since the bronze was a token currency to which a wholly artificial high value could be attached, bringing (as has already been suggested) a substantial profit to the government. Moreover, nobody was aware – and this unawareness was general in the ancient world – of the economic law which rules that, if the number of coins in circulation rises but the goods available do not, then prices are certain to increase.[27] So prices did increase, to a disastrous extent.

The relationship between Constantine's gold and bronze coinages can be illustrated by an example.[28] The public sale of wine was in the hands of a functionary known as the *rationalis vinorum*. It was his duty to account for the results of his activities to one of the emperor's principal financial officials, the *comes sacrarum largitionum*. The *rationalis vinorum*, inevitably, received most of his revenue from traders' taxes, in small payments of bronze coin. But he was not allowed to make his own subsequent payments to the imperial treasury in this form. On the contrary, he had to go out and purchase gold *solidi* with his bronze coins, and pay these to the treasury instead.

What the treasury did with them on their receipt is worthy of note. It was mentioned earlier that these *solidi* of Constantine were often regarded more as bullion than as coin. And so, when the treasury received such pieces, from the *rationalis vinorum* or similar officials, its administrators felt no compunction about melting them down. Then, later on, it made them into coins once again, when Constantine needed them for the payments that he wanted to make with gold pieces.

But even leaving aside peculiarities such as this, there were grave faults in this monetary system. For one thing, as we saw, it grossly favoured the rich against the poor. The *plebs urbana* may well have been marginally better off than the *plebs rustica*. Licinius, it is true, had tried to help the latter, to which he himself belonged by birth. But they fared badly under Constantine, and this in turn made for poor economic and agricultural conditions. True, these were patchy. For example, parts of Pannonia remained quite prosperous, and there was something of a revival round Puteoli (Pozzuoli) in Campania. But on the whole conditions were bad, and the monetary system made them worse – and contributed, therefore, to the eventual downfall of the western empire.

Moreover, it was not even comprehensive or extensive enough to provide the huge revenue from taxation which Constantine needed. This meant that taxes often had to be collected in kind instead of in cash. And this in turn meant that the principle of heredity had to be insisted upon with unprecedented strictness: people had to be told to stay where they were, so that they could not escape these impositions – that is to say, in order that they should duly pay in kind, they were bound to the soil, or to their occupation, whatever it was.

Such a development was not entirely due to Constantine. As we saw, Diocletian (if not earlier emperors as well) had already favoured a tendency to bind people to the soil, making it illegal for the rural population (*coloni*) to leave their domiciles, and probably extending this ban to their children, so that it became, in effect, hereditary – like military service. Licinius, too, adopted a similar practice. And so, therefore, with greater and more widespread effect when he came to control the entire empire, did Constantine, who, according to one interpretation, increased the hereditary compulsion of civilians, whereas it had principally concerned soldiers. For example, decurions, as we have seen, bequeathed their position to their children, as a hereditary obligation. That may (or may not) have been regarded as a privilege in decurional circles, but for the *coloni* it became a matter of grim compulsion.

Indeed, compulsion was at the heart of every aspect of the life of a *colonus*.[29] He could never get free of his lot, and was not allowed to assume any public duties which would take him away from it. The *coloni* were so firmly attached to the estate on which they worked that the landlord could not sell it without them, and they must not be moved from one estate to another, unless it could be established that the first estate had too much land, and the second too little; even the treasury itself was not empowered to break this link between estate and *colonus*. Moreover, if they did succeed in running away, *coloni* were reclaimed as forcibly as if they were slaves, and subjected to severe punishment, as was, also, the man who had given them refuge.

Here is a law of Constantine on the subject, promulgated in 332:

He with whom shall be found a *colonus* belonging to another shall have not merely to restore him to the estate on which this *colonus* was born, but shall be obliged also to pay the capitation for the time [passed with him]....

As for the *coloni* who attempt to run away, it shall be allowed to load them with chains, in the manner of slaves.[30]

By imperial oppression, then, or under the ineluctable circumstances which required such stringent measures, the Roman world had been transformed. Small farmers had ceased to exist, and in their place there was mass cultivation by slave or serf labour. Once again the rich – the large landowners – had prevailed, by mercilessly exploiting the poor, whom economic necessity had forced to flock on to their lands.

And it was Constantine who played the chief part in completing and formalizing this situation. Earlier, he had made Rome's pork-butchers, and the shipowners (*navicularii*) (314) who brought the city its grain, into hereditary castes. Moreover, not only were the sons of any army veterans brought into the same net (314/15), but so were state officials. There was a flood of laws to this sort of effect – such an extensive outpouring that one gets the impression that people were showing reluctance to comply. But by and large they were obliged to. 'The watchword was "everyone at his post," or Roman civilization would perish. It was a state of siege.'[31]

It was also a state of affairs which caused demoralization, among rich and poor alike.

The houses of the powerful were crammed full and their splendour enhanced to the destruction of the poor, the poorer classes of course being held down by force.

But the poor were driven by their afflictions into various criminal enterprises, and losing sight of all respect for law, all feelings of loyalty, they entrusted their revenge to crime. For they often inflicted the most severe injuries on the Empire, laying waste the fields, breaking the peace with outbursts of brigandage, stirring up animosities; and passing from one crime to another supported usurpers.[32]

Such was the general demoralization, but the trouble went further than social collapse: it amounted to a general unnerving of the will, a paralysis of character, a failure of strength.[33]

It was a hollow mockery, then, that each man was told he could do what his soul desired, and that Constantine and his friends repeatedly called him the 'restorer of freedom'.

What made matters even worse, a good deal worse, was the widespread corruption– 'the universality of the employment of power, public and private alike, as a source of profit'.[34]

This corruption was, of course, nothing new. It had been manifest enough in the third century, when inflation had reduced state salaries and wages to such an extent that criminal means had to be used to augment them. It was said that there had been insupportable unfairness under Diocletian, and bribery under Galerius. Maxentius had employed bribes to seduce Severus' army. Decurions, under Licinius, had corruptly gained equestrian grades. But now, under Constantine, things were no better, and indeed were even worse.

Everybody was out for what they could get. Officers treated

their soldiers dishonestly, and pay was stolen. There were bribes at church councils, and recurrent charges of handing over money in order to become a priest and gain high church office. Silvanus, the Donatist bishop of Constantina (Cirta), took bribes.[35] Rich pagans claimed exemption from civic taxes and duties on the false ground that they were Christian priests. Themistius refers to flagrant extortion by tax recorders and collectors.[36] Provincial governors, perhaps encouraged by Ulpian's dictum that a proconsul need not invariably abstain from accepting presents,[37] sold jobs and were ruinously greedy, employing *exactores* to extract their excessive requirements. There was fraud at the mints, and much false coin. The 'selling of smoke', *fumum vendere*, was the curse of the graft-ridden and patronage-poisoned law courts, handing out inefficient and brutal justice, in which state functionaries connived, taking gifts to secure judicial audiences. The *navicularii* charged with the service of the *annona* stole the grain, while they themselves were extortionately treated by the man in charge of the ports. The postal administration exploited travellers.

The officials of the imperial chancery, too, were well known to be venal, and the secret police (*agentes in rebus*) demanded fees; people did not dare to lodge complaints. Customary fraudulence, *consuetudo fraudium*, was a commonplace, in an atmosphere in which petty thefts, lies and cheating and irregular gratuities abounded, in the imperial household, as in private homes. For the court eunuchs were not guiltless, and Constantine's personal favourites played an unhappy and sinister part: as we saw elsewhere, he was 'the first of all to open the jaws of those nearest to him'.[38]

The emperor was aware of some of this corruption, and did not like it: not only was it evil, but it weakened his own authoritarian power. So he pronounced numerous edicts and laws against such wicked practices:

To all provincials: If anyone anywhere in any rank or office believes he can truly and clearly establish anything against any of my governors, counts, retinue or court, that seems not to have been properly and justly handled, let him come forward with courage and in safety, let him address himself to me.

I myself will hear everything, I myself will judge, and if the matter is substantiated, I will avenge myself. Let him speak! If the matter is proven, as I said, I will avenge myself.[39]

And then there is Constantine's famous law of 331:

The Augustus to the provincials.

The rapacious hands of the apparitors shall immediately cease, they shall cease, I say; for if after due warning they do not cease, they shall be cut off by the sword.

The chamber curtain of the judge shall not be venal; entrance shall not be gained by purchase, the private council chamber shall not be infamous on account of the bids. The appearance of the governor shall not be at a price; the ears of the judge shall be open equally to the poorest as to the rich.

There shall be no despoiling on the occasion of escorting persons inside by the one who is called chief of the office staff. The assistant of the aforesaid chiefs of the centurions and other apparitors who demand small and great sums shall be crushed; and the unsated greed of those who deliver the records of a case to litigants shall be restrained.

Always shall the diligence of the governor guard lest anything be taken from a litigant by the aforesaid classes of men. If they should suppose that anything ought to be demanded by them from those involved in civil cases, armed punishment will be at hand, which will cut off the heads and necks of the scoundrels.

Opportunity shall be granted to all persons who have suffered extortion to provide for an investigation by the governors. If they should dissemble, We hereby open to all persons the right to express complaints about such conduct before the counts of the provinces or before the praetorian prefects, if they are closer at hand, so that We may be informed by their references to Us and may provide punishment for such brigandage.

Given on the kalends of November at Constantinople in the consulship of Bassus and Ablabius.[40]

This seemed a noble programme; and in 318, 321 and 326 Constantine passed laws against counterfeiting and forging. Indeed, he became even more strident in his penalties against corruption.

Judicial severity to deal with all such offences was encouraged. His fulminations were expressly designed to terrify.

In pursuance of this same stringent policy several other categories of offender, too, were noted as liable to punishment, and capital punishment at that. They included scribes who inserted unjustified names in the lists of those entitled to immunity, tax collectors who oppressively exceeded their duties, workmen who spoiled the buildings they had been commissioned to erect or repair, creditors who had taken forcible possession of their debtors' oxen and agricultural implements, Jews who thew stones at their fellow religionists who had embraced Christianity, and diviners (*haruspices*) who had entered a private house.

But what seemed to offend Constantine most of all were offences against chastity. Slaves who had had sexual intercourse with free women were condemned to death, and so were those guilty of complicity in rape. If a maidservant assisted in the abduction of her mistress, molten lead was to be poured into her mouth. And mutilations, too, were freely prescribed. Constantine seemed concerned not so much to maintain the fabric and structure of civil society as to visit ferocious vengeance upon offences against morals. And he appeared less anxious to find remedies for the evils he deplored than to inflict punishment upon those who had been responsible for such evils. Old laws, as well as his own, were violated in the process, so that his pious but violent indignation could be satisfied.[41]

Yet the trouble was that all this severity, and all these measures to stop corruption, failed to achieve any appreciable result. Constantine's laws – ever more complicated, obtrusive and repetitive – were widely ignored and could be bought off. Even a writer as eager to see the bright side of the emperor as Eusebius had to conclude: 'Constantine spoke and acted in this way [rebuking corruption and cupidity], but he reclaimed no one from his wicked habits.... No fear of death deterred bad people from their wrongdoing.'[42] There was still rapacity and corruption everywhere. In the fifth century, it was possible to declare to an emperor, 'everything is bought'.[43] Nothing had changed; and, in his time, too, Constantine had not succeeded in changing anything at all.

But meanwhile all the resources of art were brought into play to illustrate his picture of himself as the magnificent autocrat.

They are amply deployed on the reliefs of the Arch of Constantine at Rome, the largest free-standing monument of the imperial city. These reliefs, displaying continuous narrative method, employed earlier by the Egyptians and Greeks to depict static ceremonial scenes, look like the products of a workshop which also we can see, made many sarcophagi; though the porphyry sarcophagus of Helena in the Vatican, on the other hand – originally intended for Constantine himself – displays a classicizing revolt against this 'primitive' expressionism. On the Arch of Constantine, too, there are traces of 'Constantinian classicism'. Yet, predominantly, there is a marked, and perhaps oriental, change of feeling which involved a departure from classicism – and was not entirely without late third-century precedent, as manifested on the Arch of Galerius at Thessalonica (Salonica) and a series of reliefs from Nicaea (Iznik).

The Arch of Constantine is an official war memorial, its frieze depicting four events of the war against Maxentius, together with a distribution of money to the Roman people in the Forum of Julius Caesar. The date 313/15 is usually preferred for the Arch, but arguments have been put forward for 325/6. This is the last of the free-standing triumphal arches: henceforward they are in the interiors of churches, propping up the edifice and marking off the chancel from the nave and aisles.

The reliefs on the Arch of Constantine show him in the immobile midst of a row of standardized, subordinated, symmetrized subjects, whose individualisms are replaced by uniform, mechanical, unarticulated simplification, with everything centred upon the over-lifesize, rigid figure of the emperor himself, beside whom everyone else fades into insignificance.

This is typical of late Roman art. A fiercely direct appeal is made to the people who are looking at it. In order to make contact with them, the principal figures are frontally depicted, gazing straight ahead. Crowds and groups of persons, whatever their occupation or status or rank, are displayed in flat lines, all at the same level and upon the same plane. Elegant gracefulness does not concern the sculptor, who is interested only in the message he single-mindedly conveys: it is not to be diverted or interrupted by the smallest distraction. Everything within the tableau is frozen; everyone looks the same, in a uniform presentation and role. Personal differences no longer matter, among those who surround the uniquely elevated ruler – who is on the way to transformation into the inhuman effigy that Constantine's successors duly became in the art that depicted them.

In the interests of glorifying this new, or newly formalized, type of diademed, autocratic emperor, the barrier between official and plebeian art has gone down, as a raw, vigorous, crude and forceful pseudo-primitive 'folk style' takes over to demonstrate Constantine's uniqueness.

His portraiture carries the same message. There had already been smouldering, frowning, nightmarish statues of the Tetrarchs, such as the fear-inspiring pairs in Venice and the Vatican, and a red porphyry bust of Maximinus II Daia or Licinius at Cairo. But Constantine's enormous marble head, seven times lifesize, now to be seen in the courtyard of the Conservatori Museum in Rome, is more imposing still. It was part of a statue of which the fabulous dimensions alone were deeply impressive. And, furthermore, it has mobilized the remains of classicism to infuse a sinister, imposing touch of realism into its hieratic pattern, which is reinforced by surrealistically, transcendentally huge upward-gazing eyes, and formidably aloof, exaggerated, scarcely mortal-looking features: an effort is being made to show a man in close contact with God.[44]

This Conservatori head of Constantine possibly replaced an earlier one. With its huge right hand and feet and bent left knee, the remains of what seems to have been a seated statue, it was brought, in 1486, from the Basilica of Maxentius (now completed and realigned by Constantine). In certain respects, the head looked back to the earlier empire. But much has changed. The head does display touches of realism; but they are more visible in female imperial portraits of the epoch, and in a few contemporary heads of private citizens, for example Dogmatius in the Vatican (from the Lateran).

As for Constantine, there is also a somewhat battered head at York, and a statue in the Vatican, presumably of earlier date – and possibly at one time in the Forum[45] – and a bronze head in the museum at Belgrade. Other busts are of uncertain attribution. There was also a statue at Rome, of which the 'copies', next to the old main entrance of S. Giovanni in Laterano and in front of S. Lorenzo Maggiore at Milan, are unreliable. Constantine also appears to have had a large statue in the city which he refounded as Constantinople (beside the Golden Gate); it was somewhat hastily adapted from an image of Apollo. His varied coin-portraits, too, are informative about the impression he intended to convey, though the extent to which any of them are truly realistic is disputable.[46]

What sort of a man was Constantine, behind this imposing exterior? We can at once dismiss the unrestricted encomia of his Christian admirers, Lactantius and Nazarius, who wrote that he charmed everyone at Rome by his kindliness, dignity and good humour,[47] while Eusebius could write that 'everything concerning the sovereign is noble'.[48] That is, of course, the exaggeration of professional flatterers: and we must somehow get behind their words.

When we do, we find a man of mixed qualities. There are divergent estimates of his statesmanship: was he weak-willed, or diabolically clever? At least he was, as we have seen, a superb general. He was also a masterly, coldly intelligent organizer and leader and administrator, a man of action with an immense capacity for forming schemes and carrying them out, who possessed the advantage of being absolutely tireless. 'In his dispatch of business', rightly observes Gibbon, 'his diligence was indefatigable.... Even those who censured the propriety of his measures were compelled to acknowledge that he possessed magnanimity to conceive, and patience to execute, the most arduous designs.'[49] And some of them were quite original; despite a respect for tradition, he had no objection to change.

At this point we must anticipate a little, and speak of his religious policy, which will be dealt with more fully in the pages that lie ahead. For this was the field in which his arrangements were most cunning. That is to say, although he himself, for reasons that will be indicated, became a firm adherent of Christianity, and was determined that the state and its chief representatives should ultimately embrace the same faith – as the best guarantee of imperial unity – the endeavours that he undertook to ensure that this became so were infinitely patient, and tactful, and *gradual*, since he had learnt in the hard school of Diocletian's court how not to be too impatient in pursuing his aims, and how to dissimulate. This *gradualness* was one of his principal talents and virtues.

As regards his personal habits, it is not at all certain that Julian the Apostate was correct in describing him as a victim of sensual lusts,[50] even if he was not altogether averse to the pleasures of the flesh. However, whether Eusebius was justified in stressing his gastronomic abstinence is equally uncertain.[51]

He inspired loyalty, in officers and others, and all the more so because he liked to chat with them, delighting, as Gibbon noted, 'in the social intercourse of familiar conversation'. And one of the things he worked hard at, throughout his life, was improving his education (faulty at first). And even if middle-brow – with 'an intellect not shaped for abstract argument or logical progression'[52] – he was able to speak fervently in support of the classics, and, like his father Constantius I Chlorus, deliberately combated anti-intellectual trends, as was shown by a whole series of his pronouncements, in which he encouraged intellectuals by tax immunities and offered privileges to the members of thirty-eight liberal and artistic occupations. Diocletian, too, had helped professors: and this came more easily to Constantine, who was not quite so rough.

He was a man who possessed great gifts, the gifts of a superlative emperor. Unfortunately, however, there were also other sides to the question. For one thing, not all his administrative plans, as we saw, proved successful. However, as Gibbon rightly discerned, Constantine was also unlimitedly, ruthlessly ambitious.[53] Highly emotional and religious (or superstitious, for his religious views were in a bit of a muddle), and didactically devoted to lecturing all and sundry, he was dedicated to his own personal success, and despotically determined at all costs to achieve it, even if this meant an occasionally devious approach and a tendency, despite his talent for gradualness, to make, on certain occasions, too rapid decisions on inadequate and not over-subtle grounds; since he was, perhaps, a little 'innocent' – lacking Richelieu's and Talleyrand's power of assessing human motives, although flatterers ascribed him a unique gift to pierce into the hearts of men.[54]

Constantine was not altogether lacking in tolerance and patience. But they could easily snap. His ironical humour, too, sometimes caused offence. However, he was a man who yearned to be popular, and, being vain, was nothing like as averse to flattery as Eusebius maintained[55] – this made him, sometimes, too credulous and easy to deceive, and therefore over-generous and able to be taken advantage of. Although always convinced of his rightness, he was capriciously capable of sudden, impulsive changes of mind.

He brooded in a reserved and reticent way, and dreamed at night, and believed he saw visions, and was subject to dangerous fits of suspicion and jealousy and violent fury and blind anger. Sometimes these outbursts were shortlived and mainly verbal, but on other occasions they led to murders. Eutropius and Gibbon were right in stressing his deterioration towards the end of his life, when absolute power had corrupted him, and he was 'raised by conquest above the necessity of dissimulation'.[56]

CHAPTER 6:

CONSTANTINE, CRISPUS
AND FAUSTA

EUTROPIUS declared that Constantine was responsible for many murders of his 'friends',[1] and this was unmistakably true. There was a long list of his victims. It is no use trying to excuse this in the light of an ancient civilization that had different ideals from ours, and so on, and by pointing out that other leaders such as Diocletian and especially Licinius had also committed assassinations. For Constantine's behaviour is inexcusable by any standards, and casts a blot on his reputation. Being an absolute autocrat, he believed that he could kill anyone.

One of the most shocking events of his reign was his 'execution' of one of his principal friends and advisers during his years at Constantinople, Sopater, a pagan philosopher and theosophist (331). Sopater, who went in for mystical symbolism,[2] was killed on the preposterous pretext that he had magically 'fettered' the winds and thus prevented food from arriving at famine-stricken Constantinople. But even if Constantine credulously believed in magic, as may well have been the case, this was not the real reason why Sopater met his death. He was killed because the praetorian prefect Ablabius was jealous of his power, and incited Constantine against him. The fact that Sopater was a pagan, and Ablabius was a Christian, no doubt played a part – and played a part also in the pagan Eunapius' gloomy comment: 'the entire state found misfortune through the murder of this one man'.[3] The death of Sopater certainly made Christian cohabitation with the pagans more difficult.

But something even worse, much worse, had happened five years earlier, or rather two things: Constantine's execution of his eldest son Flavius Julius Crispus, followed by the execution of his second wife Flavia Maxima Fausta as well. Fausta was not the mother of Crispus; his mother had been Minervina, who gave birth to him in *c*.305, and it has been disputed whether she was Constantine's wife (from *c*.290?) or his concubine.[4] Anyway, Minervina had disappeared from view, dead or put aside or divorced, when Constantine married Fausta, who bore him three sons, Constantine junior (II), Constantius junior (II) and Constans.

Nevertheless, Constantine's marriage to Fausta, and her production of this threefold offspring, did not by any means signify the end of Crispus (even though his enemies declared he was illegitimate). On the contrary, establishing his powerful headquarters, with his own staff and army, at Augusta Trevirorum (Trier) – where Lactantius tutored him – he was appointed Caesar, with his half-brother the new-born Constantine junior and Licinius', two-year-old son Licinius Licinianus, in 317. Then, in 320, Crispus, young though he was, was said to have fought with distinction (under the guidance of a praetorian prefect) against the Alamanni and Franks. The Tenth Panegyric, addressing his father, praised these victories highly: 'Is not your breast filled with sweet joy, O Supreme Constantine, melting to see your son after so long a time – and to see him a conqueror?'[5]

Subsequently, too, in the Second Licinian War, the naval successes of Crispus in the Hellespont region contributed mightily to his father's subsequent triumph over Licinius; Crispus' victory there was compared to the historic battle of Salamis, nearly 800 years earlier. Nor was official recognition of his glory in the slightest degree grudging. A wide array of different coin-busts celebrates his successful military roles, and upon a Lorraine milestone he is described as 'Unconquered' ('INVICTVS').[6] He was doing enormously well (and his wife Helena had given birth to a son in 322).

And yet in 326, at the age of about twenty-one, he was taken off to Pola (Pula), underwent trial there, perhaps, before the municipal senate on some trumped-up charge, and between March and October of that year was put to death – on orders issued by Constantine from Serdica or Sirmium. Upon a subsequent inscription, Crispus' name is erased.[7]

Apparently Constantine's wife Fausta had spoken to her husband against him, alleging a plot. Her motive is clear enough; she wanted to suppress Crispus in favour of her own three sons – no doubt pointing out that they were legitimate, whereas Crispus was supposedly not, and adding that civil war would follow unless Crispus was suppressed.

But why did Constantine listen to her? Fausta was the youngest daughter of Maximian and Eutropia, and in March 307, perhaps at the age of about fourteen (or younger), had been married to Constantine, on Maximian's initiative. Later, however, she revealed to her husband Maximian's conspiracy against him (just as she was later to warn him of a supposed plot by Crispus); and Constantine showed his favour by pronouncing her Augusta in 324, after the Second Licinian War (she had previously been N[obilissima] F[emina]).

Fausta appears to have inherited her father's propensity for ferocious intrigue. Anyway, Constantine was evidently prepared to believe her story of Crispus' disloyalty and potential danger. As those who are familiar with autocratic governments will recognize, this was not altogether surprising, because Crispus had done so well (Eusebius and others did not hesitate to couple him with Constantine himself). Autocrats do not like people doing *too* well – even their eldest sons: because those sons might, before long, try to supersede them.

And we must ask whether Crispus had, perhaps, taken any action, or had allowed any action to be taken, which prompted Constantine to kill him. This is a question that we cannot answer (and the Christian writers do not help us, since they embarrassedly avoid the incident altogether). We can only wonder whether there was anything in the rumour that Crispus had asked his father to retire (in his favour) after twenty years, like Diocletian;[8] or whether he had shown other signs of ambition, or anger, or disobedience; or whether Constantine had heard of unrest among Crispus' entourage, who might have been impatient for their patron to succeed to the throne.

Contemporary accounts pass over in silence the reasons for the executions marring this year 326, and later chroniclers are almost equally reticent. Eutropius notes simply, 'being forced to it by necessity, he executed that exceptional man',[9] and Victor, 'of his children, he who was born the eldest was judicially executed by his father for an undisclosed reason'.[10] Modern writers are equally puzzled. 'What precisely Crispus's crime was has never been clearly established, and is probably now unascertainable.'[11]

For the allegations against him have been obscured by legend and fabrication. Crispus could, of course, be accused of being a bastard. But another highly spiced version declared that Fausta had fallen in love with her stepson Crispus: and that when he rejected her advances, like a second Phaedra repulsed, in the myth, by Hippolytus, she accused him of trying to rape her – which is not entirely plausible. If, then, we should look to other considerations, it is worth noting that, at the same time (so it would appear), Constantine arranged for the trial and banishment of another young man of note, Ceionius Rufius Albinus, for adultery and magic. The facts behind the charges brought against him and Crispus are now impossible to recover.

However, although an edict of c.326 can be interpreted as showing Constantine's suspicions that a conspiracy was under way, there is no clear evidence, despite the conjectures mentioned above, that Crispus was guilty of anything at all. It must be repeated that Fausta, through her agents, was responsible for his downfall, in order to rid her own sons of a rival. Even if she had, earlier, officially 'adopted' Crispus as her own son[12], as she may

Gold medallion (triple *solidus*) of 326
elaborately depicting Constantine
(MAX*imus* AUG*ustus*) as consul and
honouring the Senate (SENATUS).
Minted at Thessalonica (Salonica).

Head of Constantine taken
from the vast statue that
once stood in his basilica,
but is now in the Museo
dei Conservatori.

Medallion of Constantine issued
at Ticinum (315). There has been
much controversy about a
supposed Christian symbol on the
helmet.

Gold medallion of Constantine's father Constantius I Chlorus, struck at Trier. He has conquered Allectus, usurper in Britain (successor of Carausius), and enters London as *"Restorer of Eternal Light"*.

Under Diocletian (284–305) the Roman world is ruled by four oppressive autocrats, whose outward harmony concealed great strains.

Gold medallion (10-*aureus* piece) of Diocletian, issued at his capital Nicomedia (Izmit). The figure on the reverse is Jupiter Conservator (the Preserver), who stands for an anti-Christian return to the old gods.

A view of the Milvian Bridge in Rome, the site of Constantine's victorious battle against Maxentius, after which he was converted to Christianity.

Coin of Maxentius.

The Arch of
Constantine at Rome,
the city's last triumphal
Arch, erected to
celebrate Constantine's
victory at the Milvian
Bridge. Its decoration
combines contemporary
reliefs with others taken
from second century
monuments.

Relief from the Arch of
Constantine, showing
people (no longer indi-
vidualized) listening to
his speech in the Forum
Romanum. The relief is
over the left-hand arch
on the north side.

Reconstruction of Constantine's fortress of Divitia (Deutz), across the Rhine from Colonia Agrippinensis (Cologne).

The "Basilica" at Trier showing the Audience Hall (*aula Palatina*) of the imperial palace. Though much restored, and converted into a church, it still provides a unique example of an early fourth century building.

Gold Medallion of Licinius and his son Licinius Licinianus Caesar. This is an early example of frontal portrayal and the wearing of haloes. Jupiter is described as the Preserver of them both.

Constantine with a halo. Like many before and after him, he is described as P(*ius*) F(*elix*) AUG(*ustus*).

Silvered bronze coin of Constantine showing two soldiers with the inscription "The Glory of the Army" (GLORIA EXERCITUS) and a standard bearing the letters XP (Christos). Minted at Siscia (Sisak) in Pannonia.

Sixteenth-century painting of Constantine's
Basilica of St. Peter, later replaced by the
present building. In the church of S. Martino
ai Monti, Rome.

This painted portrait from Augusta Trevirorum (Trier) is thought to represent Constantine's mother Helena. She is also shown on coins (FL. HELENA AUGUSTA).

Gold coin (double *solidus*) of Helena. She is decribed as "Augusta".

Porphyry sarcophagus of Helena, in the Vatican Museum. It may well have been originally intended for Constantine.

have, it is very possible that she had already, and deliberately, instigated rivalry between him and Constantine junior in Gaul[13] – a rivalry which is carefully contradicted by a medallion of 324 showing the two half-brothers amicably together.[14] And perhaps Crispus' removal from that country in the previous year had meant that his father was now jealous of him. This has been denied.[15] But Constantine was a jealous man, and could have been easily per-suaded that Crispus was prepared to overthrow and supplant him.

It may well be that Fausta, even if she did not stress the rape story, launched her attack on Crispus from another personal angle, complaining to Constantine that his son had abducted some girl and made her his concubine. For Constantine was strictly opposed to such practices, as part of his opposition to sexual irregularities in general, and passed a fierce law against abduction on 1 April 326, and another against concubinage (at least for married men) in the same year: whether these laws preceded or followed the condemnation of Crispus is uncertain.

Anyway, Constantine, who was extremely credulous and sus-picious, believed what he was told against the youth, although he was his eldest son. And so, seeing himself as Abraham prepared to execute his first-born Isaac – a common artistic theme – he had Crispus killed.

But a guilty conscience very soon overtook him; his Christian advisers Ossius and Sylvester may have played on this guilty conscience to tighten their hold, and it was said that the former left the court in disgust.[16] Whether that was the case or not, it was true that the emperor was liable to sudden changes of mind, and before very long he came to the conclusion that he had made a disastrous mistake, and that Crispus had not committed or planned an offence after all, so that by an appalling act of murder Constantine had deprived himself of his eldest son quite wrongly and un-necessarily: he is said to have erected a golden statue 'to the son whom I unjustly condemned'.

Who persuaded him he had made this dreadful mistake is

disputable. It was often stated to have been his mother Helena (made Augusta, like Fausta, in 324, a year when imperial ladies were briefly prominent on coins); although the Helena in question, it has been suggested, may instead have been the enraged widow of Crispus of the same name[17] – even if this remains somewhat unlikely, since the tradition that it was the older Helena, Constantine's mother, seems too strong to contradict.

Anyway, his new conviction totally changed his attitude to Fausta, and he compounded the guilt of his first execution by a second, involving the death of Fausta herself. The story that she had denounced Crispus because she loved him and he did not return her love was allowed to spring up; and it was claimed, alternatively, that she had committed adultery with a slave in the imperial stables.[18] Both were theories that might well have exercised an influence on Constantine, who was so greatly disposed to puritanical sexual legislation. And the belief that she had behaved in some such immoral way could make him feel that he was doing right by putting an end to her (a feeling that could have been confirmed by the fact that she remained a pagan). So that is what he did. He had her immersed in a scalding bath, or suffocated in a deliberately over-heated steam-room, in the Constantinian Baths at Augusta Trevirorum (Trier). Or, possibly, she killed herself, under imperial impulsion. And Ceionius Rufius Albinus was brought back from exile.

So Constantine murdered both his eldest son and his wife. The *Epitome* of Aurelius Victor was surely right in linking the two crimes,[19] and modern writers who regard them as unconnected are wrong.[20] Even if, looking at it as cold-bloodedly as we can, we are able, with difficulty, to summon up the ability to defend, or at least excuse, one or other of the two executions as justified on political, national grounds, it is impossible to justify both of them. And, indeed, neither the one nor the other can really be justified at all. It could well be argued that they are the deeds of a tyrant whose feelings had got completely out of hand.

Evagrius refused to believe that Constantine could have committed such crimes as murdering Crispus and Fausta, offering as his reason Eusebius' failure to mention them[21] – but that is no sort of a reason for disbelieving the stories, since Eusebius would not have been likely to mention anything so unfavourable to Constantine.

And there was also a curious tale that Fausta survived. But this was a fictitious effort to rescue the emperor from the charge that he had murdered his wife. For he did, undoubtedly, kill both her and Crispus, and the pagan Zosimus, accepting this, attributed his conversion to Christianity to these deeds that he had done, supposing him to have seen that the old gods could not grant him purification or forgiveness so that he had to turn to the Christian God who was, immorally, prepared to do so. This is not a very plausible account of Constantine's conversion, since his favour to Christianity, as we shall see, had started much earlier.

But what is possibly true is that the executions may, as we have seen, have upset his Christian advisers; and they may also have been the penitential cause of Constantine's dispatch of his mother Helena to the Holy Land, in the hope of expiation. As for Constantine himself, the deeds could well have helped to enhance in his personality the features of the savage, degenerate tyrant which he seemed to Julian the Apostate and Edward Gibbon, particularly in his sombre last years.

CHAPTER 7:

———

CONSTANTINOPLE

══

CONSTANTINE'S principal claims to fame, among subsequent generations, were two: his conversion of the empire to Christianity, and his creation of Constantinople (on the site of Byzantium), which was to become the capital of the eastern Roman empire and then, for many more centuries, the capital of the Byzantine empire that succeeded it.

His embrace of Christianity will be the subject of the next part of this book. But here something must be said of his establishment of Constantinople. Rome, the eternal city, was still greatly venerated, but it had long ceased to be the political centre of the empire, since it was too far removed from the frontiers and roads which guaranteed imperial defence. Panegyrists plaintively felt that Rome should once again become the imperial capital;[1] but there was no chance that this would happen. Furthermore, successive military emperors had shown no marked enthusiasm to be near the Roman senate, which might have wished to influence them, against what they considered to be their best interests. In consequence, there was a long pre-Constantinian history of the planting of imperial headquarters in other cities. As Herodian had already observed in the second century AD, 'Where Caesar is, there Rome is.'[2]

For instance, Sirmium (Sremska Mitrovica), the most important strategic centre of the Danubian region, had become for substantial periods the residence and headquarters of Marcus Aurelius (AD 161–80), Maximinus I (235–8) and other rulers. It had also profited from Probus' encouragement of viticulture (276–82). Next, when Valerian (253–60) decided to divide the administration of the empire between himself and his son Gallienus, Antioch in Syria became the capital of the eastern part of the empire. And then, after Valerian was dead, came the time when Rome began to lose its primary role in the west as well, for the need to defend northern Italy against external military threats induced Gallienus, who had now become sole ruler (260–8), to establish his residence at Mediolanum (Milan) instead. Though little is left there today, except fragments of a curved structure (*exedra*), to recall its magnificence: his military headquarters being near by, at Ticinum (Pavia).

When, subsequently, Diocletian and Maximian divided the empire again, each had a Caesar as his deputy, so that there were now, of necessity, four capitals instead of merely two. In the west, Maximian lived at Mediolanum. However, his Caesar Constantius I Chlorus, the father of Constantine, resided at Augusta Trevirorum (Trier) – where the fleet intended to put down the usurpers in Britain was constructed – and the place still contains well-preserved monuments testifying to the imperial building activities, those of himself (*c*.305) and particularly of his son. In the east, the second Caesar Galerius had resided at Thessalonica (Salonica), a convenient rear headquarters, strategically situated on the Via Egnatia – the main land route from the west to the Bosphorus and Asia – from which the Danube command could be supervised and reinforced. His new quarters and palace at that city, including an audience hall measuring 53 by 25 metres and the mausoleum which he planned for himself (now the Church of St George), were unfinished at his death. And Galerius may also for a time – notably during his hostilities against Persia – have resided at Antioch, where a fine fourth-century palace–villa, with mosaics, has been unearthed.

But the senior capital of the empire was the city where Diocletian had been proclaimed emperor and where he also chose to
reside. This was Nicomedia (Izmit) in Bithynia (north-western
Asia Minor) upon the Propontis (Sea of Marmara). And it was this
town which, according to Christian writers, Diocletian had had
the 'mad whim' of making the equal of Rome. Nicomedia enjoyed
the facilities of a good harbour, which is still the principal naval
port of the Turks today. Looking over towards Europe, the place
was safely situated outside the danger zone liable to foreign
invasion, but stood conveniently upon the main line of communication between the two embattled frontiers, on the Danube and
Euphrates.

But Nicomedia, because of its comparative remoteness, did not
perfectly meet the military needs that were important to Constantine when he considered where to plant his capital. He had lived at
Augusta Trevirorum, and at times he had also stationed himself at
Arelate (soon to be called Constantina, now Arles) and Aquileia
and Ticinum (Pavia). But it was in the pivotal area of the Balkans –
more relevant to army requirements than the region in which
Nicomedia was located – that he felt he ought, for the most part,
to reside. Within this territory he first settled, successively, in two
selected centres, both stage-points on the principal military route
between west and east.

The first of these places (c.317) was Sirmium (Sremska Mitrovica), which had been the residence of so many emperors before.
And the second was Serdica (Sofia). The town lay in a fertile plain
containing the sources of the River Oescus (Iskar), a tributary of
the Danube, and was a staging post on the main road from the
Danube and Naissus (Niş) to the Bosphorus. Serdica, which
possessed a Thracian name derived from the tribe of the Serdi, had
developed out of a military fortress during the first half of the first
century AD, and had belonged to the province of Thrace since the
establishment of that province in AD 46. In the time of Trajan
(98–117), the place become a Roman citizen town (*municipium*),
with the designation of Ulpia, the emperor's family name. Aure-

lian (270–5) made it the capital of the new province of Dacia Ripensis. Traces of buildings of second-, third- and fourth-century date have been found.

Close enough to the frontier to constitute a convenient military headquarters, Serdica appealed to Constantine, and nearly became his capital. 'Serdica', he said, 'is my Rome.'[3] But eventually he found a site which suited him even better. Rejecting Troy, so it was said, perhaps fictitiously – although he did move the Trojan Palladium to his new city – he preferred a location at the point where the road from Europe to the River Euphrates is crossed, in spectacular fashion, by the maritime passage of the Bosphorus linking the Aegean and Black Seas. Moreover, it was in this area that Constantine had won his final and historic victory over Licinius (324), at Chrysopolis (Scutari). And Victory figures prominently on the coins of the new foundation, although it had been a victory over fellow Romans and not over foreigners.

Rulers and conquerors liked to establish cities where they had won military victories, and that is what Constantine did as well. He did so with all the more enthusiasm and determination because the region on the Bosphorus where he had gained his decisive triumph over Licinius also impressed him by its strategic significance. So both these reasons combined to determine the choice of the great new city which he now established, rebuilding the ancient town of Byzantium as Constantinople.[4]

There was a legend that the Christian eunuch Euphratas influenced him in the choice of the site,[5] but it is not necessary to believe this. The dating of the new Constantinople is a little uncertain, but it seems probable that it was inaugurated in 326 and that its dedication took place in 330. The whole initiative was given an impetus by Constantine's presence on the Danube: and indeed when he made peace with the Visigoths he stipulated that they should assist, if it became necessary, in the defence of Constantinople.

The new city was fortunate to possess the magnificent harbour of the Golden Horn. It was also defensible both by land and by sea, as it had demonstrated while resisting a prolonged siege by Septimius Severus (193–5). And it enjoyed ready accessibility, again by land and sea alike, to the vital industrial and cultural centres of Asia Minor and Syria.

It was also accessible to the grain supplies of Egypt which were required in order to feed the large population which, it was hoped, this great new town would attract. From 332, the grain exported from Egypt was set aside for Constantinople, with the rest of north Africa to supply Rome, which shared the imperial grain-fleets with the new city. And Constantinople enjoyed free distributions of grain like Rome itself. This dole was eventually handed out to 80,000 persons, as at Rome (or that may merely have been a target). A short time earlier, a local famine had nearly proved disastrous: and charges that black magic had created the shortage were what brought about the death of Constantine's pagan adviser Sopater (who was alleged by John Lydus to have played a part in the city's foundation, though this, like the rival story of the Christian eunuch Euphratas, may not be true).

Constantine more than quadrupled the area of the old Byzantium. Immigrants were attracted, and encouraged to build, by grants of imperial land in Asia Minor or food rations in perpetuity. A few distinguished Romans came, but according to Eunapius most of the new arrivals were drunkards: 'for the sake of applause in the theatres, Constantine organized drinking bouts of vomiting men close to himself'.[6]

However, Constantine did spend an immense amount, probably more than he could afford, on secular, as well as religious, building at Constantinople (including a large circular Forum). And yet owing to haste, and despite the masses of carpenters, builders and other craftsmen who were employed, much of the construction was gimcrack and impermanent. But at the same time the emperor brought in huge quantities of statues from far and wide, and had others erected to represent himself and his family, and filled the city's libraries with Greek and Latin books transported from Rome. Nevertheless, by the time of his death the population is unlikely to have exceeded 50,000, and Constantinople did not become a great commercial centre very quickly. Constantine's apparent determination to make it a truly Christian place will be discussed elsewhere.

It is likely that he did not announce initially that the new city he had brought into being was to become his sole capital, and that it should therefore be entitled the New or Second Rome, *altera Roma*[7] (although the expanded city seems to have been called informally by that name as early as 324). However, this must have been his ultimate aim, based on the concept that the new foundation was a monument to his greatness; and it was not very long before this intention came into effect.[8] As a foretaste of the future, like its Italian model Rome, Constantinople was not only given free grain distribution, as we have seen, but was also endowed with a Forum and Senate of its own. The number of senators rose from 300 to 2,000 in the first three decades.

But the Senate of Constantinople consisted largely of craftsmen, unlike the landowners who filled the Senate of Rome, and they took a lower precedence, at first, than those of the ancient capital, being called *clari*, not *clarissimi* like the Roman senators. For although 'CONSTANTINOPOLIS' figured prominently on the coinage, even at Rome itself,[9] Constantine was, as usual, proceeding with circumspect caution. That is to say, Rome lost none of its privileges, and at first Constantinople did not share its traditional position, ranking constitutionally with other cities that were, or had been, imperial residences; although the grandeur of the palaces in the new city, and its proposed dimensions, promised that this would not always be so.

Still, for the time being, its inferiority to Rome was signalized by the absence of any prefect of Constantinople, which was instead subordinated to a proconsul (who also probably governed much of Thrace). Nor were there quaestors at Constantinople, or tribunes of the people, or praetors. All the same, it was possible to see where the future lay, and the new foundation marked a definitive transfer of the epicentre of the empire to the east, which was richer than Italy and the western provinces, and would house imperial rulers long after the west had gone.

PART IV:

CONSTANTINE AND CHRISTIANITY

CHAPTER 8:

CONSTANTINE AND THE CHRISTIAN GOD

THE EMPEROR Severus Alexander (AD 222–35) had been convinced of the interchangeability of deities, and was ready to look for divine authority wherever it could be found. This was a step towards monotheism, and when Constantine was growing up, there was a powerful, widespread movement in the same direction.

It was not very easy for the ancients to believe that there could be only one god, but the idea, nevertheless, became increasingly familiar, and indeed had been so ever since the time of Plato. In fact, something close to monotheism had long attracted a good many adherents, and the growth of philosophical thinking meant that the multiplicity of pagan cults was mystically reinterpreted as the symbol of a *single* overriding reality.

Hence, for example, the monotheistic beliefs which Eusebius, perhaps rightly, ascribed to Constantine's father Constantius I Chlorus,[1] and which were encouraged by doctrines such as Mithraism (in which Constantius possibly believed), and which became very apparent in a prayer which Licinius (like Constantine himself) dictated to his troops.[2] The prayer was, in fact, blandly vague and ambiguous. It may have been suggested to Licinius by Constantine – whose soldiers sang similar hymns. Yet this prayer, for all its vagueness, was distinctly monotheistic: and indeed the army may have been accustomed to shouting monotheistic invocations.

Such tendencies obviously played into the hands of the Christians. Some of them chose, hopefully, to see the prayer of Licinius' soldiers, ambiguous though it actually was, in this light, as a direct opposition to paganism, 'dictated by an angel'.[3] And Christian writers such as Eusebius, Lactantius and Firmicus Maternus took up the same monotheistic cause – like Constantine himself, for whom the restoration of the empire's unity mirrored and depended upon a *single* divine power.

Earlier, too, the spread of monotheistic ideas had favoured the Christians, although that was not the main reason why they had incurred the displeasure of the pagan Roman government. They had incurred its displeasure because they did not seem entirely loyal. Moreover, we must dispense with the view that, during the century prior to Constantine, they were a wholly insignificant minority of the population. Certainly they were a minority, but not an insignificant one: although our knowledge of them is defective, they seem to have been quite a potent and wealthy pressure group, flourishing in many centres.[4]

And they were well organized, in cohesive groups. Indeed, this was one of the things that annoyed the pagan imperial government. They were *too* well organized altogether, setting up, for example, the Council of Elvira (Illiberis) in Spain, apparently in *c.*305 – although some prefer an earlier or later dating. More will be said of their well-arranged charities and social cohesion later. But loyalty to their organization could be interpreted as an alternative to loyalty to the state, so that it seemed, indeed, to become active, unpatriotic disloyalty. The way that the government liked to express this view was to say that, by worshipping their own God instead of the pagan gods, the Christians were flouting the hallowed traditions of Rome. But what the emperors really meant was that these Christians could not be relied upon to do what the government required, preferring to accept the authority of their own bishops instead, and thus fostering disunity in the empire.

And so the government turned to 'persecuting' these Christians with varying degrees of severity. Persecution is a vague term, but it involved making things as difficult for them as possible, and trying to induce them to toe the line, pay service or at least lip-service to the traditional pagan religion, and obey the emperor. There had been instances as long ago as Nero (54–68) and Marcus Aurelius (161–80), and famous 'persecutors' were Maximinus I Thrax (235–8), Trajanus Decius (249–51) and Valerian (253–60). But far the most serious and determined persecution was that of Diocletian and his Caesar Galerius. Which of the two bore the major responsibility has been disputed. Efforts have been made to pin it on Galerius, but Diocletian evidently took the initiative (though not at the very beginning of his reign).

Two events triggered the persecutions. First, the emperors' ceremonies on behalf of the army were allegedly rendered null and void by Christians making the sign of the cross. This happened in Syria in 299, when Diocletian and Galerius were engaged in a military rite of sacrifice and divination. It was during this ceremonial that certain Christians of the imperial household made the sign of the cross, in order to keep demons away. Thereupon the official pagan diviners (*haruspices*) announced that they had failed to identify the necessary marks on the innards of the animals which had been sacrificed, so that the required and expected divination could not take place. The leader of the *haruspices* pointed to the cause of this failure: profane persons, notably Christians, were impeding the sacrifices. Diocletian and Galerius, sharing the universal contemporary belief in incantations and magic,[5] were infuriated, and directed that every member of the imperial court should sacrifice to the pagan gods. And in addition they sent letters to every military commander, ordering that all soldiers under their commands should perform a similar sacrifice, or else leave the army.[6]

And then mysterious fires broke out in the palace at Diocletian's capital Nicomedia (Izmit), which were blamed on the Christians, whether rightly or wrongly we cannot tell. In consequence, a whole series of edicts against the Christians was passed, one after another. The severity of the persecutions varied according to locality. Constantius I Chlorus Caesar, in his western dominions, was said to have kept them to a minimum, perhaps only allowing the destruction of Christian meeting-places with wooden walls, which could be repaired – though this remains uncertain.

And it cannot be decided, with any approximation to exactitude, how many Christians met their deaths and were martyred during these persecutions. The numbers of victims varied from place to place, and one can rely on the Christian apologists to make the most of all such harrowing incidents. But there is no doubt that the persecutions of Diocletian and Galerius, even if the rumours that their wives had Christian sympathies were true, were more determined than any of those that had been attempted before. Quite clearly they thought that the Christians were a major threat to the successful conduct of the empire, and in consequence determined to put an end to their religion.

The story of these persecutions initiated by Diocletian, and marked by a cumulative series of edicts, has often been told. It should be remembered that he had first persecuted the sect of the Manichaeans in 293,[7] because of his fear that they were a fifth column supporting Persia. After the Edict of Serdica of Galerius (311), restoring toleration, and the (even more permissive) Edict of Milan of Constantine and Licinius, Maximinus II Daia returned vigorously to persecution in the east, seeking to constitute a pagan church with an organization equal to that of the Christians. And these were vilified by a variety of means, including forged documents (for example the *Memoirs* or *Acts of Pilate*) and induced 'petitions' from cities (but war, drought, famine and pestilence belied his claims of pagan success, outdoing anything that the Christians could achieve). Subsequently, Licinius turned anti-Christian (removing all Christian officers from his army) because he suspected his Christian subjects of subversively favouring Constantine.

Constantine claimed that the persecutions had shocked him.[8]

Eusebius, paradoxically, regarded them as deserved and merciful, because the Christians had been behaving so badly.[9] The whole subject has been swamped by hagiographical fiction, so that the facts are hard to reconstruct. But the pre-persecution Christians had tended to attract unpopularity because they kept to themselves, would not join in customary acts of worship, and were said to shirk military duties.

What seemed most serious, however, was that they had, in effect, stolen much of the thunder of paganism, by out-talking it on both its liberal and conservative sides, and claiming to represent valid expressions of all aspects of religious consciousness. Within the bounds of its own message, that is to say, Christianity could speak with a broadness which outdid every manifestation of paganism: for example, the Mystery cults of the time, and the religious philosophies, and the officially encouraged Ruler Cult. In other words the appeal of the new faith was little short of universal.[10]

One can therefore see why rulers so greatly disliked it, and turned to persecution. For one thing, as we saw at the ceremonies which went wrong under Diocletian, the pagan priests envisaged the Christian faith as a direct impediment to the practices in which it was their duty to engage: and they therefore regarded it as imperative that this impediment should be removed. In more general terms, as we have seen, the aim of the persecutors was to restore and strengthen the traditional beliefs and institutions which had made the Roman empire great, and which Christianity clearly threatened: beliefs and institutions represented by the 'Genius of the Roman People', 'GENIVS POPVLI ROMANI', which figured largely on their coinage. For these emperors the Christian faith and Roman tradition were antithetical, and that was why they persecuted the Christians.[11] The opposite view, of course, was taken by Christian writers such as Lactantius, who sought to present his faith as compatible and harmonious with *Romanitas*, interpreting the persecutions of the past not as the policies of the usual sort of Roman emperor, but as the aberrations of 'bad' emperors or their wicked representatives – both being categories of men that could be regarded as un-Roman: a strong feature of the Christian presentation of Galerius.

Diocletian and Galerius and the like were also alarmed by the powerful cohesion of the Christian communities, which they saw as a rival and therefore a threat to the cohesion of the empire as a whole. For the Christians, despite their disunity due to 'heresies', possessed effective cult-groups, artisan associations and what might be described as retirement and funeral insurance companies, which extended right down to the humblest social classes and caused all concerned to feel greater loyalty to their Christian providers than to the government. Pagan emperors might try to emulate these in-group organizations, but did not do so sufficiently well to enable them to be regarded as anything but rivals and menaces. Even Julian the Apostate (361–3) was impressed by the organized charity and social cohesiveness achieved by the Christians, which he tried to make the pagan civil and religious authorities imitate.

Just how far, in consequence of all this, the persecutions corresponded with the wishes of the public is a matter of some interest. Since its beginnings, members of the Christian faith had stopped short of advertising themselves widely and, despite the publicity which an occasional church council must have attracted, preferred on the whole to stick quietly together. And as for the mass of the general pagan population, it was apparently content (as indeed were most educated people) not to cross the barriers of prejudice and find out more about the beliefs of their Christian neighbours.[12] But this lack of positive interest or concern also worked in favour of the Christians, when they were persecuted; because, although our evidence on the subject is insufficient, it does seem that the persecutors failed to kindle support among the rank and file of the inhabitants of the empire. And that may partly be why the persecutions before very long faded out.

From the start, Diocletian and Maximian had clearly pronounced their stand in favour of paganism by declaring themselves, with due numismatic celebration, *Jovian* and *Herculian* emperors respectively, after Jupiter the king of the gods and Hercules who had been adopted as one of their number. Jupiter figures largely on the coins of the Tetrarchy, and his prominence continued after Diocletian's abdication. Thus Licinius continued to celebrate him, and a coin of Antioch in 310 called Maximinus II Daia 'Jovius'.[13] As for Hercules, he had been closely associated with Jupiter, and was especially revered, in Diocletian's native Dalmatia. Constantius I Chlorus (and so his son Constantine as well) was in the 'Herculian' succession. Hercules' popularity can be assessed from his prominence in the mosaics of the Trifoliate Hall in the large villa at Philosophiana (Piazza Armerina) in Sicily.

There was also much talk of Mars. Diocletian's and Maximian's Caesars, Galerius and Constantius I Chlorus, had been pronounced to be under the protection of Mars and Apollo: Galerius declared that he was actually Mars's son. Mars also figures as Constantine's special patron on his early coins;[14] and his troops were at first sometimes called 'people of Mars'. Constantine also, in his early pagan days, saw himself as a protégé of Apollo (who had been the god of Augustus), and according to a Panegyrist he was accorded a vision by Apollo in his early days, in Gaul. This is the story the Panegyrist told.[15]

While on his way south to Massilia (Marseille) in 310 to deal with Maximian's unsuccessful attempt to revive his imperial claims, Constantine made a short detour to visit 'the most beautiful temple in the entire world' – at a place that has been variously identified, but was probably, since the god worshipped there was Apollo, the shrine of Apollo Grannus at Grannum (Grand, southeast of Joinville on the Marne). There, the speaker declared, Constantine experienced a vision of Apollo, attended by Victory, offering him four laurel wreaths, each of them signifying thirty years of success. In Apollo, it would seem, Constantine recognized not only the protector of his family (the Second Flavian House), but his own self: youthful, handsome, happy, a bestower of salvation, the ruler of the world whose coming was prophesied in Virgil's Fourth Eclogue. And so Constantine, after he had won his victory over Maximian's son Maxentius in 312, fulfilled the vows he had made at that point on his southward journey, and presented generous gifts to the shrine of Apollo.

It is not to be supposed that this account of Constantine's vision is authentic, or that he ever experienced such a vision at all. The Panegyrist tells the story not because it represented anything that he believed had really happened, but because he wanted to induce Constantine to extend his munificence to the cult of Apollo – and particularly, some have suggested (though this has been contradicted), the cult of Apollo at Augustodunum (Autun), the town from which the orator came. This was a famous cult, with its own grave and temple and spring, and here was a chance of securing a lavish subvention for it from Constantine. In other words, the account of Constantine's vision of Apollo can be regarded as a fiction, invented in the hope that a great temple in the Panegyrist's home town would receive financial aid from the emperor. (It was, therefore, rash of the speaker to add that the god's hot spring punishes perjury.)

On the erroneous assumption that the story was *not* fictitious, Colin Thubron has woven a dramatic tale out of the supposed happening.

Two years ago Apollo granted me a vision in Gaul. I was marching through the country of the Leuci, where his great temple stands. I had just suppressed the rebellion of my own father-in-law. . . . The temple of Apollo was very grand, as I remember it. The day was hot and the Sun blazed on its walls. I entered the inner court alone. It was built of new stone and dazzled the eyes. Everything quivered and moved. My feet made a strange echo on the pavements. And as I looked up at the face of the god, my stomach emptied. I saw myself looking back at me. His features were my own. He was riding a horse and holding out a laurel. My own divinity was offering a laurel to me. He seemed to smile. . . .

I look up at the sky and see the order and invincibility of the Sun. The Sun is pure, absolute. I too, I say, want to be pure: my life, my love, my death.[16]

Or, as observers were said to have put it,

Today Majesty had the heat-stroke bad and fell from his horse. He had it renewed times as a boy. But not since. And as a boy he holds the sides of his head. And as a boy he buries his face. Says he saw cross....

We were all aware that something momentous had happened ... For a long time Constantine looked dazed and seemed almost inarticulate. Even later, returned to his senses, he was unable to explain what had occurred. He said the same thing over and over. He had seen a cross, he said, a shining cross. Nothing more. But at the day's end he assembled all the leaders of his staff and declared that this was the symbol, and this the god, by which he would conquer.... Tonight the news is all over the army that the emperor has become a Christian.

I think he merely said 'Look! God!', and slid to the ground. In the moment before he leant against his horse I observed that his eyes were not open, as is usual with men who see visions, but were tightly closed. The Augustus is a practical man. He clearly understands the value which the troops attach to a convincing spiritual experience. And the soldiers, of course, are ecstatic. They say that their Emperor has been personally visited by God and has been granted a sign that he will conquer.... It is absurd to separate His Eternity's personal interests from those of the state. He is its guardian and its living symbol.[17]

It is a pity that this tale does not seem to be truthful, for more reasons than one. First, it made a fine and dramatic account. Secondly, it displayed the sort of legend that always clustered round Constantine, who was particularly liable, also, to visionary experiences (like his mother Helena, who allegedly saw visions in the Holy Land). And thirdly, because the student of history, although he must dismiss such legends as untruthful, has to admit that they form part of the historical picture, because they were invented and circulated and people believed in them and acted accordingly.

There is no point, therefore, in trying to rationalize the story, or distort it into rationally comprehensible terms. For the vision, if not a historical fact, is nevertheless an artistic fact, 'the creation of a particular culture at a particular period, as much removed from straight sensory perception as Picasso's *Guernica* from the news of a bombing raid in 1937'.[18] To call the tale a 'lie' then, as it would seem to be in terms of our own ways of thinking, would be a piece of secular motivation that must miss a number of valuable points. For one thing, the fourth century was an age of supposed visions. There were many self-declared visionaries, including people who were believed to be sorcerers. 'The direct intervention of God or gods, angels or demons, figured in most stories of great events, whether narrated by Christians or pagans.'[19] And the belief in visions was related to extremely widespread belief in miracles, as well as in magic (which was a charge brought against Ceionius Rufius Albinus and Sopater, in the latter case with fatal results).

Within this context, the Panegyrist's link of Constantine with Apollo was not unfelicitous. For the emperor's connections with Apollo were attested elsewhere as well. For example, plaques of the Arch of Constantine at Rome show two pictures of sacrifice to this god, as well as one each to other deities. It was not for nothing that, when Constantine became a Christian, his *Oration to the Assembly of Saints* singled out Apollo as a deity whose oracle, on an earlier occasion, had proved false: to single him out in this way proved how influential he had been.

Moreover, Apollo was equated or identified with the Sun-god, and the form of monotheism which particularly appealed to Constantine in his early years was the worship of the Sun. This was very popular in the empire at the time (Mithraism was a branch of it, and Firmicus Maternus linked astrology with Sun-worship), and may well have attracted the attention of Constantine's father Constantius I Chlorus. Anyway, it appealed to Constantine himself, who in 311 hailed the Sun as his tutelary god, and persistently portrayed the same deity on his coinage as his invincible companion ('SOLI INVICTO COMITI').[20] Coins attribute his victories to the Sun, and Julian the Apostate speaks of Constantine's special links with the Sun-god.

Sol, honoured at Rome by the city prefects Aradius Rufinus and Rufius Volusianus, remains on the coinage until 319/20, unlike the traditional pagan gods, who had vanished in 317. The Sun seems to be depicted in a brick pattern on the north wall of the church of St Gereon at Colonia Agrippinensis (Köln). Some of Constantine's troops were called *solenses*, and the city of Termessus (Göllük) in Pisidia proclaimed him to be 'the Sun'.[21] But he saw himself rather, not as the Sun, and not even as a fellow deity of the Sun, but as his 'companion' (and, perhaps, his incarnation upon earth), since the Iranian concept of kingly power as trust from God or the gods had replaced the idea of actual identification with him or them.

This connection with the Sun made Constantine's eventual transition to Christianity easier, because he may well have believed that Christ and the Unconquered Sun-god were both aspects of the Highest Divinity, and that no mutual exclusiveness existed between them or separated them. And indeed he was not, and had not been, the only man to take this view, which, with the assistance of Neoplatonism, allotted the solar religion a sort of middle ground between paganism and Christianity. Old Testament prophecy was interpreted as identifying the 'Sun of Righteousness' with Jesus Christ, who was often called *Sol Justitiae*[22] and depicted by statues resembling the young Apollo or Sol. Clement of Alexandria writes of Christ driving his chariot across the heavens like the Sun-god, and a tomb mosaic found beneath St Peter's at Rome, probably made early in the fourth century, displays him in this chariot, mounting the sky in the guise of Sol.[23] Moreover, Sol remained a Christian symbol, and on a coin of Vetranio (*c.*350), with a Christian inscription, *Sol Invictus* crowns the Christian standard, the *labarum*.[24] The Christian Sunday was manifestly named after the Sun, and Tertullian remarks that many pagans believed that the Christians *worshipped* the Sun, because it was on Sundays that they met, and prayed to the east, in which the Sun rose. Moreover, in the fourth century, in the western part of the empire at least (the date in its eastern regions is uncertain), there began the commemoration of 25 December, the Sun-god's birthday at the winter solstice, as the date for the birth of Christ.

Evidently then, in the minds of the less well informed sections of the population, Christianity and Sun-worship were easily and thoroughly entangled and merged. This was all too clear to Pope Leo I the Great (440–61), who – aware, perhaps, that people at Constantinople had sacrificed to the statue of Constantine as if it stood for Sol[25] – reprimanded his congregation for performing devotions to the Sun on the steps of St Peter's before turning their backs to it and entering the Basilica to perform Christian worship there. Nearly a century earlier, as he no doubt also knew, when Julian the Apostate had reverted to the pagan religion, this sort of feeling made it easy for many to abandon Christianity in favour of solar monotheism. The bishop of Troy was an interesting case in point. He found it possible at that time, with a clear conscience, to switch from Christian to pagan belief because, even while holding episcopal office, he had secretly continued to pray to the Sun.[26]

One of the most extraordinary events in the history of the empire, already alluded to, occurred in 311 – six years after Diocletian's abdication – when Galerius, at Serdica (Sofia), issued an edict revoking the persecution of the Christians. What actually happened was that, in every city of the empire, imperial decrees were published, in the name of Galerius, containing the following withdrawal of the edicts of persecution:

Among the other things which we have ordained for the public advantage and profit, we formerly wished to restore everything to conformity with the ancient laws and discipline of the Romans and to provide that the Christians also, who have forsaken the religion of their ancestors, should return to a good disposition.

For in some way such arrogance had seized them and such stupidity had overtaken them, that they did not follow the ancient institutions which possibly their own ancestors had formerly established, but made for themselves laws according to their own purpose, as each one desired, and observed them, and thus assembled as separate congregations in various places.

When we had issued this decree that they should return to the institutions established by the ancients, a great many submitted under danger, but a great many, being harassed, endured all sorts of death.

And since many continue in the same folly, and we perceive that they neither offer to the heavenly gods the worship which is due, nor pay regard to the god of the Christians, in consideration of our philanthropy and our invariable custom, by which we are wont to extend pardon to all, we have determined that we ought most cheerfully to extend our indulgence in this matter also; that they may again be Christians, and may rebuild the conventicles in which they were accustomed to assemble, on condition that nothing be done by them contrary to discipline.

In another letter we shall indicate to the provincial governors what they have to observe.

Wherefore, on account of this indulgence of ours, they ought to supplicate their god for our safety, and that of the people, and their own, that the public welfare may be preserved in every place, and that they may live securely in their several homes.[27]

Why had Galerius, previously an arch-persecutor, taken this remarkable step of cancelling the persecution of the Christians?

We do not know the entire truth of the matter. But we can ignore assertions by the Christian writers that, as he suffered hideously on his death-bed, he felt he must pacify the Christian God, who had inflicted his fatal illness upon him. Instead, although, like others, no doubt willing to concede that a number of different gods existed, Galerius is likely to have been moved by cold political considerations. In other words, he had decided – possibly, though not certainly, after consulting Licinius, and perhaps, also, because he wanted to avoid internal subversion while fighting the Persians – that the persecutions were a failure.

For they had not succeeded in suppressing the Christians. Indeed some of the victims had won admiration by their courageous martyrdoms. And in any case, as has already been said, there does not seem to have been great public support for the official attacks on them. So the persecutions had better be called off, in the hope that the Christians, unpersecuted, would cooperate better with the government – converted into one of many corporations or *collegia* – than when they had been subject to violent sanctions. And called off they were, as Galerius' own words clearly show (though Maximinus II Daia [died 313], after at first grudgingly accepting Galerius' recantation,[28] then entirely failed to accept it after all, and resumed the persecutions as soon as he felt he could).

What happened next, following Galerius' reversal of the persecution, was that Constantine, invading Italy, believed that he had fought and won his war against Maxentius with the backing of the Christian God. He claimed, in subsequent years (Eusebius recorded his assertion to this effect nearly a quarter of a century later), that at an earlier stage, probably in Gaul, he had been granted a vision of the Cross in the sky.

This was an epoch, as we have noted, in which visions were frequently and continually seen, or imagined to be seen, by all and sundry, especially at decisive turning points of history, and it was natural enough for someone who had played such an important part as Constantine to believe, or require others to believe, that he, too, had seen a vision, which supported his adherence to Christianity. Indeed, it is possible that he *had* had this experience: or, rather, that he had seen a cross in the sky, where the sun occasionally presents such an image, known as the 'halo phenomenon'.[29]

However, even if that was so – as some refuse to believe – there is something peculiar about Constantine's assertion that the soldiers in the army saw the cross as well. If so, they remained extraordinarily silent on the subject. And there is something peculiar, too, about Constantine's assertion that the cross he saw in the vision was accompanied by an inscription, reading 'by this sign you will conquer' ('HOC SIGNO VICTOR ERIS', on a coin of the usurper Vetranio in 350).[30] Inscriptions in the sky are not very plausible, and it is possible to look behind the polite words of Eusebius (written down only after Constantine's death) and to detect that even he, strong supporter of Constantine that he was, believed that the emperor, consciously or unconsciously, was not altogether telling the truth about his vision – which was, in fact, fictitious: or rather, the inscription and its visibility to the army were fictitious, although Constantine may perhaps have seen some natural phenomenon in the sky which he later looked back on as a heaven-sent Christian symbol.

For Constantine was extremely disposed to see visions, which was why, earlier, a pagan vision had been attributed to him. A series of visions allegedly continued throughout his life, the products of his passionate, superstitious convictions. The foundation of Constantinople supposedly produced a whole crop of visions of this kind.

And as regards this vision of the cross in the sky, it is only too probable that, in due course, Constantine came to believe that this vision has appeared to him:

A sense of mission grew in him over the years. As he neared his end, that sense worked on the incidents of his life, reshaping them according to prevailing religious and literary habits of thought. He had been helped to victory by a divine visitation and a miracle in the sky. Nothing he heard in legends about other very holy men made this seem improbable.... Constantine's miracle was a purely psychological event compressed into a form dictated by the art and mythopoeia of the day.[31]

And a man only sees in the sky, it has been suggested, what he is predisposed to notice or recall. (We need not accept the 'vision' as an imitation of a pagan vision seen in Gaul – since that vision had been fictitious.)[32]

This is how the 'vision of the cross' was reported by Eusebius:

Constantine prayed to God. He asked him and besought him to say Who He was and to stretch forth a hand to him in his present situation. As he prayed in this fashion and as he earnestly gave voice to his entreaties, a most marvellous sign appeared to the emperor from God.

It would have been hard to believe if anyone else had spoken of it. But a long time later the triumphant emperor himself described it to the writer of this work. This was when I had the honour of knowing him and of being in his company. When he told me the story, he swore to its truth. And who could refuse to believe it, especially when later evidence showed it to have been genuine?...[33]

Around noon-time, when the day was already beginning to decline, he saw before him in the sky the sign of a cross of light. He said it was above the sun, and it bore the inscription, 'Conquer with this'. The vision astounded him, as it astounded the whole army which was with him on this expedition and which also beheld the miraculous event.

He said he became disturbed. What could the vision mean? He continued to ponder and to give great thought to the question, and night came on him suddenly. When he was asleep, the Christ of God appeared to him and he brought with him the sign which had appeared in the sky. He ordered Constantine to make a replica of this sign which he had witnessed in the sky, and he was to use it as a protection during his encounters with the enemy.

In the morning he told his friends of this extraordinary occurrence. Then he summoned those who worked with gold or precious stones, and he sat among them and described the appearance of the sign. He told them to represent it in gold and precious stones....

At the time I have been describing ... he resolved to worship none but the God who had been revealed to him.[34]

It seems likely, however, that Constantine's account of his pro-Christian dream during the night before the Battle of the Milvian Bridge falls into a somewhat different and more credible category, since, despite many subsequent legendary descriptions and interpretations,[35] it was apparently based on a *real* dream, and not on a dubious visionary experience.

The ancient world, and especially the world of Constantine's epoch, was as credulous of significant nocturnal dreams as it was of other kinds of visions. 'It is to dreams', wrote Tertullian, 'that the majority of humankind owe their knowledge of God.'[36] Artemidorus of Ephesus devoted a study to the subject, the *Oneirocriticon*. Divine powers were believed to visit people very often in their dreams and give them messages, and this was thought to apply particularly to great and powerful men. Thus an angel was said to have appeared in a dream to Licinius,[37] and Constantine himself was said to have seen and talked with God in dreams,[38] as part of his lifelong relationship with the supernatural.[39] It was by this means, for example, that he was said to have learnt about the 'plot' of Bassianus.

In such circumstances it was natural that the dreamers, on awakening, should summon their advisers and try to find out from

them what the dream had meant. And that is no doubt what
Constantine did. It was hardly unexpected that such a highly
charged man should have a meaningful dream on the night before
a decisive battle: and the emperor wanted to be told what his
dream signified. The sort of man he would summon was Bishop
Ossius of Corduba (Cordova), whose influence may well have lain
behind many of Constantine's moves towards Christianity. Ossius
seems to have come from Egypt (Zosimus denounced him as an
Egyptian), and to have gone to Spain, from which he moved to
gain access to Constantine through the Christian ladies of the
emperor's court, including, perhaps, his mother Helena.

There is no need, therefore, to join Edward Gibbon in maintaining complete scepticism about the entire dream,[40] described as
'probably no more than an attempt to give Constantine's unexpected action a conventional religious explanation' – perhaps
inspired by a passage in Maccabees.[41] On the contrary, it seems
likely that he did have some sort of dream, which was interpreted
for him in the morning.

Lactantius provides one of our descriptions of Constantine's
experience.[42] His version is unsatisfactory, because he confuses
the dream with the emperor's alleged earlier vision, and only heard
of it a long time later, probably from someone in Constantine's
entourage; and he disposes of the dream rather briefly, in only
thirty-one words. But what Lactantius heard was that God had
told Constantine, in this nocturnal visitation, to inscribe the
sublime sign of God on his soldiers' shields before engaging the
enemy. And when Constantine woke up at dawn on 28 October,
we are told, he informed his friends of this portentous message.

According to Eusebius, it was now that he began to devise his
special standard, the *labarum*, which displayed the Christogram
(*Chi-Rho*: the initial letters of *Christos*) at the summit of the cross,
and which became a magical, miraculous amulet, almost the
equivalent of the Ark of the Covenant.[43] Eusebius was particularly
eager to refer to the *labarum*, because he himself had seen it, in the
emperor's private apartment, and he interpreted it as a 'sign of

salvation'.[44] But when he associates the standard with the dream, one wonders if he is not fusing together two experiences, the report he had received about the dream, and his later sight of the *labarum* itself, after it had become Constantine's standard.

The *labarum* took the form, Eusebius tell us,[45] of a long spear, covered with gold, and joined by a transverse bar which gave it the shape of the cross. At the summit of the standard was a wreath made of gold and precious stones: and it was within this wreath that the *Chi-Rho* sign was inserted. The *labarum*, then, was an amalgamation of religious banner and military *vexillum* (emblem of power), analogous to a standard earlier employed by the Mithraists. Its origins have been greatly disputed, as has the etymological derivation of the word, which continues to attract suggestions involving Celtic and Indo-European languages, though none of these explanations is entirely convincing. Moreover, the *labarum* assumed various forms, some of which are disputable (as is the meaning of the three discs which appear upon its surface on coins).[46] This standard was in existence, as a Christian emblem, in 317; but attempts to link it to the happenings of 312 may perhaps be rejected as anachronistic, or at least dubious.

A further problem is that it remains extremely uncertain whether the first two letters of Jesus' name, the *Chi* and the *Rho*, were actually supposed to have figured in Constantine's dream: the matter has been very intensively discussed, particularly in relation to his silver medallions issued at Ticinum (Pavia) in 315[47] on which the symbol occurs (what exactly did it mean at that date?) – although coins, in any case, produced only watered-down versions of current symbolism.

The *Chi-Rho* was, previously, almost unknown as a Christian emblem: no pre-Constantinian uses of the letters in such a role, or at most very few, have been identified. Certainly, the *Chi-Rho* had appeared, but in quite a different and non-Christian context, as pagan papyri indicate.[48] For the men who were writing or reading these papyri employed the sign to mark a valuable or useful passage, *Chi-Rho* standing for the Greek *chreston*, good. The symbol also bore some resemblance to the mystic Egyptian *ankh*, and others might have noted or assumed a connection with the worship of the Sun or Apollo or Mithras (though the theory of the development of the Christogram [*Chi-Rho*] from a pagan star does not seem admissible), or it might just have been regarded as a good-luck sign. Subsequently, of course, it became a Christian symbol, but how and when this transfer or transformation occurred is a matter for conjecture. It seems reasonable to suppose that it was prompted by Constantine himself or by his advisers, who were able to suggest that this not unfamiliar symbol could serve as an abbreviation for Christ, so that within a short time that is how it was, exclusively, considered.

In other words, the *Chi-Rho* had a double meaning, one for pagans and one for Christians. Double meanings were nothing new for Constantine, who had been brought up (at Diocletian's court) in an atmosphere that required dissimulation. The *Chi-Rho* may have appeared again in his statue at Constantinople, which was not only adapted from a representation of Apollo but possessed the radiate crown of the Sun-god (so familiar from the imperial coinage) and faced the Rising Sun. That is to say, the Christogram could be reverenced by both pagans and Christians: an illustration of Constantine's desire to play to both audiences.

Indeed, that may have partly been the reason why he welcomed both the *Chi-Rho* and the *labarum* – because of their ambiguity, which was convenient for his purposes. And in particular this ambiguity may have helped him to pursue his drive in favour of Christianity, to which he felt able to give vigorous expression as a result of his dream – without too greatly upsetting the pagans.

From now on, then, the Christogram, whatever its equivocal significances, became as potent a Christian symbol as the *labarum* in which it was in due course incorporated.

It was easy to confuse or assimilate it with the Cross, by which the church, accustomed to the Cross in Asia Minor and Syria, later tried to supplant it,[49] so that it is sometimes hard to distinguish between descriptions of the two symbols, especially if the Cross is depicted by a cross-like symbol known as the 'staurogram', a cross surmounted by a P-shaped loop (was the latter the supposed form of the miraculous 'heavenly sign of God' before the Milvian Bridge?).[50] Thus the Church of the Holy Apostles at Constantinople was cruciform, and the Cross appears, as a main type, on coins of Olybrius (472).[51] But a Christogram is the central feature of a sarcophagus from the Catacomb of Domitilla,[52] and was said to have been borne (surmounted by an orb) in the hand of Constantine on his statue at Rome and Constantinople; although statements to that effect have been doubted (p. 148).

The immediate result of Constantine's dream, however – a development inspired, according to legend, by the eunuch Euphratas[53] – was that he was said to have decided to inscribe the *Chi-Rho*, interpreted not only as a symbol of forthcoming victory but as a Christian symbol as well, upon the shields of his soldiers, before the decisive Battle of the Milvian Bridge against Maxentius – unless it was only a simple cross that was thus inscribed, like the 'wooden crosses' which, so Christians said, had appeared (like images of the gods) as military emblems of the third-century pagan army. Constantine may not have had time, before the battle, to arrange for the sign, whatever it was, to be engraved or chalked on *every* soldier's shield – perhaps only a few hundreds, or a few score, of those closest to him could be equipped with this providential talisman. But no matter. The message, to him, was clear. It was the Christian God who caused him, on that morning, to win the Battle of the Milvian Bridge, and henceforward it was the Christian God whom he revered.

It was not surprising that God or the gods should be believed to have appeared to a human protagonist at a critical juncture. Such epiphanies were particularly to be imagined at this epoch, when religions were so prominent. And now the violent contests between paganism and Christianity seemed to be reaching a climax. This climax took the form of the Battle of the Milvian Bridge, which was presented, on the side of the victorious Constantine, as having been the decisive clash between Christianity and paganism. At all times, and especially at such a moment, divine forces were expected to express themselves, whether by droughts or plagues or good or bad harvests, or in this case by dreams and the turning points of civil war.

Anxiety has been caused by the fact that the descriptions of Constantine's earlier vision, and his dream of 312, by Lactantius and Eusebius do not tally. But there is no reason why both events, vision and dream, should not have occurred, or have been believed to occur. There is no good reason to suppose that the descriptions refer to *one* single phenomenon. Only, Lactantius was wrong in dating the 'vision' (as opposed to the dream) as late as the night before the battle.[54]

Very possibly, the emperor's dream, on that night before the engagement, was directed and shaped by his Christian advisers. But he had the dream all the same: and what is important is not so much its exact character as the way in which it was understood. For its effect, and that of the interpretation his advisers placed on it, implanted in Constantine an absolute conviction that he was to obey the Christian God. As he declared to the Synod of Arelate (Arles) in 314,

The inconceivable goodness of our God forbids that mankind should continue to wander in the dark.... I have realised this truth from many examples outside myself, but I can also confirm it from my own experience.

There were things in my own nature which were devoid of righteousness and I seemed to see as heavenly power that I might have been carrying hidden in my breast.... But Almighty God, who watches from the high tower of Heaven, has vouchsafed to me what I have not deserved. Verily past number are the blessings that He, in his heavenly goodness, has bestowed on me, his servant.[55]

'I am absolutely persuaded', he added near the end of his days, 'that I owe my whole life, my every breath, and in a word my secret thoughts, to the supreme God.'[56]

That sounds just plain monotheism, but it was in fact Christian monotheism. For there is no doubt that Constantine became wholeheartedly converted to Christianity – and we need not be too meticulous, as some are, to avoid the term 'conversion'.[57] But the date of this event, if it was a single event, has been extensively debated. One school of thought maintains that he had undergone this conversion a good deal earlier than the Battle of the Milvian Bridge,[58] which only confirmed his decision; after all, he already had Christian bishops in his entourage as he marched on Rome. It could, for example, be conjectured that the battle was seized upon, for literary and publicity purposes, as a single dramatic concentration of what perhaps was quite a long-drawn-out process of conversion. It could also be suggested that his open avowal and the moment of psychological conviction need not necessarily have come at one and the same time, and that the latter, the first, of these two happenings may well have occurred during the course of the battle itself, at the time when victory became assured.

It seems certain, at least, that it was when this psychological moment occurred Constantine looked back on his dream and decided (perhaps after what his counsellors had told him) that it meant that Christianity must henceforward be his guide. It was during the crisis of 312, therefore, at the time of the decisive engagement of the Milvian Bridge, that this idea received its sharpest definition. The emperor at a critical point in his career had a dream that could be interpreted in the light of his needs.

It demonstrated to him, that is to say, what he had to do in order to vanquish his foes, and it identified, he believed, the divine power, capable of ensuring this outcome, as the God of Christianity. Constantine did what that power seemed to have told him to do in his dream, and victory followed. So henceforward this Christian God was for ever his Lord and Master. That is what the logic of the situation seemed to demand. For if this God had done so much for him, he had proved that he was God indeed, and he had made Constantine his servant for ever – even if, as has been suggested, Constantine did not receive much formal instruction in Christianity for some three years to come.

So he revered the Christian God, as a God of power, as *the* God of power. He was the God who had *given Constantine power*, and had enabled him at the Milvian Bridge, to defeat Maxentius (who, for this purpose, was made out to be more anti-Christian than he really was). No pagan god had ever supported his worshippers so effectively. Eusebius, doubtfully, explains that Constantine inherited this conviction from his father Constantius I Chlorus, but otherwise his analysis of how the victorious emperor came to hold this conviction – which was implanted in him most firmly, it would appear, on the eve of the Battle of the Milvian Bridge –is worthy of attention.

He considered that the assistance of God was invincible and unshakable. But on which god could he depend as an ally? That was his problem....

Of his numerous imperial predecessors, those who had put their hopes in a multitude of gods and had served them with libations and sacrificial offerings were first of all deceived by flattering prophecies, by oracles promising success to them, and still had come to a bad end. None of their gods stood by them or warned them of the catastrophe about to afflict them. On the other hand, his own father, who had been the only one to follow the opposite course and denounce their error, had given honour to almighty God throughout his life and had found in Him a saviour, a protector of his empire, and the provider of all good things.

As he pondered this matter, he reflected that those who had trusted in a multitude of gods had been brought low by many forms of death.... But the God of his father had given him clear and numerous indications of his power....

Constantine thought of all these things, and decided that it would be stupid to join in the empty worship of those who were no gods and to stray from truth after observing all this positive evidence. He decided that only the God of his father ought to be worshipped.[59]

For it was by God's grace, and by this alone, that Constantine believed he had won the victory over Maxentius:[60] the ubiquitous, winged figure of Victoria became God's angel. The Christian God had to prove himself against his rivals, and had done so – by granting that victory by which he had shown himself more potent than any of the old gods could ever hope to be.

While listening to one of Eusebius' speeches, Constantine stood: because God was the theme.[61] Otherwise, however, he was not averse to lofty comparisons between God and himself. According to Eusebius, Constantine's court reflected the heavenly court (a Hellenistic idea), and disobedience to the emperor was a sacrilege, because he ruled by the Grace of God, of whom he was an imitation (*mimesis*) upon earth.

Eusebius stressed that the favour of God had given him the title to govern, going, at this point, beyond Hellenistic theories of monarchy to interpret Constantine as the inheritor of the promise to Abraham. Arguments in favour of the emperor's power often appealed to the Old Testament, which figures largely on contemporary reliefs and catacomb paintings (Constantine was also compared to Moses). And these paintings constantly insist on the *power* of God to intervene in history: they depict the Good Shepherd, typifying the saving activity of God. Constantine believed in the Truth, the Absolute – and he became convinced that its only guarantor and repository was the God of the Christians.

However, he not only revered this God, but was afraid of him. As he declared, he feared that God's anger would descend *upon himself* if he did not do the right thing: and the same note was struck by Lactantius, whose treatise *On the Anger of God* (*De Ira Dei*) stressed the appropriateness of anger as a divine attribute, without which there could be no providence or divine jurisdiction. As for Constantine, believing in the Gospel of Matthew's allusion to eternal punishment,[62] he was convinced that God was as quick to wrath as he was himself. And, indeed, the attribution of anger to the divine power(s) was widespread, although Marcus Aurelius, for example, had deprecated the idea. But fourth-century events such as famine (in the east), and the death of Arius, were attributed to divine retribution (Orosius stressed the 'most kindly chastisements' of God).[63]

Such were the attributes of the Christian God whom Constantine venerated, and in the fetching stories about Jesus that one finds, for example, in the Gospel according to St Luke he took no interest at all. Indeed, Jesus' doings did not seem to him of any importance: nor, even, did the person of Jesus himself, since, although Constantine felt able to quote, or rather misquote, Virgil's Fourth Eclogue as forecasting the Incarnation (in his *Oration to the Assembly of Saints*, and at Nicaea), he also rebuked his half-sister Constantia for excessively revering what was believed to be a likeness of Jesus,[64] whose actual existence on earth as a human being did not seem to him a matter worth dwelling upon at all.

Nor would he have been able to see the point of Jesus's Crucifixion, at least without some mental acrobatics. It was embarrassing, to say the least, that God's own son had been subjected to this humiliating end, and contemporary Christian art avoids the whole question, because it seemed to involve such ignominy; and for this reason Constantine abolished crucifixion as a punishment. True, he dutifully deplored those who rejected the sufferings of Jesus, because they were ashamed to consider them. And he encouraged his mother Helena to obtain alleged pieces of the True Cross in the Holy Land. But he hardly ever mentions the theology which proclaimed and explained the Crucifixion, and he saw the Cross not so much as an emblem of suffering as a magic totem confirming his own victoriousness.

This sort of philosophy is excellently illustrated by sarcophagi of the time, which combine the Cross with the *labarum* and laurel-wreath – with which it was also combined on imperial standards – so that it becomes a Cross not of humiliation but of *triumph*. It is no coincidence that triumph, salvation, divine deliverance, are the favourite themes of catacomb art; and salvation is what Constantine, too, was concerned with. The Christian God, by his power, had saved him and given him victory, and that was why, from now onwards, it was the Christian God whom he would follow.

And by this means he would combat the Devil and his demons,

in whose existence and constant activity he, like everyone else, believed. The Devil seemed very real indeed, although this conception, not so far removed from the condemned dualism of the Manichaeans, must have been a puzzle to some theologians, who were obliged to believe that God was all-powerful and wholly good.[65] Constantine and his contemporaries frequently refer to the Devil,[66] and he was portrayed on the entrance gable of his palace at Constantinople.[67] The emperor believed that 'heretics' were the Devil's agents, and Lactantius wrote most eloquently of the struggle between God and the Devil, 'an adversary provided for us by God so that we may gain moral strength', against whom the Cross was believed to be a magic prophylaxis (a belief which annoyed Diocletian so much that it prompted him to launch the persecution).

On coins and paintings the Devil was represented by a dragon or a serpent. It was hoped that the Council of Nicaea 'disarmed the Devil', and that he had played no part in its deliberations. St Antony became famous for his struggles against this adversary. A recognized supernatural force, the Devil was also believed to be served by a wide army of demons throughout the world, whom Constantine was believed to have defeated and holy men such as Pachomius were able to see; Eusebius described polytheists as worshippers of demons.[68]

Constantine was one of those few and fortunate people who could back up their emotional convictions by practical considerations, and vice versa, or could mingle the two sorts of motive so they turned out to be indistinguishable: conviction and expediency became mixed and merged. For the emperor, in addition to seeing the Christian faith as God's will, also realized that it was useful. Mention has already been made of the Christians' admirable social cohesion: theirs was the only organized force in the empire, aside from the army.[69] And its enemies had come to bad ends. Edward Gibbon saw that Constantine realized the utility of Christianity, but believed that this realization was derived from his avarice and ambition.[70] Anyway, the emperor saw that it could, and would, be useful. For he liked the idea of backing Christianity because he wanted to have its effective organization on his side. That is to say, he believed firmly that by doing so he could restore to the Roman state the unity which the persecutions had shown to be so sadly lacking. Indeed, that was his dominant aim, to achieve, through the adherents of this religion, *unity* in the Roman empire – although the 'heresies' disappointed this aim.

But, it must be repeated, quite apart from this practical aim, he was deeply and fundamentally moved and impressed by the supremacy of the Christian God, and, in particular, by his own unique role as God's chosen viceroy upon earth. Such people are dangerous, and impossible to argue with. If they want to do something, they know it is with God's support. That is what Disraeli complained about Gladstone, that 'he had God up his sleeve'. Gibbon saw Constantine's 'belief' in this backing by God as mere cynical, callous politicizing.[71] Yet this conclusion was unjustifiable, since Constantine genuinely felt that he was in continuous touch with God. When he was tracing the boundaries of the new Constantinople, and someone told him he had gone far enough, he answered, 'I shall go on until He who is walking ahead of me stops.'[72]

In fact Constantine had no great taste for speculation, and not much knowledge of the Bible. But he worked hard to give his simple, emotional, somewhat weird beliefs a scriptural backing, and spent many hours in theological study, especially in his later years.[73] Yet his religion has been called a crude fetishism, and he was said to be at the mercy of any theologian who caught his ear.

Nevertheless, muddled though he may have been, he felt an absolute conviction that he was uniquely in God's confidence: that he was God's special servant and attendant and friend and representative. Basing their utterances on this conviction, flatterers even ventured to say that he was a new Jesus. Bishops dining with him felt they were like the Apostles at Jesus' table. But when an admirer actually compared him to Jesus, he objected that that was going too far. Yet Eusebius, in his *Praise of Constantine*, almost raised him to this level,[74] and even if that seemed excessive he had no objection, as the situation developed, to being ranked with Christ's Apostles, as *isapostolos*.[75] Indeed, he arranged to be buried in the Church of the Holy Apostles at Constantinople, with monuments and relics of the Twelve Apostles around him. This made it seem that he was greater than they had been; or, at the very least, that he saw himself as the Thirteenth of them. It was therefore permissible to see a resemblance between Constantine and Peter; and Christian hymn-writers likened him to Paul.

Yet Constantine understood that, despite the spread of Christianity, paganism was still the religion of the great majority of his subjects, including nearly all the members of the Senate and the dominant class at Rome, not to speak of the general public: so that he had to go carefully – paying ample tribute to the senators, for example on his coins and medallions.

That is the keynote of his entire reign: he did push Christianity, but, recalling, perhaps, that the Christians had always operated with secrecy, he pushed it by careful, ambivalent stages and periphrases. These included references to the past, such as moves to see himself as a reborn Augustus.[76] And the inscription on his Arch in Rome, designed either by Constantine himself, and his advisers, or by the Senate, offers very deliberate and definite echoes of the great pagan emperors of the past. Indeed, some of the reliefs on the Arch were actually *taken* from monuments of Trajan, Hadrian and Marcus Aurelius – so that the structure was called 'Aesop's jay', because of its borrowed plumage.

The inscription on the Arch records that Constantine had won his war against Maxentius not only through his own qualities (*mentis magnitudine*) but 'by the instinct of divinity' (*instinctu divinitatis*).[77] It was not an altogether new, or unfamiliar, phrase (or cliché). But how splendidly ambiguous! Constantine, and Christians, could take it as referring to the Christian God, but pagans, if they wished, might interpret it in some other way altogether.

And that was the keynote of Constantine's entire subsequent

behaviour. He had convinced himself that the Christian God, who gave him power, was the deity he must worship. But he had to move cautiously. In the same spirit, a Panegyrist at Augusta Trevirorum (Trier) in 313 likewise avoids more specific definitions with care, instead stressing Constantine's familiarity with the divine. Once again, he has defeated Maxentius 'advised by the divine instinct' (*divino monitus instinctu*). In July 313, the Roman Senate dedicated 'a symbol of God' (*signum dei*) to him:[78] and the Tenth Panegyric (321) refers to the same power, quoting 'the highest divinity' and its 'benign majesty' (*summa divinitas, benigna maiestas*). The 'divine mind' (*divina mens*) is another term, and Constantine himself often refers to the 'highest God' (*summus deus*). Six months after the Milvian Bridge, a Panegyrist is using similar monotheistic language:

Supreme creator of all things, who has chosen to have as many names as there are languages on earth, what name Thou Thyself preferrest we may not know – whether in Thee there resides a certain divine might and divine spirit, with which Thou dost fill the world and intermingle with all elements and, without any influence from an external impulse, does of Thyself come into operation, or whether, somewhere above all heavens, that might exists, from whence, as from a high citadel of nature, Thou regardest the work of Thy hands....

To thee I say we pray, that thou mayest preserve this our emperor for all ages.[79]

Constantine, and other Christians, could take this and similar utterances as alluding to the God of the Christians, but pagans, if they so desired, could take another view about them. The emperor did not want to cause such people offence by trumpeting his own beliefs abroad too openly or immediately.

Yet Constantine had convinced himself that the Christian God, who gave him power, was the deity to be believed in. Moreover, throughout his reign he continued to tip the scales in favour of Christianity – for instance, by bringing up his own children in the faith, so that the empire was given the prospect of a Christian succession and dynasty. As a ruler, however, he saw it as his duty to ensure harmony and order in the empire, which, by defeating his rivals, he had made a single unit once again, or so he hoped.

This meant that, even though he himself was inclined to Christianity, he had to keep the various religions in some sort of a state of balance, seeing that most of the upper classes and bureaucracy were still predominantly pagan.[80] This particularly applied to the aristocracy of Rome, with whom, therefore, his relations were distinctly complex. At first, despite evident or potential strains, he was – especially during the rise of his rival Licinius – careful to maintain friendly links with them. But his relations deteriorated – for although he favoured them with posts and honours, they were replaced as his advisers by others whose beliefs fitted in better with his own.

The 'eternal city' increasingly seemed a home of lost, outdated causes. Its prefect was virtually demoted in 321, and Constantine caused offence (in 312, 315 and 325?) by failing to celebrate the Secular Games and refusing to ascend to the Capitol to sacrifice to Jupiter. Furthermore, he made a Spanish Christian, Acilius Severus, consul in 323. Yet coinage in honour of Rome was intended to please its people – and he did not press his Christianity too hard in the city. Although the Panegyrists had ceased to stress individual pagan gods by 313, bronze coins with figures of Isis Pharia (Faria), Serapis (Sarapis) and Anubis were still, rather mysteriously, being issued at Rome, on the occasion of festivals of Isis, for half a century after the death of Constantine, and perhaps during his lifetime as well.[81] Besides, votive monuments with inscriptions to the old gods still abounded in Rome.

For it would take time, Constantine knew very well, to convince everyone else that Christianity was as desirable as he himself believed. As Edward Gibbon justly put it, 'the nicest accuracy is required in tracing the slow and almost imperceptible gradations by which the monarch declared himself the protector, and at length the proselyte, of the church'.[82]

The army also had to be treated with caution. Constantine was a popular commander, and the soldiers were disposed to like him, but they were mainly pagans (though, on the whole, mostly politically passive peasants and 'barbarians'). Like Licinius (whom he may have influenced), he got them to utter non-committal prayers to the 'supreme deity',[83] and when Eusebius observed that he taught them the 'rules of worship', he was exaggerating or over-simplifying; and so was Libanius when he remarked that the army became much more Christian in Constantine's time (Julian still found it predominantly pagan). Constantine had to be careful – remembering that Diocletian's persecution had begun in the army, and that it had been to secure army loyalty, in the first place, that it was undertaken. Moreover, although the army was too inarticulate for its views to have come down to us, there is evidence of military pressures attempting to induce him to make the sacrifices to Jupiter which he regarded with such displeasure.

Anyway, he *was* careful, and that was why his Christianization of the empire was only gradual. Its gradualness, reflecting Constantine's habit of ambiguity that has been mentioned, is reflected in the slow and for a long time minimal infiltration of the coinage by Christianity. The Christogram, in its early manifestations, seems little more than a mark of issue, or perhaps imperial rank. But it appears, as we saw, on Constantine's helmet at Ticinum in 315.[84] The *labarum*, with Christogram, stands on a recumbent serpent in 327.[85] As a main coin-type, however, the Christogram does not appear on coins until the time of Magnentius (350–3) – although he himself was not a Christian. Constantius II, who was, imitated the type.[86]

The Cross first appears, modestly, on rare coins of 314.[87] The first coins showing Constantine wearing a nimbus date from 315 (though nimbate emperors had appeared on reverses in 305).[88] Other coins show Constantine gazing upwards to heaven, as reported by Eusebius.[89] Another displays him holding the zodiac, as God's representative on earth.[90]

CHAPTER 9:

CONSTANTINE AND THE CHRISTIAN CHURCH

IN 313 CONSTANTINE and Licinius, jointly, issued the so-called Edict of Milan – building on Galerius' Edict of Toleration but going a good deal further by granting positive advantages and privileges (including the recovery of losses, and recognition of legal rights) to the Christian community.

In fact, however, the documents that have come down to us do not really constitute an 'edict' at all. What we have is, rather, a communication of some kind addressed to a provincial governor – or perhaps two of Licinius' governors (p. 164) – who was expected to convert its gist into an edict for the benefit of the people of his province. Probably what happened was that at Mediolanum (Milan), in 313, Constantine and Licinius came to an understanding, and drew up a basic list of instructions, or words of guidance, which were sent out to their various provincial representatives for promulgation in this way. One rendering of this list, probably based on the version promulgated by Licinius, was translated by Eusebius, and another transcribed by Lactantius.[1]

But even if the instructions did not, in themselves, constitute an 'edict', their general drift in favour of Christianity, evidently agreed at Mediolanum, was clear enough. A conflation of the two versions provides some such text as this:

Since we saw that freedom of worship ought not to be denied, but that to each man's judgment and will the right should be given to care for sacred things according to each man's free choice, we have already some time ago bidden the Christians to maintain the faith of their own sect and worship.

But since in that edict by which such right was granted to the aforesaid Christians many and varied conditions *haireseis*, 'heresies'] clearly appeared to have been added, it may well perchance have come about that after a short time many were repelled from practising their religion.

Thus when I, Constantine Augustus, and I, Licinius Augustus, had met at Mediolanum [Milan] and were discussing all those matters which relate to the advantage and security of the state, among the other things which we saw would benefit the majority of men we were convinced that first of all those conditions by which reverence for the Divinity is secured should be put in order by us to the end that we might give to the Christians and to all men the right to follow freely whatever religion each had wished, so that thereby whatever of Divinity there be in the heavenly seat [*quicquid divinitatis in sede caelesti*] may be favourable and propitious to us and to all those who are placed under our authority.

And so by a salutary and most fitting line of reasoning we came to the conclusion that we should adopt this policy – namely our view should be that to no one whatsoever should we deny liberty to follow either the religion of the Christians or any other cult which of his own free choice he has thought to be best adapted for himself, in order that the supreme Divinity [*Summa Divinitas*],to whose service we render our free obedience, may bestow upon us in all things his wanted favour and benevolence.

Wherefore we would that your Devotion should know that it is our will that all those conditions should be altogether removed which were contained in our former letters addressed to you concerning the Christians – these should be removed and now in freedom and without restriction let all those who desire to follow the aforesaid religion of the Christians hasten to follow the same without any molestation or interference.

Further, when you see that this indulgence has been granted by us to the aforesaid Christians, your Devotion will understand that to others also a free and unhindered liberty of religion has been granted, for such a grant is befitting to the peace of our times, so that it may be open to every man to worship as he will. This has been done by us so that we should not seem to have done dishonour to any religion.[2]

That version is a blend of what was said by Eusebius and Lactantius. Both come from communications sent by Licinius to governors of the eastern provinces, the former probably to the governor of Syria Palaestina (Judaea) at Caesarea Maritima (Sdot Yam), and the latter to his colleague at Nicomedia (Izmit) in Bithynia. As for the west, most of the provisions of the 'edict' were already recognized and in force in those regions. It is likely, however, that the surviving texts incorporate a general policy agreed at Mediolanum, and were followed, later, by a series of additional letters, and perhaps by other measures as well.

The pronouncement was based on the same sort of reasoning that had earlier lain behind the persecutions, involving the belief that the empire's troubles arose from the anger of the neglected divine power. But it tiptoes round theology, leaving a great deal vague, and deliberately obscuring differences.

All the same, the religious advantage of the Christians, designed to secure the favour of *their* supreme God for the empire, was now unmistakable. And Constantine followed up this message, with due caution indeed, but without delay. His determination to follow the God of the Christians, tempered by a prudent realization that he must not go too fast or he would offend the pagans, governed his conduct in the future. In fact, however, he went *quite* fast, granting a succession of favours to the Christians.

This policy involved a signal elevation of the clergy, who received all sorts of privileges. Already in the winter of 312/13 the emperor was making this clear in a letter to Anullinus, proconsul of Africa:

Greetings, our dearest Anullinus.

Whereas from many considerations it appears that the annulment of the worship in which the highest reverence of the most holy heavenly power is maintained has brought the greatest dangers upon the commonwealth, and the lawful revival and protection of this same worship has caused the greatest good fortune to the Roman name and exceptional prosperity to all the affairs of men, the divine beneficence affording this, it has been decided that those men who in due holiness and the observance of this law offer their personal services to the ministry of the divine worship shall receive the due reward of their labours, dearest Anullinus.

Accordingly I desire that those who within the province entrusted to you provide personal service to this holy worship in the Catholic Church over which Caecilian presides, who are commonly called 'clerics', shall be kept immune from all public burdens of any kind whatever, so that they may not be diverted by any sacrilegious error or slip from the service which is owed to the divinity, but may rather without any disturbance serve their own law, since their conduct of the greatest worship towards the Divinity will in my opinion bring immeasurable benefit to the commonwealth.

Farewell, our dearest and most beloved Anullinus.[3]

The dispensations of which, as a result, the Christian clergy became the recipients were considerable. Constantine decreed, for example, that church lands should not be subject to tax. He also commanded provincial officials to supply labour and materials for the construction of churches, for the benefit of whose members he also arranged that gifts of food should be supplied. He laid down a scheme by which allowances should be made to nuns and others who were engaged in ecclesiastical duties. All this amounted to a great deal of help to the churches, and constituted a novel development. It must have been a striking experience for the clergy to become the recipients of this unlimited generosity from Constantine, and to find a much wider and richer social life at their disposal than had been available before.

True, the emperor completely controlled the bishops himself. His dominance over them, embodied in the statement 'my will must be considered binding'[4] – which some earlier Christians would never have accepted – was a prime example of that monarchical control of the church described as Caesaropapism. Athanasius declared that the Fathers never sought imperial sanction,[5] but in Constantine's time they had to, and they did. And it was he himself who chose every bishop when a vacancy arose.

On the understanding, however, that he was in charge, the results of his favourable attitude to the church were far-reaching. The top clerics, the bishops, received special attention, and were employed to pronounce on religious issues rather as earlier emperors had used *pontifices* and augurs; and they obtained judicial powers as well. Indeed, they found themselves among the emperor's principal advisers; and, although he himself had appointed them, he treated them with respect, even asserting that 'God has given you power to judge us also'.[6] Be that as it may, he left them a great deal of responsibility for church affairs, which had come, in view of Constantine's inclinations, to fulfil an extremely important role.

The high standing of the bishops was underlined by their vast entourages visible in the churches. And it is clear from the letters (*epistulae*) they received from Constantine: he realized that they would serve him as valuable government functionaries – a significant and high ranking and privileged part of the new governing class. There were 1,800 of these bishops, 1,000 in Greek-speaking and 800 in Latin-speaking provinces. Many were vast landowners (though some were humble). Those at court dined with Constantine – like Apostles surrounding Christ in paradise, said Eusebius[7] – and some were haughty and avaricious intriguers. As the ecclesiastics took over the interests and values of the governmental hierarchy, and churches became endowed with great wealth, Christian art and architecture increasingly borrowed the grandeur of imperial ceremonial.

And it was not only bishops but the Christian clerics in general who received privileges from Constantine, who saw how valuable they could be to himself. A whole series of dispensations is recorded, including their exemption from the onerous burden of public municipal duties,[8] and their entitlement to the same immunities as pagan priests (324/6), and much else as well. Constantine's allowances to the clergy were so large that Jovian (363-4) cut them by two-thirds. Eusebius of Caesarea realized that Constantine's generosity meant that he was often imposed upon, especially by people who 'crept into the church' to secure its benefits.[9] This vastly increased inclusion of the churchmen in worldly affairs played a large part in driving people who objected to this development, and were influenced by the current fashion for secluded asceticism, to become hermits in the desert, especially in Egypt (although avoidance of heavy taxation also had something to do with the process).

This flight to hermit life started before the time of Constantine, but it was his epoch that witnessed the most eminent of all desert hermits, St Pachomius (c.292–346) at Tabennisi (c.320). Even if Constantine approved of the preaching of hermits such as St Antony (c.251–356) against the Arian 'heresy', he cannot really have applauded eremitic and monastic asceticism, which operated against his ideal of unity based on the control of the church by the state.

It was, however, a fact that gloomy otherworldliness of this kind was encouraged by the deplorable state of the empire and its society, and that Christianity 'persuaded men who might have played a part in public affairs to turn their backs on public life and enter monasteries'.[10] And by retiring in this way, it has been suggested, the monks of Egypt played as enduring a part in the history of the age as Constantine himself.[11] In any case, they certainly did not help him to fulfil his ambitions.

But even leaving these hermits out of account, the close subordination of the official church to the state – although it was very much what Constantine wanted – proved deeply disappointing to him in its outcome. Indeed (along with his condemnation of his son – which however he soon afterwards regretted), this aspect of life produced the worst disappointment that he ever suffered.

For, apart from his deep emotional involvement, the main reason why he had favoured Christianity, as we have seen, was because he believed that it would encourage unity in the empire. This was the dominant theme in Constantine's practical thinking and in his life. Unfortunately, however, the Christian faith failed to achieve that aim, owing to the dissensions between one Christian group and another. Constantine wanted an established church, to which all good Christians would belong; and those who would not belong to it were dismissed as 'heretics' – a term resounding with mutual Christian accusations, and with a long and ominous history ahead of it. Constantine deplored this ridiculous proliferation of dissension, believing that imperial unity required unity of creeds.

Constantine Augustus to Chrestus, bishop of Syracuse....

Even those who owe one another a brotherly union of spirit have engaged in a disgraceful, indeed, an abominable mutual discord. Men who are strangers in spirit to this most holy religion have been given an excuse for mockery. For this reason it has become my duty to provide that what should have been ended by voluntary agreement, as a consequence of the judgment already passed, may even now be brought to a conclusion by an assembly of many persons (at Arelate [Arles], in 313).[12]

Constantine – Victor, Maximus, Augustus – to the holy Synod of Tyre (335).

That the Catholic Church should be free of dissension is surely in accordance with and indeed befitting the prosperity of these times. The servants of God ought not now to bear the burden of any reproach. Yet some have been overcome by a passion for unhealthy quarrelling. I would not want to say that they are living as unworthy representatives of their profession. However, they are trying to cause confusion, and confusion is, in my opinion, the worst of all calamities.

I urge you, who are, as the saying goes, running forward, to come together without delay and to form a Synod.... The purpose of this will be to free the Church from all reproach, to still my anxieties, and to gain the utmost glory for yourselves by giving the blessing of peace to those who are now in conflict.[13]

And then, after the Synod of Tyre was over,

I do not know what was decided by your Council with such tempestuous tumult, but it appears that the truth has been somehow distorted by violent disorder, since, owing to your contentiousness towards your neighbours, which you desire to be invincible, you do not observe what is pleasing to God.

But let it be the work of the divine providence manifestly to convict and dissipate the horrid deeds of your quarrelsomeness, or rather fight for evil.... We who are supposed to protect (I would not say preserve) the sacred mysteries of his favour – we, I say, do nothing but what tends to strife and hatred, and, to speak plainly, the destruction of the human race.[14]

And Hilary of Limonum (Poitiers) (c.315–67), after Constantine's death, was still saying the same.

It is a thing equally deplorable and dangerous that there are as many creeds and opinions among men, as many doctrines as inclinations, and as many sources of blasphemy as there are faults among us; because we make creeds arbitrarily, and explain them as arbitrarily.... Reciprocally tearing one another to pieces, we have been the cause of each other's ruin.[15]

There was of course, it could be said, a brighter side to all this. Because the dissensions did at least mean that there were sufficient chinks in the smothering autocracy of the day to enable men to differ from one another about theological issues: that is to say, individual views could be expressed. Nevertheless, as far as the unity of the empire was concerned, these disagreements were only a dead loss.

For the history of the Christians under the later Roman empire was gravely damaged by the savage warfare which raged within their own ranks, deserved the censure of Julian,[16] and has been described as one of the most intolerable spectacles in all history.[17] 'Such events seem to many of us to cast thorough discredit upon the claim of Christianity to constitute a divine revelation.'[18] This conclusion, used by Voltaire and Gibbon to explain the fall of the western empire, can scarcely be contested except by blaming what happened upon the activities of the Devil, or by arguing – as Christians, on all sides, did in antiquity, and still disastrously do – that there was, and is, only one authentic Christian church, and that those self-styled Christians who failed to adhere to it cannot be regarded as true Christians at all.

On the credit side, as far as the historian of the later Roman world is concerned, it is necessary to counterbalance this mutual hatred and destruction between the various sects by the remarkable loyalty and cohesion within the ranks of each individual

Christian sect. Even if paganism had never suffered from the same mutual dissensions, the cohesion within Christian groups was also stronger than anything that the pagans had ever experienced. Nevertheless, it remains true that the ferocious hostility between these sects was a very powerful destructive factor, and played a massive part in the politics of the fourth and fifth centuries, which led to disaster.

Constantine was immediately confronted by these damaging dissensions. For at the very outset of his Christianizing of the empire two powerful 'heretical' bodies of Christians made themselves felt. They were the Donatists and the Arians. Between them these two sects contrived that Constantine's idea that the empire, with Christians in charge, could become a single harmonious unit was totally demolished.

The Donatists were centred for the most part in north Africa, a puritanical and perfervid country, where fanatical faiths had long since had their being (whether, and to what extent, they also existed elsewhere is disputed). This Donatist movement was brought into significance by the persecution of the Christians by Diocletian and his colleagues. The persecutors had demanded that Christians should sacrifice to the pagan gods, and surrender up their scriptural books to the pagan secular authorities: which many of them had done, in order to survive. One such person was Caecilianus, who was consecrated by Felix, bishop of Aptunga – believed, perhaps wrongly, to have been such a traitor (*traditor*) – and later won the nomination to the bishopric of Carthage. This appointment was strongly opposed by the Donatists, led by a religious leader named Donatus of Casae Nigrae, on the borders of the Sahara. It appears uncertain, however, whether the sect took its name from this man, or from the next schismatic bishop of Carthage – a very prosperous city, which contained three fine Donatist basilicas.

The Donatists set themselves up as the fierce and uncompromising enemies of all who had allowed themselves gestures towards the pagans in order to save their skins (although it was found later that some of their most vigorous opponents had done the same). As far as the empire was concerned, they stood for a deeply rooted disharmony: for they 'completely spurned traditional, classical, urban culture, and rejected the sovereignty of Constantine's official church, which they identified with this sort of hated background'.[19]

The matter came to the attention of Constantine, who did not understand such theological problems very well, or view them with great sympathy. Although he may have been made aware that the Donatists had friends at court, perhaps in the imperial family itself, the seething emotions that lay behind their movement were quite unfamiliar to him: and he was willing to offer money to those of them who might be prepared to secede from their cause. Another reason, too, why he disliked the Donatist sect was because its quarrels with the church gave the pagans cause for ridicule. Intolerance, it can be conceded, was not one of Constantine's major faults. But he did express repeated resentment of the Donatists' determination to make a breach in the national unity which he, with the support of the main Christian body, was determined to establish.

The subsequent history of the affair is tortuous. But two epoch-making events stand out. One was the fact that, at quite an early stage (311–13), the Donatists themselves *appealed* to Constantine:

We pray you, most excellent emperor Constantine, since you are of righteous stock, seeing that your father did not with the other emperors carry out the persecutions and Gaul is immune from this crime: whereas there are disputes between us and the other bishops in Africa, we pray that your piety may order judges to be given to us from Gaul.[20]

This appeal to the emperor as arbiter was based, as its wording indicates, upon his *pietas* towards his father Constantius I Chlorus, who, as we have seen, was sometimes believed to have been a Christian. But the appeal later incurred criticism from Augustine,[21] who was unimpressed by this attempt by the Donatists to shift the initiative from their own shoulders to those of the emperor.

Constantine responded to the appeal by appointing five judges – transformed into a Council or Synod by the Pope or Bishop of Rome, Silvester I, who added fourteen Italian bishops. Yet this Council, which met at Arelate (Arles) in 314, did not do much good, and the complicated story of the Donatists went on.

They now found themselves subject to the most downright condemnation from the emperor. But they instantly responded, by pressing home their accusations against the alleged traitor Felix, the bishop of Aptunga. When, however, the matter came to trial in February 315, before the proconsul of Africa, it was established that all the documents they had presented in support of their case were forged.

Before the year was over, the Donatist bishop of Carthage had died, and was succeeded by the second man named Donatus, an energetic personage who, on 10 November 316, stood firm against an edict by Constantine dispossessing his sect of their churches. Bloodshed and violence were caused by the edict – later regarded by Augustine as savage – and by the resistance it provoked.

On 3 May 321, however, the emperor wrote to his representative in Africa indicating that he was tired of maintaining this policy of forcible oppression, and that no further persecution of the Donatists should take place. And at about the same time he addressed a further communication to the African province, expressing sorrow because the measures he had taken to secure peace and create unity had not proved successful. It was for God himself, Constantine is said to have concluded, to terminate Donatism; and in the meantime the Christians in Africa must endure their hard times with patience.[22]

But the very fact that the Donatists had, earlier, appealed to the emperor proved significant. For it established, beyond a doubt, recognition of the fact that he was in control of religion – of Christian religion: that there could, or should, be no friction between church and state because the state, that is to say Constantine himself as its head, was in charge.

A second historic aspect of the Donatist schism lay in the fact that, when Constantine saw he could not get rid of it, he had employed forcible coercion (316): for he felt, at the time, that this decision was amply justified:

The insatiable plunderer, i.e. the Devil ... sends money either to seduce faith or to give an occasion for avarice by pretence of holding to the [Christian] law. But when in the face of all these enticements justice kept her course rigidly and inflexibly, judges are ordered to intervene, they are driven to put the secular power in motion, buildings are surrounded by troops, the rich are threatened with proscription, the sacraments are defiled, a mob of heathens is brought in upon us, sacred edifices become the scenes of hilarious feasts.[23]

True, as we have seen, his employment of force did not last long, because Constantine's basic tolerance reasserted itself. Moreover, it was reinforced by two considerations. One was that Diocletian's persecutions had shown that forcible treatment of Christians did not work. And the other consideration was that the Donatists themselves seemed positively to welcome martyrdom. That is why, sickened and scornful and grudging, Constantine concluded in 321: 'let things be'. Moreover, when in 330 the Donatists forcibly seized a church at Constantina (Cirta), he actually gave orders for a new one to be built for the official church which opposed them, rather than enter into further wrangles with these 'heretics'.

Nevertheless, he *had* used force: and this did immeasurable harm, and set a bleak precedent for every century to come. Moreover, as others have found since, it did not work. For the Donatists continued to exist under Constantine – and outlived him.

The second 'heresy' which put an end to his dream of imperial Christian unity was Arianism. Its founder, Arius, probably a

Libyan by birth, possessed a genius for propaganda, became a presbyter at Alexandria, and in *c.*319–22 started to propagate his views. Three of his Letters and some fragments of his *Thalia* have survived. The latter was a verse and prose popularization of his doctrines, so widely admired that it was sung in the bars of Alexandria.

But what caused all the controversy was that Arius seemed to be making the terrible observation that Jesus had not got quite the same qualifications as his divine Father. For what Arius maintained was that the Son, although created before time and superior to other creatures, was like them changeable – the Gospels represent him as subject to growth and change – and consequently different in Essence from the Father. For 'there was [a time] when Jesus was not': so that he cannot, therefore, himself be God, to whom he is in a sense posterior. That is what caused the storm, the most passionate storm that ever convulsed the Christian world, since it seemed to reduce the Son to a status that was less than divine.

But Arius' exact views, and teachings, have been the subject of extensive debate.[24] This was how Socrates Scholasticus described his opinions:

On one occasion at a gathering of his presbyters and the rest of the clergy, he [bishop Alexander of Alexandria] essayed a rather ambitious theological discussion on the Holy Trinity. But one of the presbyters, Arius by name, a man not lacking in dialectic, thinking that the bishop was expounding the doctrine of Sabellius the Libyan, from love of controversy espoused a view diametrically opposed to the teaching of the Libyan, and attacked the statements of the bishop with energy. 'If', said he, 'the Father begot the Son, he that was begotten had a beginning of existence: hence it is clear that *there was when the Son was not*.'[25]

Sabellius was a third-century theologian, known as a 'Modalist', according to whom Father, Son and Holy Spirit are 'modes' of the same being – perhaps performing temporary and successive roles adopted in order to carry out the divine plan of Redemption. And Arius also derived some of his 'subordinationist' views from his teacher Lucian, presbyter of Antioch, who, in turn, owed doctrines to Dionysius of Alexandria and Origen. But Arius' enemies maintained that such opinions undermined the entire basis of Christianity, founded on the divinity of Jesus.

There is no problem in the whole of history in which it is harder to reconstruct, with sympathy, the contestants' minds. Anyone who is a Christian today accepts that Jesus was the Son of God, without fussing about what seems the irrelevant question of when Jesus came into existence, or whether, and to what extent, he was 'posterior' to God. But apparently people of the time of Constantine felt very differently indeed. Such questions seemed to them pre-eminently important, for this was a profoundly religious epoch, in which there were no free-thinkers. The most abstruse theological controversies excited ferocious passions. Gregory of Nyssa remarked that one could not talk to a shopkeeper in the market place, or to an attendant in the public baths, without getting involved in a theological discussion,[26] and very often the discussion was about the matter mentioned above, the relationship of the Son to the Father.

As for Constantine himself, especially when church affairs in the powerful east came forcibly to his attention after the defeat of Licinius, he became aware that this problem was racking his subjects and, above all, shattering their *unity*. It was in this, as we have seen, that he was principally interested, and it was in the hope of restoring or creating this harmony – a hope that was manifestly unfulfilled – that he favoured the Christians against divided and discredited paganism.

He wrote repeatedly confirming this emphasis and preoccupation, fulminating against dissensions in the church, which were, he was convinced, displeasing to God. He called the Golden Octagon at Antioch the 'Church of Concord', and reminded the Synod of Tyre (335) that it had to restore unity. In the same spirit Eusebius, in his *In Praise of Constantine*, deliberately plays down disputes within the church and his *History of the Church* is a paean on its unity. Constantine was maintaining the tradition that the emperor had to maintain the divine peace (the pagan *pax deorum*), in the new context of Christianity, from which he hoped for mutual love and communal charity based on common membership.

And so after his victory in 324 he produced a flurry of six public statements to explain his Christian purpose. For it was his belief that Christianity was the one force which could effectively bring the jarring elements together. But it must be his own brand of Christianity, for, as we have seen, he issued laws warning against 'heresies', seeing it as his duty to banish error in religion.

His own attitude, since his Christianity was not of a particularly subtle kind, was nearer that of the commonsense person of today than that of his contemporaries who plunged themselves into this sort of controversy. In other words, he thought that any such dispute was relatively unimportant, abstruse quibbling on a point of minor importance – compared to the central problem of grasping the Truth, which meant the Truth established by the Christian God. So, in 323, he told the contestants to shut up and become united[27] (he was also concerned that they were blocking his 'road to the east', in his conflict with Licinius).

He believed he was under a moral obligation to offer this mediation in the dispute that had arisen over Arianism, just as he had, earlier, tried to mediate to calm down the Donatist 'heretics'. So that was why he composed a letter to Alexander, the bishop of Alexandria, and to his enemy Arius, requesting them to settle their disagreement in a peaceful fashion. And he gave the letter to Ossius, bishop of Corduba, to deliver. It was an entirely forlorn hope, because in fact the possibilities of an agreement or a compromise were non-existent. If Constantine really hoped that his intervention might prove effective, it can only have been, once again, because he was more concerned about imperial unity, which he regarded as all-important, than about theological principles, which seemed to him so pettifogging and pedantic.

This last point was made absolutely clear in Constantine's letter which Ossius took to Alexandria. For it repeatedly criticized both

Alexander and Arius for disputing about matters of no real significance. Bishop Alexander, indicated the emperor, had been unwise to examine his clerics about their interpretation of one single passage of the New Testament. And Arius ought to have kept quiet. Questions and answers alike, Constantine went on, were the products of a quarrelsome state of mind created by not having enough to do. As for his own ideas, convinced though he was that everyone should be Christian, he was nevertheless prepared to concede that Christians might justifiably maintain differing views on points of theological doctrine. Yet, if they were sensible people, he concluded, they could disagree about such matters in a spirit of fraternal affection.

We would do much better, therefore, he continued, to address ourselves:

to the objects within our powers and within the reach of our nature, for what persuades us in the course of a debate distracts most of us from the truth of reality, as has befallen many philosophers who exercise their wits on reasons and the investigation of the essence of things.

And whenever the magnitude of the question outstrips their enquiry, they bury the truth in methodological differences. They end up teaching conflicting opinions, and attack each other's positions, even the men who lay claim to wisdom. Hence, factious divisions among the common people too.[28]

Let each of you, sharing an equal spirit of concession, accept the just advice that your fellow servant offers you. And what is that? You ought not to have raised such questions at all, and if they were raised, not to have answered. For such investigations, which no legal necessity imposes, but the frivolity of an idle hour provokes, we should, even if they are made for the sake of a philosophic exercise, lock up within our hearts and not bring forward into public gathering or entrust imprudently to the ears of the people....

To remind your understanding by a small example, you know, I take it, that even philosophers all agree on one doctrine, and often, when they disagree on some part of their arguments, though they are divided by the keenness of their intellect, agree with one another again in the unity of their belief. If this is so, how much more should we, the servants of the great God, maintain harmony with one another?...

Give me back peaceful nights and days without care that I too may keep some pleasure in the pure light and the joy of a tranquil life henceforth![29]

Constantine may have been, intellectually, somewhat out of his depth, as he had also been when dealing with the Donatists. For in this Arian dispute, in particular, although his desire for imperial unity is clear enough, he showed himself ill-equipped to deal either with the theological principles that were involved or with the persons who were putting them forward. That accounts for the indecisiveness, displayed by reversals and changes of mind and blowings hot and cold and outbursts of bad temper,[30] which characterized the whole series of his utterances on the subject, and became especially noticeable in the 330s. Nevertheless, even if he was conscious of the intellectual disadvantages under which he laboured in dealing with these matters, he continued to remain, in his own view, wholly entitled to influence such disputes when they arose, and his determination to establish unity did not waver.

Excommunicated in 323 (by the initiative of his infuriated bishop Alexander), Arius was condemned by the Synod of Antioch (late 324), presided over by Ossius. And it was with the intention of following up this initiative that, in the following year, Constantine convoked the Christian bishops to the First Council of Nicaea, the first 'ecumenical' Council, transferred from Ancyra (Ankara), which was less conveniently situated (and too far from the possible plotting by the defeated Licinius which Constantine may at first have feared).

Unlike the previous Synod of Arelate, this First Council of Nicaea was not predominantly composed of western bishops – of whom, indeed, only six came, out of a total of 2,000 who attended the Council. They were guests of the emperor, who paid their travelling expenses; and the meetings lasted for about two months. It is not certain who was selected as chairman of the Council – probably several persons in turn, including Ossius, were appointed to preside over its meetings. Yet it was to Constantine, who held such strong views about the subordination of church to state, that everyone looked.

Various matters were discussed. But Arianism came first and foremost: and many of those present could be regarded as holding at least semi-Arian views. On somebody's advice – probably that of Ossius once again – Constantine decided to pronounce that Jesus was *homoousios* with God, 'of one substance'. This was by no means an unknown term, but it remained somewhat ambiguous and was variously interpreted. The word was distasteful to most eastern theologians, but proved welcome to Arius' opponents for the simple reason that he himself (as was intended) found it unacceptable. It might have been hoped that he could derive some comfort from its ambiguity, but although its Latin (approximate) equivalent *consubstantialis* had long been considered orthodox in the west, Arius publicly declared that *homoousios* was heretical; so he was duly excommunicated.

Later, the alternative term *homoiousios*, of *like* substance, was suggested (its supporters began to coalesce after 341), and there was a story that Eusebius of Caesarea (a middle-of-the-road semi-Arian) inserted the 'i'. Certainly he would have liked to do so, but, despite his distaste for *homoousios*, he gave in at the Council of Nicaea and accepted the term, as he explains rather lamely in his *Letter to the Church at Caesarea*.[31] It was rumoured that Constantine's stepsister Constantia subsequently suggested the insertion of the 'i', to satisfy the Arians. Edward Gibbon robustly refuses to see very much difference between *homoousios* and *homoiousios*.[32] But that is not how people felt at the time.

It must be supposed that Constantine himself, who was not very much at home in Greek, did not have a particularly clear idea of what *homoousios* was supposed to mean. But he reckoned that it would serve to obtain more or less general agreement (against Arius), and he was right: less for theological reasons than because hardly anyone had the nerve to contradict him.

So this was the Nicene Creed that eventually emerged, after redrafting to include the term *homoousios*:

We believe in one God, the Father almighty, maker of all things visible and invisible: and in one Lord Jesus Christ, the Son of God, begotten from the Father, only-begotten, that is, from the substance of the Father, God from God, Light from Light, True God from True God, begotten not made, of one substance [*homoousios*] with the Father, through whom all things came into existence, things in heaven and things on earth, who because of us men and because of our salvation came down and became incarnate, becoming man, suffered and rose again on the third day, ascended to the heavens, and will come to judge the living and the dead; and in the Holy Spirit.

To make it clear that the Arians must come to heel – if it had not become clear to them already – the following anathemas were appended:

But as for those who say, There was when he was not, and Before being born he was not, and That he came into existence out of nothing, or who assert that the Son of God is of a different *hypostasis* or substance, or is created, or is subject to alteration or change – these the church anathematises.[33]

And after the Council of Nicaea the official church took over the church of St George (S. Giorgio Maggiore) at Mediolanum (Milan) from the Arians who had constructed it.

Despite widespread doubts among those present at Nicaea, only two of them failed to accept this definition, whereupon, like Arius himself, they were condemned to excommunication – although three others, too, wrote in, shortly afterwards, to say that they wished to repudiate the acceptance of the term that they had offered at the time.

Gibbon stressed the weakness, emotionalism and ignorance of the members of religious conferences such as these:[34] of which seven more followed during the rest of Constantine's reign. Nevertheless, the emperor felt able to declare that the decisions at Nicaea were divinely inspired, and that they mirrored the judgment of God.[35] And he assured Bishop Alexander that the question of Arius was now, or should be, solved (325):

Even now will foul envy bark back with unholy sophisms of postponement? What is that to the present occasion? Do we hold other beliefs, most honoured brother, than those decided by the Holy Spirit through you all? I tell you that *Arius*, the Arius, came to me, the Augustus, on the recommendation of many persons, promising that he believed about our Catholic faith what was decided and confirmed at the Council of Nicaea by you, I your fellow-servant being present and participating in the decision.... I am that man who have dedicated my mind with pure faith to God, I am your fellow- servant who have undertaken all care for peace and harmony.... So I have sent to you, not merely suggesting but begging that you receive the men, who beg for pardon.... Aid concord, I beg you, offer the blessings of friendship to those who do not doubt the faith.[36]

Unfortunately for the emperor, however, although there had been this large and more or less compulsory measure of general agreement at the First Council of Nicaea, the question of Arianism could by no means be brushed aside in this way. For Arius still had many sympathizers. In 327 the Second Council of Nicaea readmitted him and his chief supporters to Communion, and a Synod that met at Antioch was pro-Arian. Nevertheless, Constantine himself, in 333, forgetting his own tolerance, completely lost his temper with the evidently unrepentant Arius.

Take heed, everyone take heed, how sad he sounds, when pierced by the serpent's sting [that is, the Devil's], how his veins and flesh, injected with the poison, shoot terrible pains, how his whole wasted body flows away, how he is filled with filth and dirt and wretchedness and pallor and trembling and a thousand ills, how horrible a skeleton he has grown, how disgustingly dirty and tangled his hair, how half- dead all over, how feeble the look of his eyes, bloodless his face, and how emaciated he is from his cares.[37]

Yet Arius (who had never been sent far away) did, as Constantine had earlier pointed out, at one time pay tribute to unity, though without substantially changing his mind; and he was readmitted to the church by the Council of Jerusalem (335), and rehabilitated at court.

Here one can detect the influence of Eusebius, bishop of Nicomedia (not the church historian), who was likewise a reinstated former Arian and had steadily been increasing his power.[38] He was particularly influential with the imperial family, and it was said that the emperor's stepsister Constantia, now dying, had taken the initiative in restoring Arius. As for the church historian Eusebius of Caesarea, he too, as we saw, came perilously close to adopting the Arian viewpoint, although he preferred to describe himself as 'in the middle'.[39]

Throughout this period, however, there was an extraordinary story of see-sawing dissension between Arius and his arch-enemy Athanasius (*c.*295–373). Bishop of Alexandria – in succession to Alexander – in 328, with strong Egyptian roots, fanatical but able, Athanasius despised Eusebius of Caesarea's policy of mid-line accommodation, and strongly supported the *homoousios* doctrine. But the vigour, indeed violence, of his assertions and polemics earned him no less than five periods of exile. Two of these periods of banishment were spent in the west, where he introduced monasticism. Many of his varied writings have survived. Constantine disapproved of Athanasius' policy of *exclusions*, preferring the inclusive attitude of men like Eusebius of Caesarea. Nevertheless, at times Constantine backed Athanasius, because of the latter's opposition to Arius – who, moreover, was only a presbyter, while Athanasius was a bishop. Or at least, if to back such a violent man proved impracticable, the emperor managed to tolerate him, notably in 335, when Athanasius waylaid him outside the gates of Constantinople.

A decisive point in Athanasius' fight against the Arians occurred in the same year, when Arius died in a lavatory at Constantinople: which his enemies, such as Athanasius, proclaimed as a sign of God's anger. But Arius' death did not end his influence; and indeed Arianism had destroyed imperial unity as completely as Donatism had done, though for different reasons. Constantine's idea that the adoption of Christianity would unify the empire had proved totally mistaken. And indeed Arianism itself had a significant future, being embraced by the emperor's own son Constantius II as the best means of accommodating the church to the imperial state: a view which his father could never have held.

As was mentioned earlier, Constantine was vigorously pro-Christian himself, but he had to move carefully, because so very many people in the empire, including men of great importance, were pagan.

This, as we saw, was conspicuously true of Rome, where the Senate and people were mostly adherents of paganism – which they continued to practise[40] – and it was also true of the army. But it also applied strongly to the Greeks of the east, who became more and more significant as the hub of the Roman world moved eastwards.

Constantine himself, whatever his personal feelings, was probably inclined to be relatively tolerant towards pagans, because he had seen that persecutions did not work, and because he wanted pagans as well as Christians to feel loyal to himself. Besides, he possessed many personal ties with individual pagans. Quite apart from his contacts with the leading men at Rome, such as Aradius Rufinus and Rufius Volusianus, he had special Greek (or Hellenized) friends at Constantinople, like Sopater (until his downfall was caused by the Christian Ablabius), and Nicagoras, and Hermogenes – the sort of people who particularly favoured Neoplatonism, the revived, synthetic Platonism which had been the dominant philosophy of the pagan world since the previous century.

And in their company, faithful to the predilection of his father Constantius I Chlorus for philosophers and rhetoricians, Constantine used to hold a regular 'salon', a sort of religious–philosophical debating society (the members of which, in so far as they were pagans, must have found his interest in Christianity ridiculous and perhaps humiliating). His encouragement of higher education also implied a continued toleration of paganism. He called his friend Strategius 'Musonianus', after the Muses. He even gave his churches at Constantinople the names of Greek personifications, such as Eirene (Peace) and Sophia (Wisdom), and the town itself was sometimes called 'Platonopolis', owing to his admiration of Plato. Constantine also at times described the Christian clergy and monks as 'philosophers'.

Clement of Alexandria had liked to believe that Greek philosophy was parallel to the Mosaic Law in its preparation for Christ. And Constantine's move to Constantinople obviously encouraged such thinking. But Nicagoras, mentioned above, was an Athenian who belonged to a family of Eleusinian priests, and Constantine gave funds to aid a religious function of Eleusis.

However, the emperor also felt obliged to address himself, in a far less complimentary manner, to the problem of reducing the influence of paganism. He himself, even if willing enough to allow all manner of men to feel loyal to him, had no sympathy with the ideas of the pagans, for as the somewhat contemptuous language of his utterances shows he regarded them as merely exemplifying a branch of *superstitio*. But he was well aware that a great number of people felt differently, including men of substantial importance. That is to say, he had to act cautiously. Thus we see him accepting Roman consulships, in the old traditional style, in 307 (in the west), and 312 and 313 and 315, and his Arch shows him sacrificing to the gods. Moreover, he even retained the office of *pontifex maximus*, a traditional and very pagan part of the imperial titulature. Perhaps he liked to keep the office to himself, so that it should not fall into other and dangerous hands (it was not until 379 in the east and 382/3 in the west that the title was abolished).

Moreover, Constantine also allowed people, for example at Hispellum (Spello) in 335/7, to continue their celebration of imperial cult, based on his own Second Flavian House[41] – subject only to the warning that its shrines 'must not be polluted by the deceits of any contagious superstition' (which reminds us that Christians were censured for offering sacrifice to images of Constantine).[42] And indeed, at Rome itself, eighty-three days of festivals and Games, each year, were devoted to the same imperial cult, mostly relating, once more, to the Constantinian House. The graduality of the removal of paganism from the coinage, or, to speak more exactly, the gradual conversion of pagan concepts into neutral, ambivalent coin-types and inscriptions, demonstrates the care with which Constantine proceeded.

Theoretically, he was glad to exercise, and proclaim, the toleration which he felt to be advisable:

Let those who are in error be free to enjoy the same peace and quietude as those who believe. Let no one molest another. Let each hold to that which his soul desires, and let him use this to the full.

But as for the wise – it is right that they should be persuaded that those alone will live a holy and pure life whom thou, O God, callest to find rest in Thy holy laws.... It is one thing to enter voluntarily upon the struggle for immortality, another to compel others to do so from fear of punishment.... Some think, as I hear, that the rites of temples and the power of darkness have been abolished. That indeed I would have recommended to all men if it had not been that the violent revolt of wicked error were not immoderately fixed in the minds of some to the injury of the common salvation.[33]

Even the pagans, then, said Constantine, must be spared, and allowed to do what they wish:

You who think it to your interest, go to the public altars and temples and celebrate the rights of your traditional faith: for we do not forbid the ceremonies of past practice to be performed in the light of day.

Nevertheless, while himself refusing to offer sacrifice in the temple of Jupiter Capitolinus, or promote the Secular Games, he also introduced sanctions against paganism with cautious but considerable and growing determination, passing a series of measures making life more difficult for those who adhered to its practices,[44] and in the end sending out delegates to deprive the temples of their treasures (331). Sozomen offers a good Christian view of this course of action.

It appeared to him necessary to teach his subjects to give up their rites; and this would be easy if he could first accustom them to despise their temples and the images contained therein. In considering this project, there was no need of military force; for the Christians serving in the palace carried out their instructions among the cities with the imperial proclamation. The people kept quiet out of fear that they themselves, wives and children, might suffer if they offered opposition.

The wardens and priests, deprived of the support of their majority of the populace, proffered their most precious treasures, even those icons called Heaven-Sent, and, through themselves, these objects emerged from the sacred recesses and hiding-places in the temples – and became public property.[45]

These confiscations, including the stripping of gold from cult statues, were helpful to Constantine because he was short of precious metals, and what he acquired by these measures helped him to produce an adequate gold coinage.

He also, without authorizing the shedding of blood, destroyed a few actual pagan temples themselves (not in Rome) – notably at Aegeae (Ayas) in Cilicia (to combat a demon), Heliopolis (Baalbek) in Syria, and Aphaca in the mountain region of Phoenicia – much to the glee of Eusebius[46] and other Christian writers, who agreed in finding these famous cult centres offensive because of the sexual irregularities practised there, as well as on religious grounds. Lactantius and Jerome liked to exaggerate Constantine's destruction of pagan shrines (the temple at Heliopolis was still not out of action in the sixth century), though it does seem a fact that pagan sites, in Constantine's reign, were liable to plundering attacks from Christians, notably in Britain.

There was something of a purge of prominent pagan individuals, too, including, as we saw, Sopater, on a trumped-up charge. Constantine also prohibited functionaries from performing the traditional pagan acts of sacrifice before the commencement of official business, and indeed forbade the performance of sacrifice to the pagan gods at all – and reiterated the veto when its first pronouncement aroused protests. As a result, by the end of his reign and life, it seems probable that no pagan sacrifices, on any occasion whatever, could any longer occur. Nor could the consultation of pagan oracles; and Constantine had the works of the pagan scholar Porphyry (232/3–c.305) burnt. Moreover, in 325 he abolished the gladiatorial displays which Christian writers deplored (though his action in this field – like his destruction of the temple at Heliopolis – was without permanent effect, since further laws proved necessary later in the century). Moreover, it was also said, probably with accuracy, that there was never any pagan worship at the new city of Constantinople.

As for divination or soothsaying (*haruspicina*), Constantine's laws on the subject seem somewhat contradictory and incoherent.[47] Possibly, in framing them, he was often motivated by a desire to criticize Licinius. In general, however, although hostile to *haruspices* for having triggered off Diocletian's persecution of the Christians, he did nothing much to stop *haruspicina* in private houses – or rather, having done just that, he cancelled the measures soon afterwards (and sometimes resorted to entrail divination himself).

With regard to public divination, he was, at first, distinctly tolerant. Thus he explicitly permitted the practice in 320, in relation to buildings struck by lightning. Nevertheless, he acted against public divination after 324, fearing that the secrecies involved, especially if nocturnal, could lead to political subversiveness – and indeed he declared such activities to be the work of demons and bad angels. All the same, public divination continued until at least 358.

Subversion was also suspected to be a possible outcome of astrology (about which Firmicus Maternus had a lot to say). But Constantine, being highly superstitious, did not actually proceed against the art, and duly consulted astrologers himself (for example, in 326–8). Constantine also had good reason not to dislike the Sibylline Books. They had proved his ally, by letting Maxentius down (Maxentius had the reputation of consulting sorcerers). Constantine may have shared the almost universal belief in magic and wizardry and incantations, but did not like their pagan manifestations: there are no less than eleven fourth-century regulations (*constitutiones*) condemning the practitioners of occult sciences.

Nor was this the only respect in which Constantine, despite his desire to exercise caution, was impelled by his Christian convictions to act against paganism. His aim, largely achieved, was to weaken its practices, eliminating what seemed to him and his Christian advisers its most objectionable features, but leaving its structure, nevertheless, undisturbed, until it should fade away of its own accord (which it did in the end, though only after a considerable time). Nevertheless, it could be said that, once he had defeated Maxentius in 312, Constantine patiently went on turning Roman attitudes in the direction of Christianity. And after the defeat of Licinius in 324 he began – at first in the newly acquired lands of Asia Minor and the east, and then elsewhere as well – to make decisive changes which gradually established the Christian faith as something like the official religion of the Roman empire: which is certainly how his sons and successors interpreted his actions.

To the Jews – the traditional foes of Christianity and killers of Jesus – Constantine, as a devoted new convert to the Christian faith, was openly unsympathetic (the story that his mother Helena had once been a Jew was only a rumour). Although he allowed rabbis exemption from municipal duties, there were anti-Jewish laws,[48] including one which forbade Jews to circumcise Christian slaves. Moreover, some Jews who tried to rebuild the temple at Jerusalem were brutally punished. To contrast his alleged 'tolerance' towards Jews with his sons' 'intolerance' is mistaken, even if Constantine himself did not often – apart from the instances mentioned – pass beyond vilification to actual oppression. For it was not necessary to do so: the Jews did not form a powerful enough pressure group to threaten any potent reaction to measures against them, or disturb imperial unity.

As has been suggested, however, it was a very different matter with the pagans. And, moreover, Constantine entertained considerable hopes of converting such people. Eusebius heard him say to the bishops: 'You are bishops within the church. But I have been appointed by God as bishop of what lies outside the church.'[49] He was indulging in a certain play on words, since *episkopos* meant not only bishop but person exercising surveillance. What exactly, however, did the emperor mean? It was generally supposed, following Eusebius, that he was referring to the empire's pagans, and this has, to some extent, to be accepted. But his interest in the Christian laity, outside the church hierarchy (including 'heretics'), must also be borne in mind, and Constantine may have been making the point that although he had not been consecrated as a bishop that did not mean that he was uninterested in Christian unity anywhere within the Roman empire.

But he was also concerned about people *outside* the imperial frontiers, pagan and Christian alike, in relation to whom he cherished grandiose religious ambitions. These affected two groups in particular: the pagan 'barbarians' of the north – Germans and Sarmatians – and those Christians who lived outside the other main border of the empire, that is to say within the dominions of the Persians.

As regards the former of these groups, when he made conquests of German and Sarmatian territory, the treaty agreements that ensued regularly stipulated conversion to Christianity. And when he wrote to the Persian king Sapor II he allusively, but not without a veiled threat, expressed his keen personal interest in the Christians under Persian rule, regarding himself as a divinely ordained patron and protector of Christians there.[50] As we have seen elsewhere, Sapor II cannot have liked the conversion of peoples along his frontier to Christianity in *c.*330. And he must, in particular, have felt that Constantine was too interested in the Armenian Christians, with whom the emperor made an alliance. Indeed the Persian monarch was disposed to regard all the Christians in his realm as a potential fifth column.

Constantine, on the other hand, was extremely proud of his missionary efforts there and everywhere else, as he himself declared at Nicomedia and Tyre; and many Christian writers echoed his pride. Indeed, his record in the making of conversions among foreigners was startling, and his epoch has been described as the second age of missionary evangelism, after Paul.

Some of Constantine's legislation is relevant to this point; and in any case much of it was significant. The last great lawyer had lived under Gordian III (238–44), although Diocletian (from whom a great deal of material survives) had attached great importance to the administration of justice, employing experts such as Hermogenianus and Arcadius Charisius. Moreover, it was in his reign that the first collection of imperial legal pronouncements (*constitutiones*), the Codex Gregorianus (*c.*291), appeared (although there was a steep decline of imperial rescripts at the time, partly because of the increased personal inaccessibility and remoteness of the rulers).

As for Constantine, although much of his legislation does not bear any personal stamp – as a general consideration of Roman law would confirm – some of his laws show signs of Christian thinking. Many of these declarations, it is true, contain startlingly brutal features, such as the compulsory feeding of molten lead to offenders, and the severe treatment of sexual relationships with slaves. But other laws include more humane provisions, and in these it is possible to detect Christian influence. True, this is not always agreed, and it is pointed out that intense moral fervour, and attempts to protect the weak, had already been a feature of imperial laws before the Christianization of the state. All the same, it does appear that under Constantine Christian influences were at work, as one might expect. They influenced, for example, his legislation against gladiators, and his abolition of crucifixion as a penalty (possibly because that was the fate that Jesus had suffered; but anyway the penalty seemed cruel).

Christianity, too, was apparently behind the elevation of Sunday as a public holiday and day of rest, despite a manifest solar background. 'All magistrates, city-dwellers and artisans', decreed Constantine in 321, 'are to rest on the venerable day of the Sun, though country-dwellers may without hindrance apply themselves to agriculture.... The day celebrated by the veneration of the Sun should not be devoted to the swearing and counter-swearing of litigants, and their ceaseless brawling.'[51]

Christian influences also prompted Constantine's repeated legal attempts to improve personal morality. The early church was greatly preoccupied with the defence of sexual morals: hence the emphasis on this theme by the pre-Constantinian Council of Elvira, and the widespread contemporary inclination towards asceticism. The same subject ranks high among Constantine's legislative pronouncements. There was a particular outburst of laws on chastity and related subjects in 326, and it has been much discussed whether these were related to the downfalls of Constantine's son Crispus and his wife Fausta in that year. Was Crispus said to have been guilty of a breach of the moral, sexual code? Adultery (together with magic) was one of the offences which caused Crispus' friend Ceionius Rufius Albinus to be sent into exile; and when Fausta came under suspicion for falsely incriminating Crispus, her enemies said that *she* had been adulterous.

At all events, in Constantine's legislation, adulterers and concubines are severely discriminated against; and this seems to echo Christian thought. As a result, illegitimacy was frowned upon. No one, of course, mentioned that Constantine's own mother may have been not a wife but a concubine. But in 326 the enemies of the fallen Crispus may well not have been slow to recall, and stress to others, that he, too, was said (without certainty) to have been not only an adulterer but a bastard as well. At the pagan temples at Heliopolis and Aphaca, it was ritual prostitution, as well as other sexual offences, which particularly offended the Christians.[52]

However, late Roman criminal law was in a pretty chaotic condition, and there is no reason to doubt Eutropius' conclusion that most of Constantine's legislation on such subjects proved useless, and had no effect whatsoever.[53] Nor, although he had some respect for the *sententiae* of the great lawyer Paulus, were his measures worded according to the usual traditions of Roman law, much of which – following Licinius, who had likewise preferred equity to legal correctness – he deprecated as 'quibbles of senseless verbiage'. Constantine's admiration of intellectualism, apparent in other fields, was consciously set aside here, and his laws are framed, instead, in rich rhetorical prose – influenced, often, by Greek, Hellenistic usages, rather than by Roman legal phraseology – and infused with a powerful tendency to moralize.

So it is hardly surprising that he was attacked as a disturber of ancient laws,[54] and that the emperor Julian (361–3) repeatedly suggested that he had left justice to one side. Yet that needs qualification, since Constantine had a great deal of respect for what he considered to be justice, although he did not succeed in enforcing it. Nor was his view of what was just entirely undemocratic. For despite his measures in favour of property owners he legislated, at times, on behalf of the poor and powerless, including dependants, women (including widows), children, orphans, beggars and slaves.

CHAPTER 10:

BUILDER

=====

IT WAS customary for emperors who wanted to make an impression to undertake huge and spectacular building programmes. Augustus and Hadrian had done this, and so in recent years had Diocletian and Maxentius. Constantine acted similarly, on a vast scale, and emphasized how proud he was of this activity.

For one thing, he constructed many secular buildings, restoring prosperity, or the appearance of it, to Rome and numerous other towns. His creation of churches overshadowed, in later tradition, his secular buildings, but the latter, too, were imposing – perhaps deliberately grandiose, in order to show the pagan world that Constantine was not only a builder of churches: 'a showy extravagance', they have been called, 'aimed at a mass audience'.

At Rome Constantine built baths (their entrance flanked by statues of horse-tamers, now in front of the Quirinal Palace). And there were his mother Helena's baths, too, standing 270 yards north-east of the church of S. Croce in Gerusalemme, as well as her Mausoleum (near the Via Casilina), which Constantine originally intended for himself. The quadrifrontal Arch of Janus, intended as a meeting-place for the merchants of the cattle market (Forum Boarium), is also likely to be Constantinian, perhaps designed to celebrate the emperor's triumph over Maxentius. A decagonal structure of the same period, now known misleadingly as the Temple of Minerva Medica, but probably a throne room and state banqueting hall, or fountain building, still stands in what were the Gardens of Licinius. Constantine also created fine effects by his restorations at Rome. Outstanding, in this respect, was his completion and reorientation of the Basilica of Maxentius, a vast building, with an apse and gigantic exedras (like side-chapels), which took its shape from the central halls of imperial baths. And Constantine also restored the Circus Maximus, after its partial collapse, and a city gate, the Porta Asinaria, as well.

Outside Rome, Constantine built at Puteoli (Pozzuoli), and reconstructed an aqueduct on the Cumaean Gulf (Bay of Naples). Reference has been made elsewhere to his numerous and massive edifices at Constantinople, and to his fortifications, notably the camp at Divitia (Deutz) on the Rhine. Moreover, as mosaics found at Carthage record, he spent a lot of money on construction work in north Africa, after the area had been ravaged by Maxentius when he put down the revolt of Domitius Alexander there.

The Basilica of Augusta Trevirorum (Trier), which had been the capital of Constantine's father Constantius I Chlorus, who had started systematic building projects there, is of particular interest because the main lines of its construction by Constantine can, unusually, still be seen. It was the Audience Hall, the *aula Palatina*, of his palace there (and has been a Lutheran church since 1856). The building was begun in *c.*306, and was praised by a Panegyrist in 310.

More than 2,400 metres square, with no aisles but an apse, its walls pierced with pipes to provide heating, and equipped with a space under the floor to secure the luxurious circulation of hot air, the walls of the Basilica are constructed of brick, which was originally, in the interior, concealed behind marble slabs and a plaster covering; and this covering was painted, around its two tiers of windows, with Cupids and ochre-tinted tendrils of vines, against a red background. Above the windows, too, the plaster was decorated with painting, and the arches which crowned the windows were adorned with mosaics; while geometric designs of multi-coloured marble and gilt glass covered the lower parts of the walls.

The building was very lofty, with its vault one hundred feet above the ground, and was no less than 250 feet long. Its pavement displayed a honeycomb pattern in black and white, and a similar design was to be seen in the narthex. In the middle of the apse was a platform, on which stood the emperor's throne. It was here that he sat for ceremonial celebrations, designed to announce victories or new laws, or to receive envoys from foreign lands. The eyes of his audience lifted into this massive, ornate space, rich in every tint of gold and red and green and yellow, and moved on to the climactic point of the imperial throne within the apse. Planned so as to show off the platform on which Constantine sat, this apse was resplendent with mosaics, under a coffered and gilded ceiling.

Constantine also built many-roomed baths at Augusta Trevirorum, with apses, cross-vaults, domes and half-domes. But in the summer months when he was residing at this city, Constantine and his court moved five miles out of the town, to a new fifty-room villa–palace on the River Mosella (Moselle).

In the field of secular building, therefore, Constantine was by no means inactive.

However, his most conspicuous achievement was the creation of Christian churches, not matched by any similar establishment or repair of pagan temples. And this forms highly significant evidence of his pro-Christian policy, and tangible, conspicuous proof of his attachment to the Christian faith.

Moreover, the churches of which he directed the creation assumed many different forms. Indeed, the variety of Constantinian ecclesiastical architecture is extraordinary. Those who sponsored and planned these buildings – often the emperor himself, advised, in the east if not elsewhere as well, by architects including Eustathius, presbyter at Constantinople, and Zenobius (probably a Syrian), although his strong personal influence was always apparent as well – tried out every conceivable design. Some of the churches have side-aisles, some do not. Some have apses and transepts, and others dispense with them.

Other buildings are centralized (like the slightly earlier secular edifice known as the Temple of Minerva Medica) – domed polyhedrons and rotundas, including especially the baptisteries and *martyria* that were the counterparts of pagan *heroa*, Constantine being particularly devoted to the cult of martyrs.[1] And in some cases these centralized constructions were attached at the end of longitudinal basilicas. Or the longitudinal edifices are reduplicated, making a double cathedral. There were also considerable possibilities of variation in regard to exteriors. Certain basilicas were preceded by atria, although it was also possible to do without them. And there could be precinct walls, too, though once again these were not indispensable.[2]

Quite a number of Christian churches had existed before the Constantinian revolution, and they were not by any means all humble house–churches, although these, following the New Testament pattern, had continued to exist: for example, there was a house–church of the early second century AD at St Prisca in Rome. Similar house–churches, too, are recorded at Rome in the 230s, and we learn that Aurelian (270–5) allowed Christian bishops to control them.[3] However, house–churches were not the whole story, since San Crisogono in the same city was quite a rich pre-Constantinian building;[4] and the tombs in the fore runners of the church of Sant' Eustorgio at Mediolanum (Milan) point to the existence of an ecclesiastical centre before Constantine. There was also a large new church at Nicomedia at the time when Diocletian began his persecution.

But it was Constantine who multiplied such buildings throughout the empire. Despite all variety, the most frequent, indeed the standard, pattern was that of the basilica, which, in one form or another, displayed much expansion and development, establishing a new set of images and patterns for the changed world. These basilicas were oblong buildings, containing – according to the most usual pattern – side-aisles, divided off from the central nave by arched colonnades (inside and not outside the church, which was thus like a Greek temple turned inside out). Since the nave was higher than the aisles, the internal colonnades of these basilicas were surmounted by brick walls, which rested directly upon their arches and usually contained windows. At the end of the nave, when there was an apse, as was usually the case, it was entered through an arch, carrying triumphal implications, and stood behind the altar (crowned by a canopy); in the case of episcopal churches, it contained the bishop's throne (*cathedra*), rather as the secular Audience Hall at Augusta Trevirorum had contained the throne of the emperor – and the pattern was repeated in the palace created for Diocletian's retirement, at Salonae (Split).

The roofs of these basilicas did not normally consist of cross-vaulting. Instead they were flat and made of wood, which was either visible or concealed by a ceiling. The great vaults of earlier Roman secular buildings (including the Basilica of Maxentius, though not other pagan basilicas) seemed too worldly and redolent of un-Christian times. Besides, they would have impeded the axial flow of naves and aisles which was planned to attract the gaze of Christian worshippers towards the apse and its altar.

Nevertheless, these splendid churches, which set such a stamp on the future, owed a great many other features to the pagan basilicas of the past, which had served at one and the same time as market, meeting-place and law court (with a tribunal where the imperial and then episcopal thrones were placed later). Indeed, the new Christian buildings owed these pagan basilicas the main lines of their entire structure, including the arrangement of the windows. And yet the whole ineluctable tide of the churches' direction, leading so potently towards the apse and the altar, was not the same as the more passive and relaxed, circumambient and counter-flowing, orientation of the pagan basilicas of the past.

The interiors of the churches as a whole were spacious, dignified and designed to encourage spiritual elevation. They accomplished two things at one and the same time: they recalled the disciplined Roman past which lay behind them – and they spoke for the noble glories of heaven. It was usual, moreover, for a Constantinian basilica to be entered from the west, so that the rising sun poured its rays of light upon the celebrating priest as he stood in front of the altar facing the worshippers.

For the essence of this whole dramatic arrangement was light. Incorporeal and insubstantial, as it shone through the windows of the nave, this shining light left what lay below in reverent penumbra, while bathing all the rest of the building, and the congregation, in its luminous radiance. And in all Christian basilicas, throughout the empire, this light of the sun was enhanced by brilliant internal colouring, provided by paintings and mosaics and precious metal objects and jewelled robes, of which oil-wicks and candles prolonged the shimmerings and glintings into the night. The poet Prudentius rhapsodizes, too, about the 'ceilings with gilded beams that make the whole chamber seem like a sunrise. And in the windows glows stained glass, so that they look like fields studded with gorgeous flowers.' Nor does he forget the exteriors of the churches, which although less elaborately decorated than the interiors, displayed 'paints of every colour reflecting their gold, which the water blends with green reflections in the ornamental pools'.[5] Later in the century, some priests were complaining about the excessive magnificence of all this decoration.

The turning of worshippers' eyes towards the apse and the altar was encouraged and heightened by every means. All possible architectural devices were brought into play to achieve this single-mindedness of intent: 'the measured pace of columns, the trajectory of horizontals, the side-lighted tunnel of space, the enframing arch, the terminal apse'.[6]

When the church had a centralized plan, the architects were no less ingenious in their creation of magical effects. The congregation was concentrated in a central pool of space, grouped radially around the altar in the middle. Once again, there was a powerful mobilization of transcendent light, which brilliantly struck the central area of the building, leaving a sombre penumbra all round, so that the human beings at the foot of the illuminating shaft were surrounded by darkness. The old order had aimed at serenity. What the new order was intended to do was to stimulate dramatic tensions.

The creation of these churches required an interplay of many forces and resources, some of which applied at all points throughout the Roman empire, whereas others depended on local and regional factors. In the former category the emperor's own insistence on magnificent monumental edifices prominently figured, balancing the new Christian image against the traditions of Rome, and seeking to achieve his revolutionary aims without disturbing the framework already established by centuries of Roman tradition. In the second category came the actual provision of the required materials, from adjacent sources (or imported from abroad). And there was also, of course, the personality and taste of the architect himself to be considered, whether he was a man from the neighbourhood or brought in from outside. He must obey the instructions laid down for him, but much also depended on his own background, and, in particular, on whether he knew, by personal observation or hearsay, about the other great churches which were being, or had been, erected elsewhere in the empire.

Constantine's prolific erection of Christian basilicas and other buildings, on a scale which, despite respect for antique traditions, amounted to an architectural revolution, meant that the whole empire did not contain enough architects and builders to construct what he wanted them to construct, as he himself complained in letters. Deliberately encouraging the arts and sciences as he did, he offered particular privileges to architects and constructional engineers (*mechanici*) and surveyors (*geometrae*). Architecture was the great art of an otherwise somewhat sterile cultural age – and it was especially well adapted to displaying the boundless power of the absolute ruler.

Despite, therefore, the gifts that were showered on the churches by individuals – gold and silver chandeliers, lamps and candlesticks, chalices, jugs and patens and jars – the creation and maintenance of these churches required enormous imperial endowments, and the expenditure of a great deal of money, much of which had to be found from the already oppressive taxation that Constantine imposed on the empire.

However, there is an irritating and disappointing feature in any study of Constantinian ecclesiastical architecture. It resides in the fact that, with the exception of what can be seen at Augusta Trevirorum, nearly all Constantine's churches have totally, or almost totally, disappeared – vanished off the face of the earth. This is partly because, although they represented such a major achievement, and were replete with expensive objects and materials, they were often poorly constructed,[7] due to the fact that, as we have seen, there were not enough good architects and builders to cope with this immense programme. But another reason for their disappearance is that in many cases they and their sites were so greatly revered that later emperors, for their own glory, replaced them with their own new constructions.

Nevertheless, by recourse to literary descriptions and archaeology, we can get quite a good idea of what Constantine's massive and extravagant ecclesiastical building programme amounted to – we can see roughly, that is to say, what most of his churches were like.

One of the most notable features of the programme is the exceptional prominence of Rome. Although the city had not, for some time, been an imperial capital (except under the now discredited Maxentius), it was still the home of the Senate, and enjoyed exceptional veneration. The city was still, however, largely pagan, in spite of which (or because of which) Constantine covered it with great and wealthy churches, although he did locate most of them outside Rome's walls, often near the graves of martyrs, to whose cults he was so especially devoted – hence the establishment, in his reign, of many funeral halls of massive dimensions. The sites outside the city on which he constructed these Christian buildings were mostly on land owned by himself, no doubt so as to avoid annoying the pagans by taking over properties that were theirs.

But his Lateran Basilica at Rome, 'the mother and head of all churches' (*mater et caput omnium ecclesiarum*), was *inside* the walls.[8] Perhaps as early as 313 he presented the imperial palace of the Lateran, the home of his wife Fausta, to the church as a residence suited to the lofty standing of Miltiades, the bishop of Rome or Pope (311–14). Constantine's adjacent cathedral, the Basilica Constantiniana or Lateranensis, dedicated to Our Saviour (S. Giovanni in Laterano) – probably the first large Christian ecclesiastical building – was erected, by means of the endowment from twenty-nine estates, upon the site formerly occupied by the barracks, now razed to the ground, of the cavalry guard (*equites singulares*), who had fought for Maxentius against Constantine. A further dedication of the Basilica took place in 324, under the papacy of Silvester I (314–35). In this church – one of the many which have now almost entirely disappeared and have been completely replaced, although traces of the original walls and of two windows survive – a spacious nave, flanked by two aisles on either side, was supported by rows of huge columns. The aisles were separated by lower arcades, resting on twenty-two columns of green marble.

The present wide transept is a medieval addition. But Constantine's church already had a lofty apse, where there were seats for the bishop and his clergy. This apse was separated from the main body of the church by a silver screen resting upon a double row of columns, and silver statues of Jesus stood on either side of the screen: an image of the Resurrected Christ, between four angels, facing the clergy, and a statue of Christ as Teacher facing the congregation – which could add up to several thousand people in a church of this size. Seven golden altars stood in the apse and the sacristies, and the 115 chandeliers and 60 candlesticks which illuminated the Basilica at night were made of gold and silver as well. The church, later dedicated to St John the Baptist and St John the Evangelist, was destined to be frequently rebuilt and restored from the fifth and eighth centuries onwards. The luxurious adjoining baptistery also goes back to a Constantinian original, although the present octagon is of later fourth- or fifth-century date. But the red porphyry columns belong to Constantine's original foundation.

Another, different kind of Roman church, not far away, was the building now known as S. Croce in Gerusalemme, created in the Sessorian Palace, which owed its original foundation to Elagabalus (AD 218–22). It may well have been Constantine's mother Helena who had a palace church built on that spot – legend indicated that it was founded to celebrate the victory over Maxentius – and who presented it with relics including what was believed to have been a part of the True Cross, acquired during her journey to Palestine (and now to be seen in a side-chapel). A large rectangular hall with big square windows was adapted for the purpose, and divided into a nave and two narrower aisles. An apse was added at one of the building's short ends. This was, as usual, where the clergy officiated, while the rest of the church comprised three separate sections, two for the servants and the court and the other containing the altar. The building was reconstructed in 1144 and 1743/4.

But Constantine's most astonishing construction at Rome was St Peter's, though once again it has been so thoroughly replaced by later churches that we have to rely partly on archaeological research, but more particularly on old descriptions and paintings, notably the late sixteenth-century picture by Domenico Tasseri or Filippo Gagliardi, the architect, in the church of San Martino di Monti, to obtain some idea of what the original building was like. As a prime part of Constantine's attempt to give a Christian stamp to Rome, the new church was designed to house vast numbers of pilgrims, coming to venerate the place where St Peter was believed to have met his death and been buried. The decision to build this combined Basilica and *martyrium* was probably taken between 324 and 326, and construction was begun in *c*.332.[9]

Although it is now so very hard to distinguish perceptible Constantinian elements in St Peter's, something is known about how it came into existence. In the second century, a shrine and monument (*memoria*) of Peter had been established on the site. It was surrounded by pagan tombs, belonging to an extensive necropolis. When Constantine began to build his Basilica, the chambers of those tombs were filled in with earth, and their tops were levelled down. On the flat area thus created, a large terrace was brought into existence, incorporating parts of the Circus of Caligula (37–41) and Nero (54–68), and running deep into the slope of the Vatican hill, which was cut away for the purpose – an enormous task.

On this terrace the huge Constantinian Basilica of St Peter was erected, enclosing the saint's shrine. In order to overcome the difficulties presented by the uneven site, the walls of the church's nave and aisles had to be built up over a foundation extending some twenty-five feet above the downward slope of the hill, while the walls on the north and west side had correspondingly to be driven down into the uphill part of the slope. The immense cost and labour involved in conquering the problems of this difficult site show how much weight Constantine attached to siting his church at the precise spot where Peter was supposed to have been buried.

This was also demonstrated by the dual nature of the building that came to be erected. For the nave and aisles did not simply terminate in a chancel, according to the more normal basilica pattern. Instead they were prolonged by an enormous transverse structure, a sort of transept, towards which the eyes and steps of the worshippers were led. It was this transverse structure which enshrined the earlier monument of St Peter, and was therefore the focal point of the entire building. Surrounded by a bronze balustrade, the monument was also surmounted by a splendid canopy (*baldacchino*), resting on four spiral columns bearing reliefs of vine scrolls.

This was, therefore, a church combined with a very special *martyrium*, the shrine of the martyred Peter himself, and it was destined in consequence to retain its exceptional fame and sanctity throughout subsequent generations. As in all Constantinian architecture, the interior of the building was studded with precious objects and furnishings, and rich materials of every kind. It also displayed marble columns brought from many pagan temples, including six imported by Constantine from Greece.

However, this mighty edifice took a long time to build, and by the time of Constantine's death in 337 only the portions that stood above the monument to Peter had been completed – together with the triumphal arch linking the Basilica with this monument, which bore an inscription reading: 'Because of your leadership the glorious universe has reached to the furthest stars: victorious Constantine dedicated this church to you.' (The rest of the building was not finished before 360, the atrium in *c.*390, and the murals of the nave in *c.*450; and the subsequent history of St Peter's involved numerous complexities and rebuildings.)

Revering the biblical and Apostolic and post-Apostolic past, Constantine was said to have placed the entire resources of the state at the disposal of the papacy, and particularly in the hands of Pope Silvester, for purposes of the construction of Roman churches; and, indeed, besides the Lateran and St Peter's, the emperor had at least five other churches in the city built as well. Among them were SS. Marcellino e Pietro (a large basilica with a splendid cemetery, in which the mausoleum of Constantine's mother Helena was located), and S. Sebastiano and S. Lorenzo. (Against the sixth-century, and later, Liber Pontificalis, however, the round church of S. Costanza, built for Constantine's daughter Constantia or Constantina, is post-Constantinian [dating from *c.*345], and so is the adjacent church of S. Agnese.)

At Augusta Trevirorum (Trier), where as we have seen the Audience Hall (Basilica) of the imperial palace has survived, a 'double cathedral' – of which the left part was subsequently converted into the Liebfrauenkirche and the right part into the modern cathedral – was begun in 326 or soon after, on a scale that befitted this important capital. And, indeed, an imperial residence had existed on the site before, to house Constantine's mother Helena (according to her anonymous *Life*); perhaps it was destroyed after the executions of Crispus and Fausta in 326.

The two main sections of the 'double cathedral', each a basilica in itself, were linked to one another by connecting buildings, one of them a regular baptistery. The 'double cathedral' was still not finished in *c.*340, when Athanasius attended Easter Mass in the uncompleted edifice; and it was reconstructed some forty years later by Gratian.

Many fragments of the walls and ceilings of Constantine's 'double cathedral' have survived. They include a number of painted ceiling coffers (augmented by new discoveries in 1967 and 1968), displaying frescoes of imperial women (of much disputed identity), which recall the adaptation of the church from a palace, and seem to have been knocked to the ground after the destruction of the secular building. Helena, who was thought to have been responsible for the transformation of the palace into a church, and whose architects later used it as a model for buildings in the Holy Land, sent the supposed Cloak of the Virgin to be housed in the choir; and the 'Holy Coat of Trier', which she was also believed to have presented, was said to have been the seamless robe of Jesus himself.

Moreover, the exercise hall of the Constantinian baths at Augusta Trevirorum was converted into the Church of SS. Gervasius and Protasius.

Some of Constantine's other major building activities were centred upon his foundation of Constantinople, on the site of the old Byzantium, which was the occasion for so many stories and myths.

Although it was not yet a major architectural centre, Constantine built important churches there (and wrote to Eusebius requesting fifty copies of the Bible to be lodged in them),[10] but scarcely a trace of these buildings has survived. About his cathedral at Constantinople, the church known as Santa Sophia – the Holy Wisdom with which Jesus was identified,[11] but which was also a virtue claimed by Constantine, as his coins show—our knowledge is particularly deficient, because the edifice was burnt down in 404 and totally rebuilt, on a massive scale, in the sixth century by Justinian, whose magnificent construction survives today. But the first church, completed in 360, had been started by Constantine and was endowed in his will. Probably his architect designed it as a basilica with double aisles and galleries, approached through a propylaeum and an atrium.

Another building at Constantinople replaced by Justinian was that of the Holy Trinity, soon dedicated, instead, to the Holy Apostles, on which work was probably started after 330 by Constantine himself (as a *mausoleum*) and which was finished, too, within his lifetime. This building, like the church and which was of the Holy Wisdom, has gone. But we have a sort of description of it from Eusebius. It seems to have been built as a Greek cross, with arms of approximately equal length. This shape was owed to the intention that Constantine himself should eventually be buried under the central drum, beneath its conical roof, where he was to be surrounded by the emblems of the Twelve Apostles (including coats and cloaks that were said to have belonged to St Luke and St Andrew). So the church was planned not only as a *martyrium* of the Apostles but also as a mausoleum and *martyrium* of the emperor himself, as their thirteenth member. Indeed, according to one recent view, Constantine planned it as a mausoleum, and it only became a church after his death. Eusebius adds the following information about the appearance of this edifice, after it became a church:

He had the church built to a vast height, and he decorated it splendidly with slabs of various colours which covered it from the foundation to the roof. And over the roof he put finely fretted work and overlaid it everywhere with gold. The outside portion which protected the edifice from rainfall was of bronze rather than tiles, and this too gleamed with an abundance of gold. It brilliantly reflected the rays of the sun, and it dazzled the distant onlooker. A well-carved tracery of bronze and gold encircled the entire dome.

The church was thus splendidly adorned by the generosity of the emperor.

Around it was a very large open area, the four sides of which were bordered by porticoes. These porticoes enclosed the church and the open area, and nearby there were royal apartments, with baths and promenades, in addition to others which had been prepared for those in charge of the place.[12]

This church of the Holy Apostles was extensively copied elsewhere in the fourth and fifth centuries, but was subsequently obliterated by the Turkish conquerors of Constantinople, to make room for the Fatih Mosque, approximately on the same site.

There are also records of other churches at Constantinople attributed to Constantine. Sozomen mentions a shrine of St Mocius (a martyr of Diocletian), assigned to the Constantinian period by tradition. It replaced a temple of Zeus or Heracles, on a site that is no longer identifiable. Another pagan building was made into a church of St Menas. The date of the patriarchal cathedral of Holy Peace (St Irene; Küçük Aya Sofya) is uncertain, but Sozomen attributed this, too, to Constantine, and legends attributed the project (as well as the Holy Apostles) to the influence of the eunuch Euphratas.[13] Constantine also built a church of Holy Power (Dynamis) at Constantinople. And chroniclers added basilicas of St Agathonicus and St Acacius. Moreover, Constantine founded a church of the Virgin at Blachernae nearby. Eusebius may have been right to say that all his religious building at Constantinople was of a purely Christian character.[14]

Antioch in Syria was also the site not only of a Constantinian cathedral, of which little is known, but also of another important church of the same epoch. This was the lofty Golden Octagon, next to the imperial palace upon an island in the River Orontes, adjoining the centre of the city. Begun in 327 (but not completed until after Constantine's death), the Golden Octagon was dedicated to Harmony or Concord, the concept to which the emperor was so greatly devoted, uniting, as he hoped, empire and church. Although, as so often, no trace of the building survives, once again we can form some idea of its appearance, this time by combining written descriptions with a picture on a floor mosaic, now in the Archaeological Museum at Antakya. As its name the Golden Octagon indicates, the church was centred upon an eight-sided core, which was surmounted by a pyramidal or domed wooden roof, covered with gilt; and it was enveloped, on all sides, by two-storeyed, colonnaded aisles, containing niches.

The Golden Octagon was not, as it has been sometimes called, a *martyrium*, because it does not appear to have housed any significant relic. Instead, as its formal dedication to Harmony and its proximity to the palace suggest, it was pre-eminently a palace church, like Helena's Sessorian building at Rome; but in this case it was more personally related to its imperial founder himself, though his visits to Antioch were rare.

The place, however, where a Constantinian basilica and *martyrium* were most obviously combined was Jerusalem, at the very place where Jesus himself was believed to have met his death and to have received the burial that preceded his Resurrection: the Church of the Anastasis or the Holy Sepulchre on Mount Golgotha, upon the site of a Jewish burial chamber and beneath a Temple of Aphrodite. Constantine's mother, Helena (Augusta since 324) was responsible. Although our only contemporary source is Eusebius' unreliable *Life*, it was believed that she was shown the correct location in a vision, and by 326/7 the idea of a church had taken shape. Constantine himself ordered Bishop Macarius of Jerusalem to build on the site 'a basilica more beautiful than any on earth',[15] without sparing money, craftsmen, labourers or materials; and work began in 328. The centrally planned building that emerged from this instruction is shown on an apse mosaic (384–417) in the church of Santa Pudenziana of Rome. It inspired a long series of other churches of similar design.

This and all other Palestinian projects were given great encouragement by Constantine's dispatch to the Holy Land of his mother Helena. It was said that her journey was a sort of pilgrimage to compensate for, and distract attention from, Constantine's murder of Crispus in 326, which Helena had reputedly countered by denouncing the emperor's wife Fausta, who had been the cause of Crispus' downfall and death. But that cannot be verified, and indeed it is equally uncertain when Helena, inspired, no doubt, by Constantine's conversion, had first become a Christian (it was rumoured that she had been a Jew before). She especially venerated Lucian, presbyter of Antioch – and the teacher of Arius.

While in Palestine, Helena committed her son, who encouraged and prompted her, to the payment of enormous sums for building churches. And when she left the country, she took with her some pieces of wood which, she was told and believed, had formed the True Cross – a fortunate, though dubious, discovery. In order to find them, she had made enquiries among the local people, who advised her to proceed to a place where 'ancient persecutors' had built a shrine of the pagan goddess Aphrodite.

Stimulated by visions, she ordered that the site should be excavated, whereupon, according to St Ambrose's work *On the Death of Theodosius (De Obitu Theodosii,* 395), three crosses were disinterred, together with the inscription which Pontius Pilate, according to the New Testament, had set up, on the occasion of the Crucifixion of Jesus, in Hebrew, Greek and Latin.[16] It next remained to discover which of the three crosses was the one on which Jesus had died. Here Bishop Macarius of Jerusalem came to Helena's help, by undertaking, with a prayer for God's help, to place a sick woman on each of the crosses in turn, so that it could then be seen what happened to her on each of the three occasions. When she was placed on the first two crosses, nothing happened. Next, however, she was made to lie on the third cross, whereupon she was healed.[17] That, it was concluded, must have been the True Cross on which Jesus had met his death.

In consequence, Helena built a church on the spot, and lodged parts of the Cross there in silver caskets. The remaining parts she sent to Constantine, together with nails from the same Cross, which he incorporated in the bit of his war-horse. He was profoundly affected by Helena's discoveries. And he himself was said to have intended, as the climax of the building programme in the Holy Land, to be baptized in the Jordan – although this may be a myth, and in any case he never got there, as his strength began to fail before he could make the journey.

Although Helena's visit to the Holy Land was rapidly engulfed in myth, she had certainly been phenomenally active. With the assistance of the natives, who no doubt did not go unrewarded, she had located, to her own satisfaction, all the spots where every important event in the recorded career of Jesus at Jerusalem supposedly took place.[18] She had arranged for each of these places to be dug up, and promptly identified what was found there to her own satisfaction. The authenticity of these finds, dating back, as was alleged, to a so much earlier time – the tomb, Golgotha, the True Cross and the locations where Jesus was born and ascended to heaven[19] – has aroused scepticism, which is hardly surprising. A scholar has commented that her thrilling discoveries were made 'with miraculous aid seldom now vouchsafed to archaeologists'.[20] A few others, lately, have been less sceptical (1991), pointing to a ring from the Cross found at Golgotha (or did Helena put it there herself?).

What was significant, however, was not so much, or not only, the authenticity or otherwise of what she had found as the immense impression that these supposed triumphs made on the general public of the empire. Helena could be described, in fact, as the most popular and successful archaeologist who has ever lived. Not only, as we saw, was her son Constantine profoundly impressed by what she had allegedly recovered, but her discoveries, and especially the discovery of the Cross, passed rapidly into legendary form,[21] in which they were recorded, for example, in the *Church History* of Rufinus of Aquileia (*c.*400). Some of these remains are still to be seen in a side-chapel of the church of S. Croce in Gerusalemme at Rome.

Helena's deeds inspired an immense flood of further pilgrims to

Jerusalem. She herself had not been the first of such pilgrims (as the earlier graffiti of a pilgrims' ship found on the wall of a chapel beneath the Church of the Holy Sepulchre shows), but she was regarded as their archetype. Jerusalem was already prepared for this development by the great flowering of Christian liturgy and art which the city had begun to experience after Constantine's conversion. And now, attracted to the town by the news of Helena's finds, the pilgrims flocked in, to offer thanks or walk where Jesus had walked, filled with devoutness and zeal. They wholeheartedly accepted and admired the identifications of sites which Helena had proposed, and went on to invent fresh identifications of their own. They came from far and wide, precursors of modern touristic parties; and they created a new sort of literature, travelogues of the pious, mixing together legends and facts, the writings which still continue to be produced today. The earliest extant itinerary is by a man from Burdigala (Bordeaux), who went to Jerusalem in the spring of 333.[22]

As to the Church of the Holy Sepulchre at Jerusalem, which had been commissioned before Helena's visit, it was consecrated in 336 by a gathering of bishops, summoned to Jerusalem from the Synod of Tyre. The church building had to include not only the tomb of Christ but the rock of Calvary some ninety feet away to the south-east. The building itself was a five-aisled basilica preceded by a columnar atrium. But the basilica terminated, at its western extremity, in a circular, domed structure containing twelve columns, the rotunda of the Resurrection (Anastasis), which housed the shaft grave that was identified with the Holy Sepulchre itself, and was covered by a canopy. Work on this memorial may not have begun until after Constantine's death, but the edifice as a whole, in its original form, may be justly described as Constantinian. Another church, too, was erected at Jerusalem, upon the supposed (though much debated) site of Jesus' Ascension to heaven, on the Mount of Olives. This building was known as the Eleona.[23] Like the Church of the Holy Sepulchre, it is depicted on a mosaic at Santa Pudenziana in Rome.

In Bethlehem, a further great ecclesiastical building was constructed on Constantine's orders. Its focal point was the rock-cut grotto, which was supposed to be the birthplace of Jesus (and pagan women had come there on a fixed date every year to mourn for the death of Adonis).[24] Over this revered spot, surrounded by a railing, was constructed an octagonal *martyrium*. It may have had an opening in the centre of its room, like the Pantheon at Rome, and its floor, too, was pierced by a circular aperture, through which pilgrims could look down into the place where it was believed that Jesus had been born. Beyond the *martyrium*, to the west, was a new basilica with its nave flanked by two aisles on either side, where Constantinian construction is still to be seen. The *martyrium* was approached through a colonnaded atrium, to which a forecourt was appended, providing processions with a lengthy progress from end to end.

At Mambre, too (Ramath-el-Khalil, two miles north of Hebron), where Jesus had taught the disciples, a small church was built at the order of Constantine, shortly before 330. It adjoined the terebinth or oak tree (known as Ogyges), venerated from very ancient times, and was enclosed in a precinct wall beneath which God was believed to have spoken to Abraham, who was said to have erected an altar beside the tree. And a church was also built at Maiuma-Constantia (El Minah) in the Gaza Strip – because its inhabitants, unlike those of Gaza itself, were Christian. What a wealth of churches Constantine had commissioned in the Holy Land! Evidently an immense impetus had been given to this programme by the visit of Helena to the country.

Constantine built churches in other parts of the empire as well. Thus a basilica at Nicomedia commemorated his victories. A lavish cathedral at Tyre, too – of which the account by Eusebius is our earliest extant description of a Christian church – was approached from an atrium reached through a monumental colonnade, 'massive and raised aloft, attracting the gaze even of strangers to the faith'.[25] Aquileia in north Italy likewise received a new church in 313–19. It was created by Bishop Theodore out of three buildings (including a palace of Maximian) to make a 'double cathedral', with two parallel main halls containing chancels flanked by rows of side chambers, and a huge spread of colourful mosaic floors.

Elsewhere, also, churches were constructed on Constantine's orders, often at great expense. They are recorded, for example, at Ostia, Albanum (Albano Laziale), Capua (Santa Maria Capua Vetere), Neapolis (Naples), Constantina (Cirta), Arelate-Constantina (Arles) and Castellum Tingitanum (Orléansville in north Africa). And there was also a new church at Drepanum (near Nicomedia in Bithynia), refounded in 318 as Helenopolis, in honour of Helena who had been born there. The church was named after St Lucian, whom Helena so greatly admired; and Constantine himself went to hot springs at the place.

Inspired by the emperor, others, too, not only donated rich gifts to churches, but built them as well.[26] One such benefactor was Marcus Julius Eugenius of Laodicea Catacecaumene or Combusta (Yorgan Ladik) in Lycaonia (Asia Minor).

PART V:

THE END AND
THE AFTERMATH

CHAPTER 11:

BAPTISM, DEATH AND SUCCESSION

In 337, at the very end of his life when he knew he was about to die, Constantine had himself baptized in a village near Nicomedia, by its bishop Eusebius (not the ecclesiastical historian Eusebius of Caesarea). Before baptism, Constantine was required, theoretically, to spend a period as a catechumen, a convert under instruction. The Synod of Elvira had fixed a minimum of two years for this process, but it was no doubt waived in favour of Constantine.

Ever since New Testament times baptism had occupied a position of great importance in the Christian community and was regarded as essential to the new birth and to membership of the Heavenly Kingdom. In the words of the Gospel according to St John, 'Unless one is born of water and the spirit, he cannot enter the Kingdom of God.'[1]

The questionnaire employed at baptism in c.AD 200, if not earlier, ran as follows: 'Do you believe in God the Father Almighty? Do you believe in Jesus Christ, the Son of God, who was born by the Holy Spirit from the Virgin Mary, who was crucified under Pontius Pilate and died, and rose again on the third day living from the dead, and ascended to the heavens, and sat down at the right hand of the Father, and will come to judge the living and the dead? Do you believe in the Holy Spirit in the Holy Church?'[2]

Nowadays Christians are generally baptized in their infancy, but in the ancient world adult baptism was common. Surprise has often been expressed, however, that Constantine, who had displayed his adherence to Christianity so much earlier, postponed his baptism until what was virtually his death-bed. Some members of the church deplored the lateness of this decision. But in fact late, last-minute baptism – like adult baptism in general – was not an infrequent phenomenon, because it was strongly felt that after baptism one ought not to commit a sin, and the only way to ensure this was to become baptized when one was not going to live for very much longer. In the words of Edward Gibbon:

The sacrament of baptism was supposed to contain a full and absolute expiation of sin; and the soul was instantly restored to its original purity, and entitled to the promise of eternal salvation.

Among the proselytes of Christianity, there were many who judged it imprudent to precipitate a salutary rite, which could not be repeated: to throw away an inestimable privilege, which could never be recovered.[3]

Constantine was one of the men who evidently held this view. He delayed his baptism not, as was reported, because his earlier attempts to take the step had been thwarted by clergymen on account of his past sins, and not, as was also said, because he eventually hoped to be baptized in the River Jordan, when he could manage to get there, and not through mere indifference or procrastination, and not because of a desire to refrain from offending pagans, or in order to keep a foot in both camps (despite his assiduous expertise in this respect), or, alternatively, because as God's special servant he did not feel that baptism was necessary. The truth was different. He delayed his baptism through fear of God. Believing, as he did, in divine anger, he (in common with others, as we have seen, who likewise delayed their baptisms) was terrified about the future of his soul, which would be imperilled if, after baptism, he did anything wrong.

Eusebius of Caesarea offers a long account of the speech Constantine allegedly made to the bishops when his baptism did finally take place – knowing that he could not postpone the riteany longer, because his health was declining. No doubt the actual speech, in the form in which it is recorded, cannot be accepted as historical. 'It must – however reluctantly – be admitted that it is unlikely that he recorded his ... words with enough accuracy for a minute analysis of them to be a valid exercise.'[4] All the same, when he is quoted as saying, 'let there be no further delay' (*amphibolia*), although the exact meaning of the word is disputed, his request strikes a convincing note: he is giving a characteristically peremptory order, 'arranging everything just as it pleased him'. And so Constantine took off the purple robe of imperial power, was baptized naked (as was the custom) by Bishop Eusebius of Nicomedia, and put on the white vestment which Christian converts wore for a week after their baptism.

Catholics became uncomfortable about baptism at the hands of Eusebius of Nicomedia – who was practically an Arian – and invented a story that he was instead baptized by Pope Silvester I of Rome, which is repeated on the inscription upon the Egyptian obelisk in the Piazza di San Laterano.[5] That this is entirely fictitious is one of the certainties in the long but obscure papacy of Silvester (314 – 35). Constantine had evidently met Silvester, probably more than once, and had greatly enriched his Roman church, but it was not Silvester who baptized him. Nicomedia was not in Silvester's diocese, and, in any case, at the time of the emperor's baptism Silvester had already been dead for two years.

After his baptism, Constantine proceeded to a state-owned villa at Achyrion near Nicomedia, and lay down on a white couch, and died. We owe the details to an unusually vivid account by Eusebius.[6] It was on Whit Sunday of the year 337 that the emperor breathed his last, at about midday. His personal staff and bodyguards mourned his death unofficially, and there were lamentations in Nicomedia. Then followed the appropriate solemn ceremonial in honour of the dead man. The body was laid in a coffin made of gold and covered with purple draperies. Next, it was taken to the city to which he had given his own name, Constantinople.

There, in the central hall of the palace, the dead Constantine, lying in state in imperial robes and wearing his diadem, received the homage of the principal members of his empire. Each man came up in due order of precedence to perform obeisance (*proskynesis*) to the corpse: the functionaries of his household, the army commanders, the senators and lesser officials. Placed upon an elevated dais, the coffin was surrounded by an array of lighted torches and attended day and night by members of his bodyguard, while a countless line of men, women and children filed through the hall to pay their respects for the last time.

In due course the second son of the late emperor, Constantius II, arrived in Constantinople, and the final rites began to take place. Led by Constantius, the funeral procession made its way through the streets of the city to the Church of the Holy Apostles. And there the proceedings underwent a solemn and significant transformation. For Constantius and his attendant soldiery stepped back, and so did all the other secular leaders of the empire. Their part in the ritual was finished, and henceforward everything was in the hands of the church.

So the clergy moved forward, and took over the task of commemorating their brother in the faith. Burial prayers were intoned, and the body of the recently baptized emperor was interred in the mausoleum which he had built for himself, flanked by monuments of the Twelve Apostles, of whom he had not been ashamed to declare himself the Thirteenth. His remains were laid under the central drum of the building (though in 356/7 they were removed to a separate adjoining mausoleum, so as to leave his earlier burial place to the Twelve Apostles themselves). These arrangements, it seems, had involved a change of plan. For Constantine had first intended to be buried in the family mausoleum on the Via Labicana at Rome, or perhaps in the mausoleum in the same city in which his mother Helena was buried, while the porphyry sarcophagus originally, it would appear, designed for him (with military reliefs) was instead employed to house Helena's body; it was found in the mausoleum where her remains were placed, and is now in the Vatican museum.

Then Constantine was deified (made *divus*), as his coinage records: a curious indication that his adoption of the Christian faith did not prevent this pagan custom from being retained. The coins celebrating his deification show him, veiled, in a quadriga[7] (reminiscent of the ascent of Elijah – but the chariot was also an attribute of Apollo and the Sun). A hand descends from heaven. Eusebius records the issue of these coins.[8] There was also a dedicatory inscription describing Constantinus as a deified figure, *divus*: 'Divo ac Venerabili Principi Constantino Patri Principum.'[9] And even in his lifetime, in 326, a bronze medallion had shown one of his sons presenting him with a globe surmounted by a phoenix, indicating rebirth and immortality.[10]

Earlier still, in *c.*318, Athanasius had alluded to the apotheosis of deceased emperors as still occurring.[11] Coins were issued in honour of Divus Maximianus, Divus Constantius (I Chlorus) and Divus Claudius (II),[12] and Firmicus Maternus wrote about the divinity of the emperor[13]– which could be regarded, perhaps, as a matter of honouring rather than worshipping him, but was a pagan heritage all the same.

In his last years, after he had killed his eldest son Crispus (326), Constantine had to think again about the eventual succession to his throne; and he finally formed an extraordinary plan to arrange this. As his wife Fausta, when she falsely denounced Crispus, had been well aware, the obvious candidates were her sons by Constantine who were Crispus' half-brothers, namely Constantine junior (II), Constantius junior (II) and Constans – born in 316, 317 and 323.

And they had not been made to suffer for her evil act and sad end, but had, on the contrary, been steadily introduced to the realities of regional government. Constantine junior (though his detractors, following a well-worn practice, spread the word that he was illegitimate) and Constantius junior had already been made Caesars before Crispus' death, in 317 and 324. Subsequently, after Crispus was dead, Constantine junior was installed at Augusta Trevirorum (Trier) by his father in 328, and Arelate (Arles) was renamed Constantina after him in the same year. Moreover, their brother Constans, again denounced by some as a bastard (although this report may only be an echo of rumours about Crispus or Constantine junior) was likewise made Caesar in 333, when he was only a small boy, which is what his brothers, too, had been when they received similar honours.

Then, in 335, the thirtieth year after his accession (that is to say, when his *tricennalia* were celebrated), Constantine the Great, looking towards the future, when he himself would have disappeared, divided the empire into four parts. Constantine junior (II) was to reign in the western provinces, Constans in Italy and Pannonia and north Africa, and Constantius junior (II) in the east; though Constantine's step-nephew Delmatius (or Dalmatius) was to rule as another Caesar in Thrace, Macedonia and Achaea, and although his capital was probably Naissus (Niş), it is possible (though not certain) that his sphere was meant to include Constantinople, so that the city should not become a bone of jealous contention between the emperor's sons.

Each of these Caesars was given a quasi-imperial establishment, with a praetorian prefect to guide his youthful steps, just as Crispus had earlier had a prefect beside him in Gaul. Moreover, the easternmost provinces were allotted to Delmatius' brother Hannibalianus (or Hanniballianus), though they were detached from the empire, technically, for the purpose, since he was given an un-Roman, royal position of his own.

Delmatius and Hannibalianus were the sons of Delmatius the elder, the emperor's stepbrother who had been the son of Constantius I Chlorus and Theodora, the stepdaughter of Maximian. This branch of the family had earlier been persecuted by Helena (who succeeded Theodora as Constantius' partner) and remained secluded, but were once again in favour now that Helena was dead (and appeared on coins after the death of Constantine).[14] The younger Delmatius had successfully put down a revolt by Calocaerus in Cyprus in the previous year.

As for his brother Hannibalianus – married to Constantine the Great's daughter Constantia or Constantina – the full title by which he was henceforward know was 'King of Kings and of the Pontic peoples', the former part of this strange designation being no doubt directed against the king of Persia – as was the figure of the River Euphrates on his coins.[15] With his capital at Caesarea (Kayseri) in Cappadocia, Hannibalianus was evidently put in titular control of the eastern imperial frontier. However, Constantine I, no doubt in order not to furnish the Persians with too plausible a pretext for moving against him, took no steps to install Hannibalianus in his kingship, other than allowing him the issue of coins to which reference has been made.

Within the empire, on the other hand, there were to be four rulers, Constantine I's three surviving sons and his step-nephew Delmatius. In other words, there was to be a sort of reversion to the Diocletianic Tetrarchy, modified by the emperor's manifest leaning towards hereditary rule, since the four rulers-to-be comprised three sons and a nephew of his own.

How did his mind work? Ever since the time of Carinus and Numerian (283–4) – and indeed earlier, too, under Valerian and Gallienus (253–60) – the empire had been under divided rule. Diocletian's Tetrarchy had formalized and sanctified the arrangement; and the empire had remained divided until Constantine I made himself the sole ruler of the entire Roman world by his final defeat of Licinius (324).

While Crispus was alive, it is not impossible that Constantine envisaged him as his sole successor, though this solution would have been strenuously resisted by the emperor's wife Fausta, who was pushing her own three sons forward as Crispus' rivals. After the removal of both Crispus and Fausta, Constantine, as we have seen, did nothing to discourage the continued advance of her sons, leading to their ultimate promotion to what was virtually joint emperorship.

But why, in that case, did Constantine I not designate his eldest surviving son Constantine junior (II) as the future sole emperor, such as he was himself? Probably because he did not think that Constantine junior was capable of the role. Certainly, he himself had, in the end, ruled over the entire empire. But over the previous half-century and more it had never been believed that the empire could be controlled by a single pair of hands, and Constantine I probably felt that what he had achieved could not be repeated or maintained by Constantine junior: which was evidently correct.

The alternative, then, was to leave the empire jointly to all his three surviving sons – although Julian later remarked that he made no real attempt to improve their inferior qualities[16]–with Delmatius perhaps added to revive the appearance of a Tetrarchy, and Hannibalianus (in his extra-imperial role) in order to provoke the Persians. This multiple subdivision at least served the purpose of diminishing the danger of a plot against Constantine I himself, while he was still alive and in charge. But can he seriously have thought that such a joint arrangement would work? In fact, it failed to work, very quickly and completely and abysmally and explosively, and it seems to us inevitable that that was what was going to happen. If we can see, now, that that was undoubtedly going to be the course of events – and Julian, too, saw, not long afterwards, that this had been bound to be so – surely Constantine I must have seen it too, at the time?

It is not very plausible to suppose that he delegated his powers in order to have more time to concentrate on his religious duties. If that argument is left aside, he can scarcely be acquitted of the charge of cynically losing heart and thinking, *après moi le déluge*. Or, at best, he must have felt that he could not backseat drive and provide, completely, for the future – which must be left to its own devices and to chance, for his sons to sort out as well as they could: without any of them being capable of ruling as single emperor, as his own exceptional self had done (though one of his sons,

Constantius II, did manage this sixteen years later). Eusebius of Caesarea, seeking to exalt Constantine's authority and foresight, politely suggested that he was splitting up the empire like a private citizen dividing his patrimony.[17] Yet the arrangement, it must be repeated, was manifestly unworkable, and scarcely lasted at all, and remains a deeply unsatisfactory conclusion to his reign.

This came to an end when Constantine the Great died on 22 May 337. Delmatius failed to arrive at Constantinople in time to preside over his funeral, a serious lapse if the city was within the sphere of his control – as is not certain. It also, in view of his absence, raises the question whether his position was exactly comparable to that of the other Caesars; perhaps it was not so regarded. Anyway, as we saw, it was Constantius the younger (II) who arrived to preside over the funeral. There is some slight evidence that his father had considered him the most competent of his sons; and indeed he foreshadowed his later dominance, not only by arriving in the city before his brothers and relatives, but also by immediately beginning to undermine their power.

The first to go were Delmatius and Hannibalianus. This happened during a brief period when, after Constantine's death, his appointed heirs rather strangely delayed claiming their inheritance, and, according to Eusebius, the dead man himself continued for a time to be regarded as the ruler.[18] It looked rather as though his successors were just paralysed by the sheer impracticability of the joint rulership that had been bequeathed to them. But there was more to it than that, for the delay belonged to a plan, on the part of the late emperor's sons (and particularly Constantius II in the east), to arrange the murders and massacres of Delmatius and Hannibalianus and their supporters while exonerating themselves from these events – since they were not yet technically on the throne.[19]

At all events, Delmatius and Hannibalianus quickly perished at the hands of the army, which thus showed itself keen to stress the exclusive rights of Constantine's sons. The father of the two murdered men, Delmatius the elder (the son of Theodora), died as well – it was alleged that he had tried to poison his half-brother Constantine I – and so did Delmatius the elder's brother Julius Constantius (who had probably received some honours with the rest of his family in 335), and a number of other senior statesmen, including the praetorian prefect Flavius Ablabius (although he had been with Constantius junior [II] in the east).

So now the three sons of Constantine were the joint rulers. Yet, despite over-optimistic coinages inscribed 'The Peace of the Emperors' ('PAX AVGVSTORVM'),[20] their joint rulership predictably, and quickly, fell apart. In 340 Constantine II was killed at Aquileia by Constans. In 350 Constans was killed in Gaul by the usurper Magnentius. And then, in 353, at Mursa Major (Osijek), Magnentius was put down by Constantius II, who re-established his father's sole rule of the empire until his death in 361.

During the next three years Julian the Apostate and then Jovian managed to maintain this imperial unity. But in 364 Valentinian I redivided the empire between himself and his brother Valens, and with the exception of a fleeting reunification under Theodosius I in the 390s the Roman world remained divided until the fall of the last western emperor, Romulus Augustulus, in 476. So it had been Constantine who pursued the policy which led to this ultimately fatal division.

CHAPTER 12:

THE SIGNIFICANCE OF CONSTANTINE

CONSTANTINE is, of course, best known as the first Christian emperor, and it is predominantly for his conversion of the Roman imperial state to Christianity that he became famous. But it is from this undoubted fact that most of our difficulties arise, because some of our ancient literary authorities applauded his Christianity and others attacked it: so that no balanced view is forthcoming.

As Gibbon, who deplored his adherence to the Christian faith, was obliged to observe: 'Greeks, Russians and in darker ages Latins, have ranked Constantine as a saint.'[1] His baptism brought him into medieval Christian poetry.[2] He has been described as the founder of Christian chivalry, though this has been contradicted.[3] He has also been seen as presenting the first image of a medieval sovereign.[4] His Christianity has understandably been seen as a vast turning point, 'even if only accelerating an inevitable development'.[5] Not inevitable at all, say others, declaring that his religious policy was one of history's great surprises. And on the other side there were, of course, as we have seen, hostile pagan legends denouncing the lifework of Constantine as the greatest of all evils. Here, then, are some of the reasons why it is so singularly hard to obtain a truthful estimate of what happened.

Certain points, however, do emerge. One is that he was a Christian of a very peculiar type, a type that would hardly be recognized as Christian at all today. For the God he believed in was a God of power, who had given him victory, and he would have had little sympathy with the idea that Christianity meant love, or charity, or humility, of which his 'middle-brow' view of religion did not have the slightest comprehension. Furthermore, he was utterly confident that he himself was the man of God, God's servant and representative who was constantly in touch with him and was told by him what to do – and how, by doing accordingly, he could avoid divine anger. This made Constantine a difficult man for other mere human beings to deal with, being on a direct line with God, he must always be right.

Cynical views, then, that Constantine became a Christian only because there was political advantage to be gained from this policy are misdirected. He became a Christian because he formed the overwhelming conviction that the God of the Christians was all-powerful and had given him power and victory. And yet, at the same time, his mind moved on a more practical level as well. For there was, in his view, advantage to be gained from the change. He had witnessed the persecutions, and they had failed. And Christianity enjoyed a close-knit tightness of organization which, as his Christian advisers no doubt informed him, it was much better to employ as the friend of the state than as its enemy. The Christian community, that is to say, should be brought in as the ally and close component of the government, and should be amalgamated with it, so as to achieve the *national unity* which the persecution had so conspicuously failed to supply.

And there lay Constantine's great failure. For it became clear, very soon, that Christianity was hopelessly divided within itself, and that its recognition merely magnified these chronic divisions, by setting them on a larger canvas. It was the greatest setback of Constantine's life. While the process unfolded itself, he did his best to encourage Christianity (setting a hideous precedent by his forcible coercion of Christians who failed to toe the line – although this coercion was admittedly shortlived).

But he moved very cautiously and skilfully in regard to the

pagans, who formed the majority of his population, and particularly of his upper class and army. He was able to exercise this caution because, although an impulsive man, he also had a keen eye for what was politically possible, and his whole reign is an object lesson in how to get Christianity accepted, firmly yet cunningly, without attempting too much speed. One question, however, which cannot fail to disconcert Christians today is his ability to reconcile his new faith with appalling murders, including those of his own kin.

Another question which arises is whether, although Constantine regarded himself as the linear descendant of earlier emperors, Edward Gibbon was right to suppose that his conversion of himself and his subjects to Christianity was one of the principal causes of the fall of the western Roman empire, which ceased to exist 139 years after his death. It was Constantine, according to this view, who made this shipwreck inevitable, or, to change the metaphor, opened all the gates to destructive forces.[6]

It is true that his Christianization of the Roman world, accompanied by an unprecedented outburst of church construction, meant the undermining and collapse of many of the antique traditions which, according to Diocletian, had held the state together. But they were collapsing anyway, and it is hard to see how, even without Constantine, they could have survived very long. For this was a crucial era of violent transition, in which world history was changing direction.[7] The Roman epoch was coming to an end. It is also true that many eminent and intelligent men were deciding to serve the church instead of the state – or they decided to become hermits. But there were many other causes of the forthcoming collapse, and Christianity can hardly be ranked high among them. The most that can be legitimately said for Gibbon's thesis is that Christianization perhaps accelerated the process.

Yet meanwhile Constantine's position as the first Christian ruler of the empire made him, as we have seen, a legend, and the subject of many legendary stories[8] – which are, indeed, significant to the student of history: hardly less significant, indeed, than what actually happened. For these legends exercised an enormous influence on the minds and thoughts of subsequent leaders and writers, and people in general.

Hardly anyone, at that time or in the centuries to come, made the smallest honest attempt to differentiate between what was fact and what was myth – which is why it is so difficult to do so now, for example in relation to Constantine. And even when a historical incident had been correctly handed down, it was habitually distorted and altered for propagandist and rhetorical reasons – so much so that fictitious documents were actually manufactured to ram home points of view which no authentic document could confirm. Incentives to embellish Constantine's career with touches of imagination were, from the first, very strong. The forged 'Donation of Constantine', of the eighth century – intended probably to justify Frankish independence of Constantinople – is a particularly blatant example.[9]

Although our sources concentrate so mightily on religion, they could not of course fail to notice one secular development, which was Constantine's creation of Constantinople. Something has been said about its foundation in an earlier chapter. Thereafter, the western empire disintegrated. But the eastern, Byzantine empire, centred upon Constantinople, survived, for many centuries to come. And that was the work of Constantine. For although the western empire succumbed to the Germans in 476, Constantinople remained as the capital of its eastern, Byzantine counterpart until 1453. During the greater part of that period (as most of us were not taught at school) it was by far the most important city in Europe.

So Constantine, who created it out of Byzantium, clearly lived in an epoch of sensational change, which he himself helped decisively to promote. Was he then, it is often asked, the last Roman or the first Byzantine emperor? But the query may also be raised in another form: was he, by founding Constantinople, responsible for the downfall of the western Roman empire (a suggestion that has already been mentioned), or should he rather be thought of as the founder of the new empire which lasted, for the most part in such splendour, throughout the entire Middle Ages?

True, he cannot be held responsible for the eclipse of Rome itself as the empire's capital, since this had already taken effect during the previous half-century or more. But his creation of Constantinople certainly initiated a new and longlived era.[10] The epicentre was decisively moved in an eastward direction, and to that extent Constantine's foundation of Constantinople struck a death-blow to the Roman west, which during the next century ceased to exist.

Other secular developments of Constantine's reign, however, have tended to be neglected owing to the concentration by our literary sources on religion. Such, for example, was his reconstruction of the administrative machine, in regard to which, despite his extraordinary abilities in this field, he can be blamed for over-taxation, extravagance, failure to prevent corruption, and coinage which favoured the rich against the poor – although, once again, this coinage also proved fundamental to the development of the Middle Ages (whether this was a good thing or bad).

Also subject to criticism, despite his military talents, is Constantine's reorganization of the army. From now on, it was divided between a frontier force and a striking force. There had been signs of this division before, but Constantine made it definitive. And there are reasons to suppose that it was a mistaken and disastrous decision, which helped to let the Germans in.

Another thing that let them in was the increased admission of Germans into the army, both as top generals and as very numerous rank-and-file soldiers – again not a new development, but again now apparent on an unprecedented scale. And, above all, Constantine enlarged and extended earlier policies that allowed German civilians to immigrate into the empire in thousands. Whatever the justifications for all these steps, and justifications can be found (and were blared forth by coinage announcing frequent victories over the Germans), these permissions to immigrate, and the taste they gave the 'barbarians' for settlement instead of nomadism or mere raiding, inevitably prepared the way for the epoch, not so far ahead, when the Germans would take over the western empire.

In all these circumstances, it seemed curious that Constantine should deliberately pick a quarrel, as he appears to have done, with the only substantial state which bordered on the empire, namely the kingdom of the Persians beyond its eastern frontiers. This quarrel, unnecessarily as it would seem, caused vast expenditure and loss of life under Constantine's successors.

And indeed, now that we are talking of his successors, what a mess he had brought about! It is difficult to believe that in dividing the empire among his three surviving sons, and two of his nephews, he can seriously have believed that this arrangement would prove effective: and, in fact, it did not, and caused years of bloodshed.

So Constantine had a lot to answer for. An effort has been made, in this book, to assess his character, and it contained evil as well as good. Evil, it can be argued, is indispensable in a successful chief, and Constantine, despite his defects, enjoyed a great deal of success, both as a military commander and as a leader in civil life.

But he was also murderous, and the many whom he murdered, or executed, included not only his rival Licinius (to whom he had promised survival) but also his own eldest son and his own second wife Fausta. There is no excusing those deaths, at any time or in any society. Certainly, it can be explained, as was suggested above, that powerful people are hardly ever nice, and that autocrats can do as they like, and if they want to commit murder, at the bidding of circumstances that seem to them to demand such action, then that is what they do. But this is no excuse. There are, and remain, certain absolute standards, and by his death-dealing Constantine offended signally against them.

It is a mocking travesty of justice to call such a murderer Constantine the Great. Or, perhaps not: for what does Greatness mean? Constantine was, as we have seen, a superlative military commander, and a first-rate organizer. He was also an utterly ruthless man, whose ruthlessness extended to the execution of his nearest kin, and who believed that he had God behind him in everything he did. That, surely, it must be repeated, is the stuff of which the most successful leaders are made.

CHRONOLOGICAL TABLE

c. 272/3 or *c.* 282	Birth of Constantine I
284	Accession of Diocletian
286	Maximian Augustus in the west
293	Tetrarchy: Constantius I Chlorus and Galerius made Caesars
303	Persecution of Christians begins
305	Abdication of Diocletian and Maximian. Constantius I Chlorus and Galerius become Augusti. Severus and Maximinus II Daia become Caesars
306	Constantine I leaves for west. Death of Constantius I Chlorus. Constantine I hailed Augustus, recognized as Caesar by Galerius. Maxentius proclaimed Augustus in Rome
307	Maximian resumes title of Augustus: his daughter Fausta marries Constantine I
308	Conference of Carnuntum. Licinius made Augustus
310	Rising and death of Maximian

311	Toleration Edict of Galerius at Serdica (Sofia)
312	Constantine wins Battle of Milvian Bridge. Death of Maxentius
313	Edict of Mediolanum (Milan) by Constantine I and Licinius. Licinius defeats Maximinus II Daia at Campus Serenus
314	Synod of Arelate (Arles)
315	Arch of Constantine at Rome
316 (or 314 and 316)	First Licinian War
317	Crispus, Constantine junior (II) and Licinius Licinianus made Caesars
318–20	Donatist and Arian disputes
320	Crispus' victory over Alamanni
323, 328, 332	Wars against Visigoths
324	Second Licinian War
325	Council of Nicaea
326	Execution of Crispus and Fausta
327–8	Helena in Palestine
332	Inauguration of Constantinople
334	War against Sarmatians
335	Plans to divide empire among Constantine's sons and nephews
336	Preparations for Persian War
337	Death of Constantine I

SOME LATER ROMAN EMPERORS

193–211	Septimius Severus
244–9	Philip the Arab
253–60	Valerian
253–68	Gallienus
268–70	Claudius II Gothicus
270–7	Aurelian
276–82	Probus
282–3	Carus
283–4	Carinus and Numerian
284–305	Diocletian
286–305	Maximian
305–6	Constantius I Chlorus
305–11	Galerius
306–37	Constantine I 'the Great'
308–24	Licinius
337–61	Constantius II
362–3	Julian the Apostate
364–75	Valentinian I
364–78	Valens
379–95	Theodosius I 'the Great'
408–50	Theodosius II
475–6	Romulus Augustulus
527–65	Justinian I 'the Great'

GENEALOGICAL TABLE

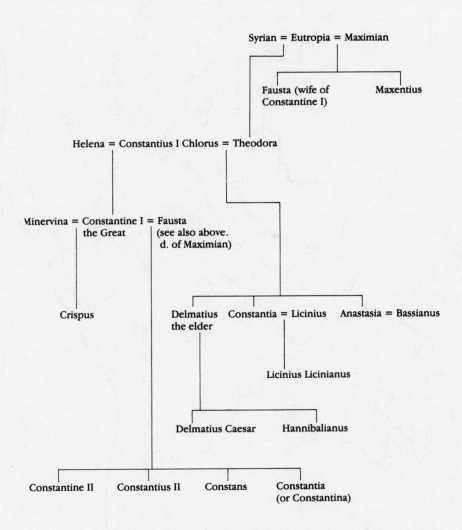

Syrian = Eutropia = Maximian

Fausta (wife of   Maxentius
Constantine I)

Helena = Constantius I Chlorus = Theodora

Minervina = Constantine I = Fausta
        the Great   (see also above.
                    d. of Maximian)

Crispus

Delmatius   Constantia = Licinius   Anastasia = Bassianus
the elder

Licinius Licinianus

Delmatius Caesar   Hannibalianus

Constantine II   Constantius II   Constans   Constantia
                                                            (or Constantina)

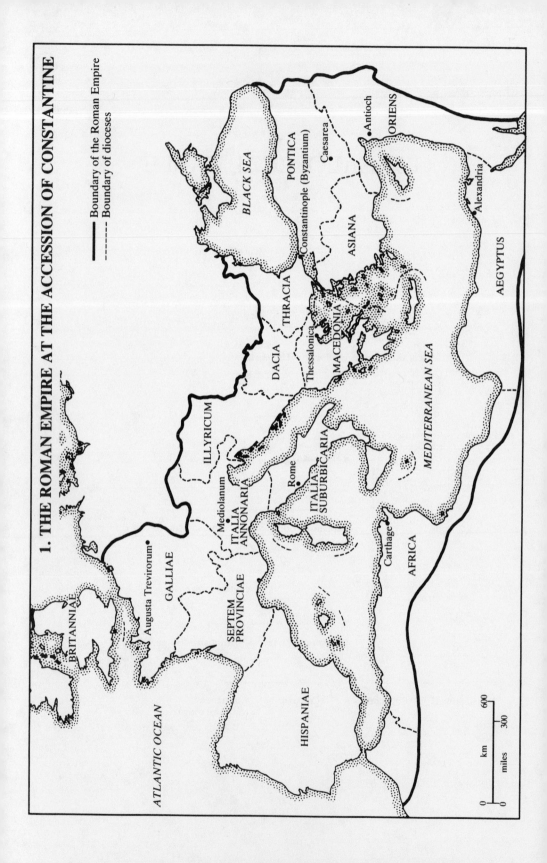

1. THE ROMAN EMPIRE AT THE ACCESSION OF CONSTANTINE

Boundary of the Roman Empire
Boundary of dioceses

BRITANNIAE

ATLANTIC OCEAN

GALLIAE

Augusta Trevirorum

SEPTEM
PROVINCIAE

HISPANIAE

ITALIA
ANNONARIA

Mediolanum

ILLYRICUM

Rome

ITALIA
SUBURBICARIA

Carthage

AFRICA

MEDITERRANEAN SEA

BLACK SEA

DACIA

THRACIA

Thessalonica

MACEDONIA

Constantinople (Byzantium)

PONTICA

Caesarea

ASIANA

Antioch

ORIENS

Alexandria

AEGYPTUS

km
0 · · · 300 · · · 600
miles
0

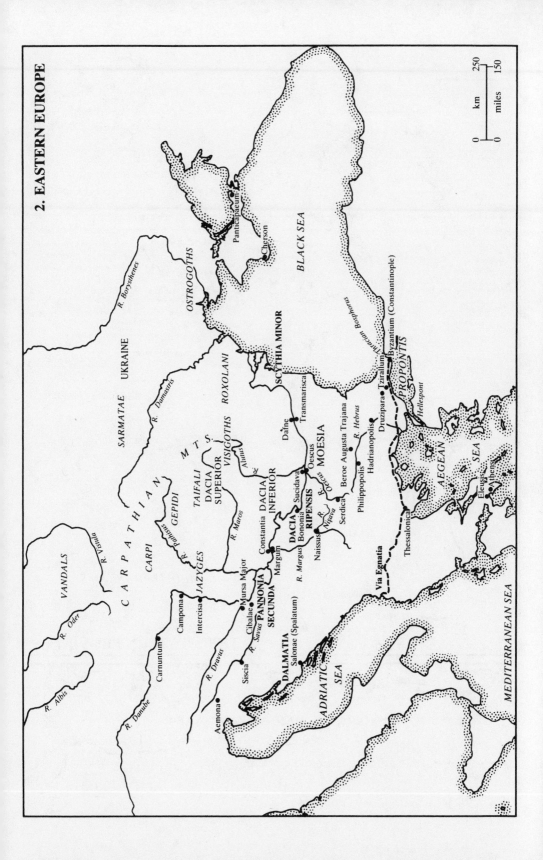

2. EASTERN EUROPE

km
miles
0   250
0   150

R. Albis
R. Oder
VANDALS
R. Visula
R. Danube
R. Dravus
Carnuntum
Aemona
Siscia
Campona
Intercisa
R. Savus
Mursa Major
Cibalae
PANNONIA SECUNDA
DALMATIA
Salonae (Spalatum)
ADRIATIC SEA
JAZYGES
CARPI
C A R P A T H I A N   M T S.
GEPIDI
SARMATAE
UKRAINE
R. Borysthenes
R. Danastris
R. Maros
Tibiscus
R. Pathissus
TAIFALI
DACIA SUPERIOR
VISIGOTHS
Alutus
ROXOLANI
OSTROGOTHS
Panticapaeum
Cherson
BLACK SEA
SCYTHIA MINOR
DACIA INFERIOR
Constantia
Margum
R. Margus
Bononia
DACIA RIPENSIS
Naissus
Nisava
Serdica
Sucidava
Oescus
Oescus
Daphne
Transmarisca
MOESIA
Beroe Augusta Trajana
Philippopolis
R. Hebrus
Hadrianopolis
Druzipara
Tzirallum
Byzantium (Constantinople)
Thracian Bosphorus
PROPONTIS
Hellespont
AEGEAN SEA
Eleusis
Athens
Thessalonica
Via Egnatia
MEDITERRANEAN SEA

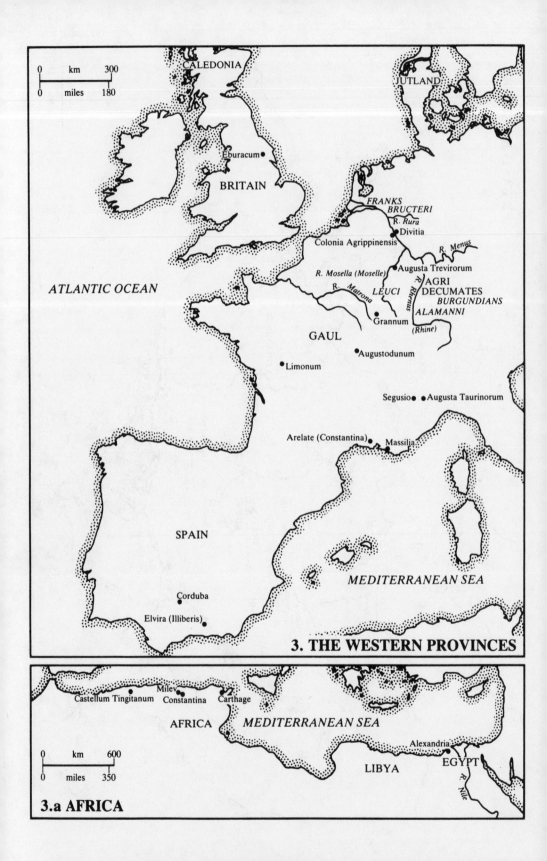

3. THE WESTERN PROVINCES

3.a AFRICA

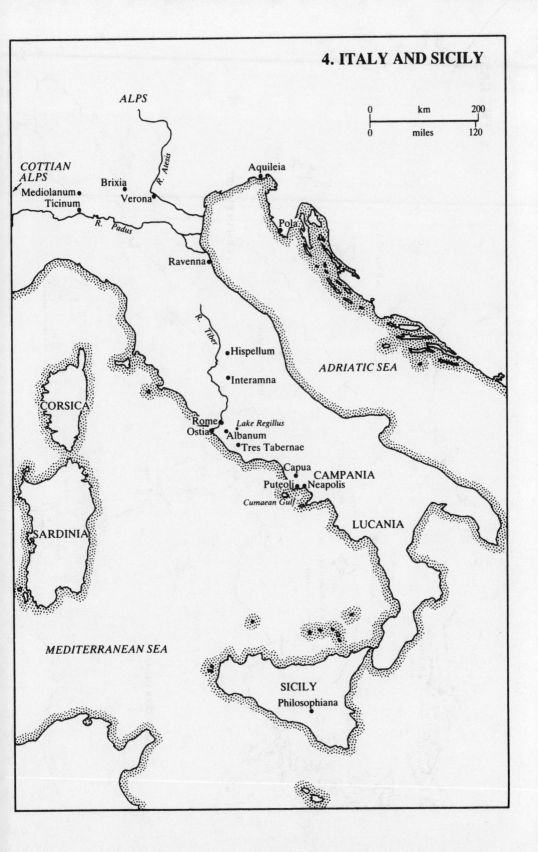

4. ITALY AND SICILY

ALPS

COTTIAN ALPS

Mediolanum
Ticinum

Brixia
Verona

R. Atesis

Aquileia

Pola

R. Padus

Ravenna

R. Tiber

Hispellum

Interamna

ADRIATIC SEA

CORSICA

Rome
Ostia
Albanum
Tres Tabernae

Lake Regillus

Capua

CAMPANIA

Puteoli
Neapolis

Cumaean Gulf

SARDINIA

LUCANIA

MEDITERRANEAN SEA

SICILY
Philosophiana

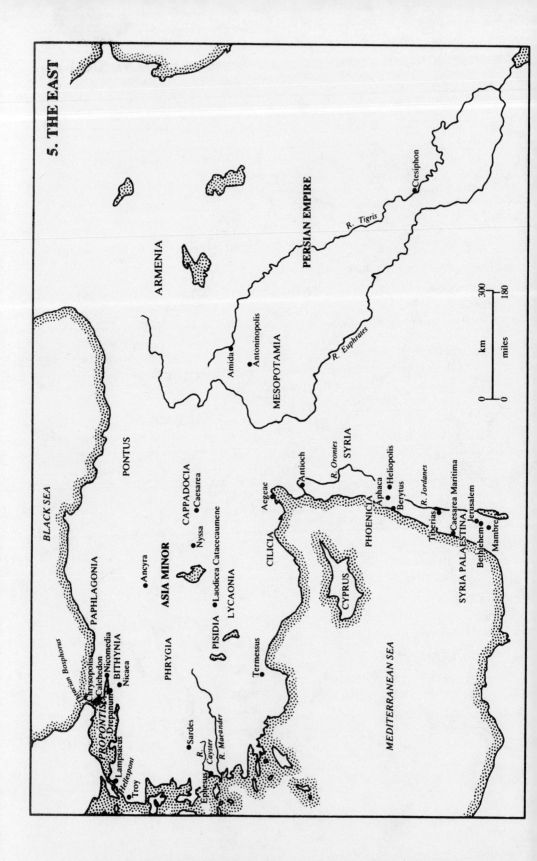

5. THE EAST

BLACK SEA

PERSIAN EMPIRE

ARMENIA

R. Tigris

Ctesiphon

MESOPOTAMIA

Amida
Antoninopolis

R. Euphrates

PONTUS

PAPHLAGONIA

BITHYNIA

Thracian Bosphorus

Chrysopolis
Calchedon
Nicomedia
Nicaea
Drepanum
PROPONTIS
Lampsacus
Hellespont
Troy

Sardes

R. Cayster
R. Maeander

Ephesus

Ancyra

ASIA MINOR

PHRYGIA

CAPPADOCIA

Caesarea

Nyssa
Laodicea Catacecaumene

PISIDIA

LYCAONIA

Termessus

Aegeae

CILICIA

Antioch

R. Orontes

SYRIA

Aphaca
Heliopolis
Berytus

PHOENICIA

CYPRUS

R. Jordanes

Tiberias

Caesarea Maritima

Jerusalem

Bethlehem
Mambre

SYRIA PALAESTINA

MEDITERRANEAN SEA

km   0   300
miles 0   180

ABBREVIATIONS

Alföldi	A. Alföldi, *The Conversion of Constantine and Pagan Rome*, 1948, 1969
Baker	G. P. Baker, *Constantine the Great and the Christian Revolution*, 1931
Barnes	T. D. Barnes, *Constantine and Eusebius*, 1981
Baynes	N. H. Baynes, *Constantine the Great and the Christian Church*, 1931, 1972
Bruun, *SCN*	P. Bruun, *Studies in Constantinian Numismatics: Papers from 1954 to 1988*, 1991
Eus.*HE.*	Eusebius, *Historia Ecclesiastica* (History of the Church)
Eus.*LC*	Eusebius, *Laus Constantini* (Praise of Constantine)
Eus.*VC*	Eusebius, *Vita Constantini* (Life of Constantine)
Gibbon	E. Gibbon, *The Decline and Fall of the Roman Empire*, 1766–88 (references to abridgment by D. J. Low, 1960)
Holland Smith	J. Holland Smith, *Constantine the Great*, 1971
Jones	A. H. M. Jones, *Constantine and the Conversion of Europe*, 1949, 1972
Lact.*DMP*	Lactantius, *De Morte Persecutorum* (*On the Deaths of the Persecutors*)
MacMullen	R. MacMullen, *Constantine*, 1970
RIC	H. Mattingly, E. A. Sydenham, C. H. V. Sutherland and R. A. G. Carson (eds), *Roman Imperial Coinage*, I–IX, 1923–1951

REFERENCES

PREFACE

1   Evelyn Waugh, *Helena* (1950), p. x
2   Baynes, p. 3
3   A. Manaresi, *L'impero e il cristianesimo* (1914), p. 513
4   MacMullen, p. 16

PART I: INTRODUCTORY

CHAPTER 1: THE SOURCES

1   T. D. Barnes, *Journal of Roman Studies*, 1973, p. 29; R. Syme, *Ammianus and the Historia Augusta* (1968), p. 205 and n. 3
2   K. M. Setton, *Christian Attitude towards the Emperor in the Fourth Century* (1941), p. 42
3   A. H. M. Jones, *Journal of Ecclesiastical History*, V, 1954, pp. 196–200
4   J. Moreau (ed.), revised by V. Velkov, *Excerpta Valesiana*, 2nd edn (1968)
5   F. Halkin, *Analecta Bollandiana*, LXXVII, 1959, pp. 63ff., LXXVIII, 1960, pp. 5ff
6   *Cf.* M. Hadas, *History of Latin Literature* (1952)
7   *RIC*, VII, p. 111 nos 220ff.; p. 314 nos 143ff., etc.
8   Bruun, *SCN*, p. 198
9   Eus. *VC*, 4.9
10 *Cf.* MacMullen, p. 215
11 Gibbon, p. 261; *cf.* F. Paschoud, *Historia*, XX, 1971, pp. 334ff.

CHAPTER 2: THE RISE TO SUPREMACY

1   *RIC*, VII, p. 323 nos 248 and 250
2   J. P. C. Kent and M. and A. Hirmer, *Roman Coins* (1978), no. 588
3   Aurelius Victor, *Epitome*, 41
4   *Panegyric* X (II), 11, 2
5   Gibbon, p. 226
6   C. H. V. Sutherland, *Roman Coins* (1974), p. 264 nos 520f.
7   Lact. *DMP*, 19.1–4 (tr. J. L. Creed)
8   *RIC*, VI, pp. 48, 58, etc.
9   MacMullen, p. 32
10 *RIC*, VI, pp. 338ff., 367f., 370, 418, 431; *cf.* M. Cullheid, *Opuscula Romana*, XVII, 1989, pp. 9–19
11 J. Lafaurie, *Comptes Rendus de l'Académie des Inscriptions*, 1965, pp. 192–210
12 Lact. *DMP*. 32.1ff.
13 *RIC*, VII, pp. 310ff., p. 180 nos 203, 207
14 A. Alföldi, *Cambridge Ancient History*, XII, pp. 149, 723
15 *Cf.* W. Ennslin, *Cambridge Ancient History*, XII, p. 94

PART II: CONSTANTINE AT WAR

CHAPTER 3: CIVIL WARS

1   E.g. D. De Decker, *Byzantium*, XXXVIII, 1968, p. 496
2   J. L. Creed, *Lactantius: De Morte Persecutorum*, p. 117 n. 7
3   *Panegyric* XII (IX), 9.3
4   Barnes, p. 305 n. 144, against Aurelius Victor, *Caesars*, 40.29
5   *RIC*, VII, p. 235 no. 13, p. 237 no. 33
6   *Ibid.*, p. 340 no. 361
7   *Ibid.*, p. 305 no. 67; *cf.* T. Grünewald, *Historia Einzelschrift*, LXIV, 1990
8   Barnes, pp. 66f.
9   *Excerpta Valesiana*, 1, 5, 14f.
10 *RIC*, VII, p. 368 no. 54 (AD 316)
11 *Ibid.*, Index II, s.v.
12 *Ibid.*, p. 604 nos 26, 27
13 *Ibid.*, p. 645 and n. 16
14 Socrates Scholasticus, *Historia Ecclesiastica*, 14
15 Zonaras, 13.1
16 For Licinius' possible good points, see Barnes, p. 68

17 Jones, p. 135
18 *RIC*, VII, pp. 62, 64, 567; P. M. Bruun, *Arctos*, n.s. III, pp. 21ff.
19 Julian, *Caesars*, 329

CHAPTER 4: FOREIGN WARS

1 See *Romanobarbarica: Contributi allo studio dei rapporti culturali tra mondo romano e mondo barbarico* (vol. XI was in 1991)
2 MacMullen, pp. 39f.
3 Baker, pp. 22f.
4 T. S. Burns, *A History of the Ostrogoths* (1984), pp. 33f.
5 J. D. Randers-Pehrson, *Barbarians and Romans* (1983), pp. 38f.
6 Baker, pp. 220f.
7 P. J. Heather, *Goths and Romans 332–489* (1992), p. 15
8 J. D. Randers-Pehrson, *loc. cit.*
9 *Excerpta Valesiana*, 5.27
10 Wolfram, *History of the Goths*, p. 60; unlike most, Wolfram believes these stories
11 P. J. Heather and J. Matthews, *The Goths in the Fourth Century* (1991), pp. 44f. n. 98
12 Julian, *Caesars*, 329c
13 J. B. Firth, *Constantine the Great* (1905), p. 124
14 *RIC*, VII, p. 331 no. 298
15 *Ibid.*, pp. 574f. nos 36f.
16 *Ibid.*, p. 333 no. 306
17 The name of Geberic can be left out, because he does not belong to this period; P. J. Heather, *op. cit.*, pp. 78f.: against Wolfram, *op. cit.*, p. 62
18 Baker, pp. 270ff.
19 H. Opitz, *Zeitschrift für neutestamentliche Wissenschaft*, XXXIII, 1934, pp. 1438f.
20 *RIC*, VII, Index II, s.v.
21 *Ibid.*
22 Eus.*LC*, III, etc.
23 J. B. Firth, *op. cit.*, p. 129
24 MacMullen, p. 147
25 P. J. Heather and J. Matthews, *op. cit.*, pp. 23f. and n. 30
26 *Cf.* MacMullen, pp. 41f.; H. Wolfram, *Gotische Studien*, I, pp. 4–12; *History of the Goths*, p. 62

27 J. P. Kent and K. S. Painter, *Wealth of the Roman World AD 300–700* (1977), p. 25 no. 11

28 J. Porteous, *Coins* (1964), p. 18

29 Alföldi, p. 93

30 *RIC*, VII, Index II

31 *Ibid.*

32 *Ibid.*, p. 167 no. 34ff.

33 P. J. Heather and J. Matthews, *op. cit.*, pp. 24, 39 n.80; and A. Dauge, *Le Barbare* (1981), pp. 307, 378, 413ff.

34 Gibbon, pp. 262b

35 E. M. McCormick, *Eternal Victory*, p. 186

36 *RIC*, VII, Index II, s.v.

37 C. Thubron, *Emperor* (1978), pp. 5, 23

38 R. MacMullen, *Corruption and the Decline of Rome* (1988), p. 176

39 Lact. *DMP*, 7.2

40 M. Grant, *The Fall of the Roman Empire* (1976, 1990), p. 36

41 Zosimus, *Historia Nova*, II, 34 (tr. Buchanan and Davis)

42 Eus. *VC*, II, 28f.

43 T. D. Barnes, *Journal of Roman Studies*, 1985, p. 131

44 J. C. Rolfe, *Ammianus Marcellinus*, XXV, 4.23 (Loeb ed.); *cf.* George Cedrenus, *Chron. Anno XXI Constantini*, p. 295f.

45 *RIC*, VII, p. 368 no. 54 (AD 316)

46 J. Burckhardt, *The Age of Constantine the Great* (1852, 1949), p. 292

47 *RIC*, VII, pp. 26, 75: 'King' on his coins, *ibid.*, pp. 589f.

48 Ammianus Marcellinus, XXV, 4.23

PART III: CONSTANTINE AND THE STATE

CHAPTER 5: THE GOVERNMENT AND CHARACTER OF CONSTANTINE

1 *RIC*, V, 1, p. 299.305f. '[IMP.] DEO ET DOMINO NATO AVRELIANO AVG.)

2 *RIC*, V, 2, pp. 19, 108f.,114

3 Gibbon, p. 250

4 Eus. *LC*, V,. 6; *cf.* H. A. Drake, *In Praise of Constantine* (1975), p. 162 n. 13

5 *RIC*, VII, pp. 36f.

6 *Ibid.*, p. 489

7 Gibbon, p. 127

8   MacMullen, p. 53

9   P. M. Bruun, *Numismatic Notes and Monographs*, 146, 1961, p. 47

10   *Cf.* MacMullen, pp. 47, 233; A. Piganiol, *L'empire chrétien*, p. 355 and n. 3; Barnes, p. 255

11   *Cf.* J. B. Firth, *Constantine the Great* (1905), pp. 331f.

12   Zosimus, *Historia Nova*, V, 32

13   Eus. *VC*, IV, 1

14   *RIC*, VII, p. 238 nos 49ff.

15   E.g. Julian, *Orationes*, VII, 227c

16   Ammianus Marcellinus, XVI, 8–12

17   Lact. *DMP*, VII, 4

18   Eus. *VC*, 4.2

19   A. H. M. Jones, *The Roman Economy* (1974), pp. 170f.; *cf. ibid.*, p. 205

20   F. Lot, *The End of the Ancient World* (1931, 1966), p. 174; *cf.* Lact. *DMP*, 23

21   Libanius, *Contr. Florent.*, p. 427; *cf.* F. Lot, *loc. cit.*

22   H. I. Bell, *Jews and Christians in Egypt* (1924), pp. 73f.

23   *Cf.* F. Lot, *op. cit.*, p. 175

24   Gibbon, p. 260; *cf. Codex Theodosianus*, II, 7, 3

25   *Cf.* F. W. Walbank, *The Awful Revolution* (1969), p. 99

26   J. P. C. Kent and M. and A. Hirmer, *Roman Coins* (1978), p. 46

27   M. Grant, *The Fall of the Roman Empire* (1976, 1990), p. 18

28   J. Porteous, *Coins in History* (1969), pp. 16ff.

29   E. Garsonnet, *Histoire des locations perpétuelles et des baux à longue durée* (1879), p. 15

30   *Codex Theodosianus*, V, 91

31   F. Lot, *op. cit.*, p. 100

32   Anonymus, *De Rebus Bellicis*, II, 2f.; *cf.* E. A. Thompson, *A Roman Reformer and Inventor* (1951), p. 32

33   F. De Coulanges, *L'Invasion germanique et la fin de l'Europe* (1891), p. 224

34   R. MacMullen, *Corruption and the Decline of Rome* (1988), p. x; *cf.* pp. 167f.

35   Optatus of Milevi, App. 1

36   *Ibid.*, p. 162

37   Ulpian, *Digest*, I, 16, 6.3; *cf.* R. MacMullen, *Corruption and the Decline of Rome* (1988), p. 127

38   Ammianus Marcellinus, XVI, 8, 12

39   *Cf.* MacMullen, p. 198

40   *Codex Theodosianus*, I, 16.7 (tr. C. Pharr)

41 J. Naudet, *Des Changements opérés dans toutes les parties de l'administration de l'empire romain sous les règnes de Dioclétien, de Constantin et de leurs successeurs jusqu'à Julien* (1817), II, pp. 141f.

42 Eus. *VC*, IV, 30 (tr. C. Luibhéid)

43 F. Lot, *op. cit.*, p. 176

44 P. Brown, *The World of Late Antiquity* (1971), p. 82 no. 61

45 Bruun, *SCN*, pp. 64f n. 40

46 *Ibid.*, p. 193 n. 18; *cf. ibid.*, pp. 107, 151ff.

47 *Cf.* J. B. Firth, *Constantine the Great* (1905), p. 90

48 Eus. *VC*, Prologue

49 Gibbon, pp. 266f.

50 Julian, *Caesars*, 318A, 329A, 336A

51 Eus. *LC*, V, 7

52 MacMullen, p. 237

53 Gibbon, p. 215

54 *Panegyric*, V (VIII), 518C

55 Eus. *LC*, V, 5f.

56 Eutropius, X, 7.1; Gibbon, p. 267, *cf.* 298

CHAPTER 6: CONSTANTINE, CRISPUS AND FAUSTA

1 Eutropius, X, 6

2 Johannes Lydus, *On the Months*, 4.2; *cf.* Alföldi, pp. 57, 105, 114

3 Eunapius, *Lives of the Sophists*, VI, 2

4 T. D. Barnes, *Classical Philology*, LXXI, 1976, p. 267, *pace*, H. A. Pohlsander, *Historia*, XXXIII, 1984, p. 80

5 Nazarius, *Panegyric*, IV (X), 36

6 A. Billorel, *Revue archéologique de l'est*, XX, 1969, pp. 222ff.

7 *Corpus Inscriptionum Latinarum*, X, 517

8 *Cf.* A. Vogel, *Der Kaiser Diokletian* (1857), p. 71

9 Eutropius, X, 6

10 Aurelius Victor, *Caesars, Epitome*, 41.11; stressed also by Julian, *Caesars*, 336

11 Holland Smith, p. 207

12 Julian, *Orationes*, I

13 *Cf.* E. Horst, *Konstantin der Grosse* (1964, 1965), p. 250

14 *RIC*, VII, p. 203 no. 442

15 E. Horst, *op. cit.*, p. 251

16 *Cf.* Barnes, p. 384 n. 10

17 Baker, p. 255
18 Philostorgius, *Historia Ecclesiastica* II, 4
19 Aurelius Victor, *Epitome*, 41
20 Jones, p. 230
21 Evagrius, *Historia Ecclesiastica*, III, 41, 374

CHAPTER 7: CONSTANTINOPLE

1 *Panegyric*, IV (X), 3.3, 6.1, 6.4
2 Herodian, *Histories*, I, vi, 5
3 *Fragmenta Historicorum Graecorum*, IV, 189
4 See A. Alföldi, *Journal of Roman Studies*, 1947, pp. 10ff.
5 F. Halkin, *Analecta Bollandiana*, LXXVIII, 1960, p. 5
6 Eunapius, *Lives of the Sophists*, VI, 3.1; *cf.* MacMullen, p. 189; Holland Smith, pp. 224f.; A. Piganiol, *L'empire chrétien*, p. 54, believes Eunapius
7 Socrates Scholasticus, *Historia Ecclesiastica*, I, 16
8 Jones, p. 83
9 *RIC*, VII, pp. 335f., etc.

PART IV: CONSTANTINE AND CHRISTIANITY

CHAPTER 8: CONSTANTINE AND THE CHRISTIAN GOD

1 Eus.*VC*, I, 13–17 (too ready to see Constantius I Chlorus as Christian); *cf.* N. H. Baynes, *Cambridge Ancient History*, XII (1939), p. 629
2 Tr. H. A. Drake, *Eusebius: In Praise of Constantine* (1976), pp. 23f.
3 Jones, p. 98; R. Lane Fox, *Pagans and Christians* (1986), p. 62
4 P. Brown, *The Making of Late Antiquity* (1978), pp. 57ff., 62
5 V. J. J. Flint, *The Rise of Magic in Early Medieval Europe*, (1991) p. 13
6 Barnes, pp. 18f.
7 M. Grant, *The Climax of Rome* (1968), p. 202; S. N. Lieu, *Manicheanism* (1985)
8 Constantine, *Oration to the Assembly of Saints*, 25
9 Eus.*HE*, VIII, 1.7ff.
10 D. Winslow, in S. Benko and J. J. Rourke (eds), *The Catacombs and the Colosseum* (1971), pp. 249f.
11 P. S. Davies, *Journal of Theological Studies*, XL, April 1989, p. 92; *cf.* Aurelius Victor, *Caesars*, 39, 45

12   R. MacMullen, *Christianising the Roman Empire AD 100–400* (1984), pp. 104f.

13   *RIC*, VI, p. 28, no. 1273

14   *Ibid.*, VII, p. 236 nos 23ff., etc.

15   *Panegyric*, VI (VII), 21.4ff.

16   C. Thubron, *Emperor* (1978), pp. 13f.

17   *Ibid.*, pp. 161ff.

18   MacMullen, p. 67

19   C. E. Coleman, *Constantine the Great and Christianity* (1914), p. 133

20   *RIC*, VII, Index II, s.v.

21   F. Cumont, *Textes et monuments*, I, p. 290; Alföldi, p. 59, n. 3

22   Eus.*LC*, VI, 20, etc.

23   J. Lees-Milne, *St Peter's* (1967), p. 27 (illustration)

24   R. A. G. Carson, *Principal Coins of the Romans*, III: *The Dominate AD 294–498* (1981), p. 54 no. 1391

25   Philostorgius, *Historia Ecclesiastica*, II, 17; Eus.*VC*, I, 3

26   H. Chadwick, *The Early Church* (1967), pp. 126f.

27   Eus.*HE*, VIII, 17.6–10 (tr. A. C. McGiffert and B. C. Richardson)

28   *Ibid.*, IX, 9A.1–9

29   M. Cary and H. H. Scullard, *History of Rome*, 3rd edn (1975), p. 523

30   R. A. G. Carson, *Coins of Greece and Rome* (1962, 1970), pl. 24 no. 363

31   *Cf.* MacMullen, pp. 77f.

32   Alföldi, p. 18 n. 3

33   Eus.*VC*, I, 28 (tr. C. Luibhéid)

34   *Ibid.*, 28–32; *Panegyric*, VI (VII), 43ff.

35   F. Halkin, *Bibliotheca Hagiographica Graeca*, 3rd edn (1937), 396–397C, and *Analecta Bollandiana*, LXXVII, 1959, p. 70 n. 6

36   Tertullian, *De Anima*, 1472

37   Lact.*DMP*, 46.1

38   Eusebius, *On Christ's Sepulchre* (*LC*), 18.1

39   P. Brown, *op. cit.*, p. 63

40   Gibbon, p. 306

41   2 Macc. 15

42   Lact. *DMP*, 44.12ff.

43   Eus.*LC*, 9.12

44   Eus.*VC*, I, 28ff., 44

45   *Ibid.*, 45

46   M. Rostovtzeff, *Journal of Roman Studies*, 1942, p. 104; *RIC*, VII, p. 64 n. 1

47   *RIC*, VII, p. 364 n. 36; *cf. ibid.*, p. 62; Bruun, *SCN*, pp. 53ff., 59 n. 27

48 Bruun, *SCN*, p. 67 n. 53, 73, 74 n. 50; *cf. ibid.*, pp. 35, 62

49 Alföldi, p. 42 n. 4; Bruun, *SCN*, p. 74

50 Bruun, *SCN*, p. 67; *cf. ibid.*, p. 71 n. 1

51 H. Mattingly, *Roman Coins* (1928, 1962), pl. LXIII, no. 12, R. A. G. Carson, *Principal Coins of the Romans*, III: *The Dominate AD 294–498*, p. 86 no. 1561

52 M. Gough, *The Origins of Christian Art* (1973), pp. 108f., fig. 91

53 F. Halkin, *Analecta Bollandiana*, LXXVIII, 1960, p. 5

54 R. Lane Fox, *Pagans and Christians* (1986), pp. 615ff.

55 Optatus of Milev, App. V; *cf.* Alföldi, pp. 8, 124

56 *Cf.* J. Lees-Milne, *op. cit.*, p. 56

57 E.g. T. G. Elliott, *Constantine's Conversion: Do We Really Need It?*, Phoenix, XLI, 1987, p. 421

58 J. Szidat, *Gymnasium*, XCII, 1985, pp. 514–25

59 Eus.*VC*, I, 27 (tr. C. Luibhéid); Eus.*HE*, IX, 9.12ff.; Lact.*DMP*, 36.3 and 37.1; Alföldi, p. 37

60 Optatus of Milev, App. III, V

61 Eus.*VC*, IV, 33

62 Matt. 25:46

63 Orosius, *Clementissimae Admonitiones*, I, 6.5; II, 1

64 *Cf.* H. A. Drake, *In Praise of Constantine* (1975), p. 153 n. 50

65 *Cf.* J. Blair, *English Historical Review*, CVII, 1992, p. 378

66 E.g. Eus.*VC*, III, 12; Eus.*HE*, X, 4,14; Lactantius, *Divine Institutions*, II, 16.1; *cf.* V. Cilento, *Transposizione dell' antico* (1961), pp. 180ff.

67 H. Dörries, *Constantine the Great* (1972), p. 59

68 Eus.*LC*, VII, 2

69 J. Burckhardt, *The Age of Constantine the Great* (1852, 1949), p. 345

70 Gibbon, p. 299

71 *Ibid.*, pp. 289, 295, 302

72 Philostorgius, *Historia Ecclesiastica*, II, 9

73 Eus.*VC*, I, 32

74 *Cf.*Barnes, p. 254

75 *Cf.* Holland Smith, p. 283

76 Orosius, *op. cit.*, I, 6.5; II, 1

77 *Corpus Inscriptionum Latinarum*, VI, 1139

78 *Panegyric*, XII (IX), 25

79 *Ibid.*, 26; *cf.* Alföldi, p. 71

80 *Cf.* C. Roebuck, *The World of Ancient Times* (1966), pp. 702f.

81 A. Alföldi, *Dissertationes Pannonicae*, XI, 7, 1937, p. 80; A. Alföldi, *A*

Festival of Isis at Rome under the Christian Emperors of the Fourth Century (1937); H. Mattingly, *Roman Coins* (1928, 1960), pp. 226f.

82 Gibbon, p. 284
83 Eus.*LC*, IX, 10
84 *RIC*, VII, p. 36 and n. 36;*cf.* note 47 above
85 *Ibid.*, p. 572 no. 19
86 *RIC*, VIII, pp. 123, 163f., 188f., 217f., 268 (Magnentius); pp. 165, 252, etc. (Constantine II)
87 A. Alföldi, *Journal of Roman Studies*, p. 14
88 *RIC*, [v5]vii, p. 43
89 Eus,*VC*, IV, 15
90 H. Mattingly, *op. cit.*, pl. LXI no. 13

CHAPTER 9: CONSTANTINE AND THE CHRISTIAN CHURCH

1 Eus.*HE*, X, 5.1ff., Lact.*DMP*, 48; J. E. L. Oulton, *Eusebius: Ecclesiastical History* (Loeb edn), II, pp. 444f. n. 1
2 N. H. Baynes, *Cambridge Ancient History*, XII (1939),pp. 689f.
3 Eus.*HE*, X, 5.15–17 (tr. Jones, p. 88)
4 Jones, pp. 142f.; another version is in Holland Smith, pp. 191f.
5 MacMullen, p. 237
6 *Ibid.*, pp. 168f.
7 Jones, pp. 169f.; another version is in Holland Smith, p. 242
8 *Inscriptiones Latinae Selectae*, 705
9 Eus.*VC*, II, 68; Baynes, pp. 18f.; MacMullen, p. 165
10 T. D. Barnes, *Journal of Roman Studies*, 1985, pp. 130f.
11 P. Brown, *The Making of Late Antiquity* (1978), p. 80
12 Eus.*HE*, X, 5.22 (tr. C. Luibhéid)
13 *Ibid.*, IV, 42
14 Jones, pp. 190ff.
15 Hilary of Poitiers, *Ad Constantium*, II, 4, 5
16 Julian, *Letters*, 52, etc.
17 MacMullen, p. 169
18 C. E. M. de Sainte Croix, *The Class Struggle in the Ancient Greek World* (1981, 1983), p. 497
19 M. Grant, *The Fall of the Roman Empire* (1976, 1990), p. 201
20 Optatus of Milev, *De Schismate Donatistarum*, I, 22
21 Augustine, *Epistles*, 89.2
22 R. M. Grant, *Augustus to Constantine* (1970, 1990), pp. 268f.

23 *Sermo de Passione Donati*, 3; J. P. Migne, *Patrologiae Cursus Completus, series Latina*, VIII, 952–8

24 P. J. Heather and J. Matthews, *The Goths in the Fourth Century* (1991), p. 136

25 Socrates Scholasticus, *Historia Ecclesiastica*, I, 5

26 Gregory of Nyssa, *Oratio de Deitate Filii et Spiritus Sancti*; J. P. Migne, *op. cit.*, *series Greca*, XLVI, 557

27 MacMullen, p. 169

28 *Ibid.*

29 Jones, pp. 142f.; another version is in Holland Smith, pp. 191f.

30 MacMullen, p. 237

31 Eusebius in C. Luibhéid, *The Essential Eusebius* (1966), pp. 217ff.

32 Gibbon, pp. 316f.

33 Tr. J. N. D. Kelly, *Encyclopaedia Britannica* (1971 edn), VI, p. 719

34 Gibbon, p. 310

35 Eus.*VC*, III, 20

36 Socrates Scholasticus, *Historia Ecclesiastica*, I, 26; *cf.* Jones, pp. 169f.; another version is in Holland Smith, p. 242

37 MacMullen, p. 182

38 L. W. Barnard, *Journal of Church and State*, XXIV, 1982, pp. 337ff.

39 Eus.*HE*, X, 4.1

40 *Inscriptiones Latinae Selectae*, 4146, 3409

41 *Ibid.*, 705

42 Philostorgius, *Historia Ecclesiastica*, II, 77

43 Eus.*VC*, II, 68

44 *Cf.* T. D. Barnes, *Journal of Roman Studies*, 1985, pp. 130f.

45 Sozomen, *Historia Ecclesiastica*, II, 5; *cf.* R. MacMullen, *Christianising the Roman Empire AD 100–400* (1984), pp. 49f.

46 Eus.*VC*, III, 53–8; Eus.*LC*, VII, 5–7

47 Barnes, pp. 52f. (references)

48 F. Lucreci, *Atti dell'Accademia delle Scienze morali e politiche* (Naples), XCVII, 1981, pp. 171ff.

49 Eus.*VC*, IV, 24

50 *Ibid.*, 56–60

51 *Ibid.*, IV, 8, 14: T. D. Barnes, *Journal of Roman Studies*, 1985, p. 131

52 *Codex Justinianus*, III, xii, 3; *Codex Theodosianus*, II, viii, 1

53 Eutropius, X, 7; Alföldi, p. 74

54 Ammianus Marcellinus, XXI, 10, 8

CHAPTER 10: BUILDER

1   Eus. *VC*, IV, 23
2   R. Krautheimer, *Early Christian and Byzantine Architecture* (1965), p. 42
3   Eus. *HE*, VII, 30.19
4   R. Krautheimer, *op. cit.*, p. 15 and fig. 5
5   J. Lees-Milne, *St Peter's* (1967), p. 64
6   P. E. Brown, *Roman Architecture* (1961), pp. 47f.
7   *Cf.* J. Burckhardt, *The Age of Constantine the Great* (1852, 1949), p. 352
8   H. von Schoenebeck, *Klio*, Beiheft XLIII, 1939, pp. 87ff.
9   J. Lees-Milne, *loc. cit.*
10 Eus. *VC*, IV, 36
11 1 Cor. 24:30
12 Eus. *HE*, IV, 58f.
13 F. Halkin, *Analecta Bollandiana*, LXXVIII, 1960, p. 5
14 Eus. *VC*, III, 48
15 *Ibid.*, 25ff.
16 John 19:20
17 R. M. Grant, *Augustus to Constantine* (1970, 1990), pp. 342f.; *cf.* Rufinus, *Historia Ecclesiastica*, X, 7–8
18 A. Elon, *Jerusalem* (1990), p. 121
19 E. Waugh, *Helena* (1950), pp. 225–60
20 S. Runciman, *Byzantine Civilisation* (1933), p. 26
21 P. Devos, *Analecta Bollandiana*, CI, 1983, pp. 407ff.
22 A. Elon, *op. cit.*, pp. 120f.
23 Eus. *VC*, 41–3
24 D. Bowder, *The Age of Constantine and Julian* (1978), p. 63
25 Eus. *HE*, X, 4, 38
26 R. MacMullen, *Corruption and the Decline of Rome* (1988), pp. 51, 235

PART V: THE END AND THE AFTERMATH

CHAPTER 11: BAPTISM, DEATH AND SUCCESSION

1   John 3:5
2   J. N. Davidson-Kelly, *Encyclopaedia Britannica*, VI (1971 edn), p. 718
3   Gibbon, p. 303

4   Holland Smith, p. 293
5   F. Halkin, *Analecta Bollandiana*, LXXVII, 1959, p. 71
6   Eus. *VC*, IV, 65–70; *cf.* H. St. L. B. Moss, *Cambridge Medieval History*, IV, part I, p. 1
7   R. A. G. Carson, *Principal Coins of the Romans*, III: *The Dominate AD 284–498* (1981), p. 32 no. 1339, p. 48 nos 1362, 1363
8   Eus. *VC*, IV, 68
9   *Corpus Inscriptionum Latinarum*, VI, 1151
10   *RIC*, VII, p. 328 no. 279; *cf.* A. Alföldi, *Journal of Roman Studies*, 1947, p. 15
11   Athanasius, *Against the Pagans*, 9
12   *RIC*, VII, p. 180, etc.
13   Firmicus Maternus, *Mathesis*, II, 30, 5–6
14   *RIC*, VIII, 139, 248, 446
15   *RIC*, VII, pp. 584, 589f.
16   Julian, *Orationes*, VII, 238ff.; *cf.* J. Burckhardt, *The Age of Constantine the Great* (1852, 1949), p. 344
17   Eus. *VC*, I, 1, 9
18   *Ibid.*, IV, 67
19   Barnes, p. 267
20   H. Mattingly, *Roman Coins* (1928, 1960), pl. LV, no. 3 (*c.*AD 340)

CHAPTER 12: THE SIGNIFICANCE OF CONSTANTINE

1   Gibbon, p. 303b; *cf.* C. E. Coleman, *Constantine the Great and Christianity* (1914), pp. 99f., 102
2   Baynes, p. 37
3   E. Horst, *Konstantin der Grosse* (1984, 1988), pp. 312ff.
4   H. Wolfram, *Constantin als Vorbild für den Herrscher des hochmittelalterlichen Reiches*, *Mitteilungen des Instituts für Österreichische Geschichtsforschungen*, LXVIII, 1959, pp. 226ff.
5   Alföldi, p. 7
6   D. P. Jordan, *Gibbon and his Roman Empire* (1971), p. 193
7   *Cf.* C. N. Cochrane, *Christianity and Classical Culture* (1940, 1957), pp. 212, 217
8   *Cf.* F. Halkin, *Analecta Bollandiana*, LXXVII, 1959, LXXVIII, 1960
9   W. Ullmann, *A History of Political Thought: The Middle Ages* (1965), pp. 81–5, 97f.; R. E. McNally, *Encyclopaedia Britannica* (1971 edn), VII, p. 580
10   N. H. Baynes, *Cambridge Ancient History*, XII (1939), p. 699

SOME BOOKS

A. ALFÖLDI, *The Conversion of Constantine and Pagan Rome*, 1948, 1969

M. T. W. ARNHEIM, *The Senatorial Aristocracy in the Later Roman Empire*, 1972

H. W. ATTRIDGE AND G. HATA (eds), *Eusebius, Christianity and Judaism*, 1992

G. AULEN, *Christus Victor*, 1970

R. BAINTON, *The Penguin History of Christianity*, vol. I, 1964, 1967

G. P. BAKER, *Constantine the Great and the Christian Revolution*, 1931

I. BARNEA AND O. ILIESCU, *Constantine cel Mare*, 1982

T. D. BARNES, *Constantine and Eusebius*, 1981

T. D. BARNES, *The New Empire of Diocletian and Constantine*, 1982

P. BATTIFOL, *La paix constantinienne et la catholicisme*, 1954

N. H. BAYNES, *Constantine* (*Cambridge Ancient History*, vol. XII, ch. XX), 1939

N. H. BAYNES, *Constantine the Great and the Christian Church*, 1931, 1972

H. BERKHOF, *Die Theologie des Eusebius von Caesarea*, 1939

G. BONAMENTE AND N. ALTO, *I cristiani e l'impero nel quarto secolo*, 1988

D. BOWDER, *The Age of Constantine and Julian*, 1978

G. W. BOWERSOCK, J. CLIVE AND S. R. GRAUBARD (eds), *Edward Gibbon and the Fall of the Roman Empire*, 1977

H. BRANDENBURG, *Roms frühchristliche Basiliken des vierten Jahrhunderts*, 1979

P. BREZZI, *La politica religiosa di Costantino*, 1964

P. BROWN, *Power and Persuasion in Late Antiquity*, 1992

P. BROWN, *The Making of Late Antiquity*, 1978

P. BROWN, *The World of Late Antiquity*, 1971

P. BROWN (ed.), *Society and the Holy in Late Antiquity*, 1982

P. M. BRUUN, *The Roman Imperial Coinage*, vol. VII: *Constantine and Licinius AD* 313–337, 1966

P. M. BRUUN, *Studies in Constantinian Chronology*, 1961

P. M. BRUUN, *Studies in Constantinian Numismatics: Papers from* 1954 to 1988, 1991

V. BURCH, *Myth and Constantine the Great*, 1927

J. BURCKHARDT, *The Age of Constantine the Great*, 1852, 1949

S. CALDERONE, *Costantino e il Cattolicesimo*, vol. I, 1962

A. CAMERON, *Christianity and the Rhetoric of Empire*, 1991

C. CECCHELLI, *Il trionfo delle croce*, 1954

H. CHADWICK, *The Early Church*, 1967

H. CHADWICK, *Heresy and Orthodoxy in the Early Church*, 1991

G. F. CHESTNUT, *The First Christian Histories*, 1977

R. CHRISTLEIN, *Die Alamannen*, 1978

C. E. COLEMAN, *Constantine the Great and Christianity*, 1914

P. COX, *Biography in Late Antiquity: A Quest for the Holy Man*, 1983

B. CUNLIFFE, *Greeks, Romans and Barbarians*, 1988

G. DAGRON, *Naissance d'une capitale: Constantinople et ses institutions de* 330 à 451, 1974

J. G. DAVIES, *The Early Christian Church*, 1963

V. DE CLERCQ, *Ossius of Cordova*, 1954

L. DE GIOVANNI, *Costantino e il mondo pagano*, 1977, 1982

E. DEMOUGEOT, *La formation de l'Europe et les invasions barbares*, vol. II (284–476), 1979

A. DI BERNARDINO (ed.), *Encyclopaedia of the Early Church*, 1991

H.-J. DIESNER, *The Great Migration: The Movement of Peoples across Europe AD* 300–700, 1982

E. R. DODDS, *Pagan and Christian in the Age of Anxiety*, 1965

H. DÖRRIES, *Constantine and Religious Liberty*, 1960

H. DÖRRIES, *Constantine the Great*, 1972

H. DÖRRIES, *Das Selbstzeugnis Kaisers Konstantins*, 1954

G. DOWNEY, *The Late Roman Empire*, 1969

J. N. DRIJVERS, *Helena Augusta*, 1991

P. DUCREY (ed.), *Gibbon et Rome à la lumière de l'historiographie moderne*, 1977

C. DUPONT, *Le Droit criminel dans les constitutions de Constantine: Les infractions*, 1953; *Les peines*, 1955

J. W. EADIE, *The Conversion of Constantine*, 1977

R. FARINA, *L'impero e l'imperatore cristiano in Eusebio di Caesarea: la prima teologia politica del Cristianesimo*, 1966

A. FERRILL, *The Fall of the Roman Empire: The Military Explanation*, 1983, 1988

J. B. FIRTH, *Constantine the Great*, 1905

A. M. FORCINI, *Lettori bizantini di Zosimo*, 1987

R. LANE FOX, *Pagans and Christians*, 1986

W. H. C. FREND, *The Donatist Church*, 1952, 1985

W. H. C. FREND, *The Early Church: From the Beginning to 461*, 1965, 1991

G. GERLAND, *Konstantin der Grosse in Geschichte und Saga*, 1937

E. GIBBON, *The Decline and Fall of the Roman Empire*, 1766–1788 (abridgment by D. M. Low, 1960)

C. GILL AND T. P. WISEMAN (eds), *Lies and Fiction in the Ancient World*, 1993

W. GOFFART, *Caput and Colonate: Towards a History of Late Roman Taxation*, 1974

A. GRABAR, *Christian Iconography*, 1961

M. GRANT, *The Climax of Rome*, 1968, 1974

M. GRANT, *The Fall of the Roman Empire*, 1976, 1990

M. GRANT, *Readings in the Classical Historians*, 1992

R. M. GRANT, *Augustus to Constantine: The Rise and Triumph of Christianity in the Roman World*, 1970, 1990

R. M. GRANT, *Early Christianity and Society*, 1977

R. M. GRANT, *Eusebius as Church Historian*, 1980

R. M. GRANT, *Gods and One God*, 1986

S. L. GREENSLADE, *Church and State from Constantine to Theodosius*, 1954

S. L. GREENSLADE, *Schism in the Early Church*, 1953

R. C. GREGG AND D. E.L GROH, *Early Arianism: A View of Salvation*, 1981

T. GRÜNEWALD, *Constantinus Maximus Augustus: Herrschaftspropaganda in der zeitgenössischen Überlieferung*, 1990

J. M. HARRIES, *Religious Conflict in Fourth Century Rome*, 1982

J. M. HARRIES, *Towards a New Constantine?*, 1985

W. HARTMANN, *Kunst des Konstantins als Christ und Philosoph in seinen Briefen und Erlassen*, 1902

P. HEATHER, *Goths and Romans 332–489*, 1991

P. HEATHER AND J. MATTHEWS, *The Goths in the Fourth Century*, 1991

P. V. HILL AND J. P. C. KENT, *The Bronze Coinage of the House of Constantine*, 1956

J. HOLLAND SMITH, *Constantine the Great*, 1971

K. HÖNN, *Konstantin der Grosse*, 1940, 1945

E. HORST, *Konstantin der Grosse*, 1984, 1985

L. HOULDEN (ed.), *Judaism and Christianity*, 1988, 1991

E. P. HUNT, *Holy Land Pilgrimage in the Later Roman Empire*, 1982

M. A. HUTTMANN, *The Establishment of Christianity and the Proscription of Paganism*, 1914

P. JOHNSON, *A History of Christianity*, 1976, 1978

A. H. M. JONES, *Constantine and the Conversion of Europe*, 1948

A. H. M. JONES, *The Decline of the Ancient World*, 1966, 1975

A. H. M. JONES, *A History of Rome through the Fifth Century*, vol. II: *The Empire*, 1970

A. H. M. JONES, *The Later Roman Empire (AD 284–602)*, 2 vols, 1964, 1986

A. H. M. JONES, *The Roman Economy* (ed. P. A. Brunt), 1974

D. P. JORDAN, *Gibbon and the Roman Empire*, 1971

W. E. KAEGI JR, *Byzantium and the Decline of Rome*, 1968

A. KANIUTH, *Die Beisetzung Konstantins des Grossen: Untersuchungen des religiösen Haltung des Kaisers*, 1941

M. KAZANSKI, *Les Gothes (I–VII s. après J.C.)*, 1991

H. C. KEE, *Constantine versus Christ: The Triumph of Ideology*, 1982

P. KERESZTES, *Constantine: A Great Christian Monarch and Apostle*, 1981

E. KLEINBAUER, *Early Christian and Byzantine Architecture: An Annotated Bibliography and Historiography*, 1992

H. KRAFT, *Kaiser Konstantins religiöse Entwicklung*, 1955

H. KRAFT (ed.), *Konstantin der Grosse*, 1974

M. KRAŠENINNIKOV, *Prodromus Syllages Vitarum Laudationum-que Sanctorum Constantini Magni et Helenae*, 1915

R. KRAUTHEIMER, *Early Christian and Byzantine Architecture*, 1965

R. KRAUTHEIMER, *Three Christian Capitals*, 1987

B. KRUGER (ed.), *Die Germanen*, 2 vols, 1976, 1983

R. LAQUEUR, *Eusebius als Historiker seiner Zeit*, 1929

J. LEES-MILNE, *St Peter's*, 1967

L'église et l'empire au IVe siècle (Fondation Hardt), 1989

S. N. LIEU AND M. L. H. DODGSON, *The Roman Eastern Frontier and the Persian Wars AD 226–363*, 1991

H. LOEWENSTEIN, *Konstantin der Grosse*, 1983

F. LOT, *The End of the Ancient World and the Beginnings of the Middle Ages*, 1931, 1966

L. LUCAS, *The Conflict Between Christianity and Judaism: A Contribution to the History of the Jews in the Fourth Century*, 1910, 1992

S. T. MCCLOY, *Gibbon's Antagonism to Christianity*, 1933

A. C. MCGIFFERT AND B. C. RICHARDSON, *The Nicene and Post-Nicene Fathers*, 1890–1908

R. MACMULLEN, *Christianising the Roman Empire AD 100–400*, 1984

R. MACMULLEN, *Christianity in the Roman World*, 1974

R. MACMULLEN, *Constantine*, 1970

R. MACMULLEN, *Corruption and the Decline of Rome*, 1988

R. MACMULLEN, *Enemies of the Roman Order*, 1966

R. MACMULLEN, *Paganism in the Roman Empire*, 1981

R. MACMULLEN, *Soldier and Civilian in the Later Roman Empire*, 1967

J. MAILAÜ, *Les états barbaresques*, 1973

A. MANARESI, *L'impero romano e il cristianesimo*, 1914

R. A. MARKUS, *Christianity in the Roman World*, 1974

R. A. MARKUS, *The End of Ancient Christianity*, 1991

S. MAZZARINO, *Antico, tardoantico ed era costantiniana*, vol. I, 1974

S. MAZZARINO, *The End of the Ancient World*, 1966

R. MILBURN, *Early Christian Art and Architecture*, 1988

A. MOMIGLIANO (ed.), *The Conflict between Paganism and Christianity in the Fourth Century*, 1963

C. R. MOREY, *Christian Art*, 1955, 1958

A. A. MOSSHAMMER, *The Chronicles of Eusebius and Greek Chronographic Tradition*, 1979

B. MÜLLER-RETTIG, *Der Panegyricus des Jahres 310 auf Konstantin den Grossen*, 1990

L. MUSSET, *The Germanic Invasions*, 1975

J. NEUSNER, *Judaism and Christianity in the Age of Constantine*, 1987

F. OWEN, *The Germanic People: Their Origin, Expansion and Culture*, 1960, 1990

R. PARIBENI, *Da Diocleziano alla caduta dell'impero di occidente*, 1941

F. PASCHOUD, *Cinq études sur Zosime*, 1975

S. PEROWNE, *Caesars and Saints: The Evolution of the Christian State AD 180–313*, 1962

S. PEROWNE, *The End of the Roman World*, 1966

E. PETERSON, *Monotheismus: Eis Theos*, 1926

R. PICHON, *Lactance: étude sur le mouvement philosophique et réligieux sous le règne de Constantin*, 1901

J. N. PIETERSE (ed.), *Christianity and Hegemony: Religion and Politics as the Frontiers of Social Change*, 1992

A. PIGANIOL, *L'Empereur Constantin*, 1952

A. PIGANIOL, *L'Empire chrétien*, 1947, 1972

J. D. RANDERS-PEHRSON, *Barbarians and Romans: The Birth Struggle of Europe, AD 400–700*, 1983

L. RICHARDSON, *A New Topographical Dictionary of Ancient Rome*, 1992

J. B. RUSSELL, *Satan: The Early Christian Tradition*, 1981

H. VON SCHOENEBECK, *Beiträge zur Religionspolitik des Maxentius und Constantin* (Klio Beiheft 43, NF 30) (1939, 1962)

H. SCHRÖRS, *Konstantins des Grossen Kreuzerscheinung*, 1913

H. SCHUTZ, *The Romans in Central Europe*, 1985

E. SCHWARTZ, *Kaiser Constantin und die christliche Kirche*, 1913, 1936, 1969

K. M. SETTON, *Christian Attitude towards the Emperor in the Fourth Century: Especially as Shown in Addresses to the Emperor*, 1941

D. V. SIMON, *Konstantinisches Kaiserrecht*, 1977

R. C. SMITH AND J. LOUNIBUS (eds), *Pagan and Christian Anxiety*, 1984

M. SORDI, *The Christians and the Roman Empire*, 1986

J. STEVENSON, *A New Eusebius*, 1957, 1987

U. SÜSSENBACH, *Christuskult und Kaiserliche Baupolitik bei Konstantin*, 1977

H. TEMPORINI AND W. HAASE (eds), *Aufstieg und Niedergang der römischen Welt*, II, 9.1–2 (1976, 1978), 16.1–2 (1978), 23–8 (1979, 1980)

C. P. THIEDE, *The Heritage of the First Christians*, 1992

E. A. THOMPSON, *Romans and Barbarians: The Decline of the Western Empire*, 1982

M. TODD, *The Early Germans*, 1992

F. VALLETT AND M. KAZANSKI (eds), *L'armée romaine et les barbares du IIIe au VIe siècle* (Actes du Colloque International, S. Germain-en-Laye, 1990), 1993

D. VAN BERCHEM, *L'armée de Dioclétien et la reforme constantinienne*, 1952

L. VOELKL, *Der Kaiser Konstantin*, 1957

J. VOGT, *Constantin der Grosse und sein Jahrhundert*, 1949, 1960, 1973

J. VOGT, *The Decline of Rome*, 1967

M. WAAS, *Germanen im römischen Dienst im vierten Jahrhundert nach Christus*, 1972

F. W. WALBANK, *The Awful Revolution: The Decline of the Roman Empire in the West*, 1969

D. S. WALLACE-HADRILL, *Eusebius of Caesarea*, 1960

J. B. WARD PERKINS, *Studies in Roman and Early Christian Architecture*, 1993

SOME BOOKS

———

E. M. WIGHTMAN, *Roman Trier and the Treveri*, 1970
R. WILLIAMS, *Arius: Heresy and Tradition*, 1987
H. WOLFRAM, *History of the Goths*, 1979, 1988, 1990

INDEX